LEGAL WRITING:
Sense and Nonsense

LEGAL WRITING:
Sense and Nonsense

David Mellinkoff

Professor of Law, University of California, Los Angeles

West Publishing Co. St. Paul, Minnesota

Library of Congress Cataloging in Publication Data

Mellinkoff, David.
    Legal writing.

    Includes indexes.
    1. Legal composition.   2. Law—United States—
Language.   I. Title.
KF250.M44   1982   808'.06634   81-14688
ISBN 0-314-63275-1 (pbk.)   AACR2

To Ruth, my closest critic

Acknowledgements

This book draws heavily, and with gratitude, on what I have learned from law students and from fellow professionals in the practice and in academe. The debt is too large to list them all by name, but each is fondly remembered. For helpful comment and suggestion, my thanks go to Professors of Law Benjamin Aaron, Jesse Dukeminier, Robert Jordan, William Klein, Melville Nimmer, Gary Schwartz, Murray Schwartz, and Kenneth York. My thanks, too, to Mrs. Marilyn Schroeter, who must often have wished that the manuscript were as perfect as her rendering of it.

Above all, my special thanks to Professor of English Richard Lanham, who tried to save me from error, and often succeeded.

Contents

Preface

In the days of King Edward III, a new law said that lawyers had to use English in the courtroom. This law was to cure a very old trouble: People *"have no knowledge or understanding of that which is said for them or against them."*

Six hundred years later the complaint is as fresh as a stinkweed.

Even worse. After six hundred years of lawsuits caused by language atrocities, a terrible suspicion is born. Maybe the lawyers don't understand each other.

Too often it's not a maybe. Too many lawyers are long on law and short on English, especially writing it. They don't even like to think of themselves as writing at all but only *drafting*. To those who love her, *drafting* is not confined to *legislative drafting*. If it's about the law, you don't write it, you *draft* it. That comforting old word suggests the precision of another draftsman, who works with compass and rule, drawing lines of incomparable accuracy. Legal drafting isn't like that. *Drafting* is another name for *writing*, and only serves to let some lawyers feel that they can ignore the language and grammar of mere *writers*.

Most law can be expressed in ordinary English. Most of it is. But by the time lawyers get through mushing up ordinary English, very few English speakers and only some lawyers can recognize it. They throw in words that were headaches before the age of steam. They try to get by, stuffing law into sentences that aren't built to take the load. Instead of rejecting the rubbish and keeping the good in the language of the law, they swallow it whole. And end up with *lawsick*.

That's the way it is in the law books. That's the traditional way. That *must* be the precise way. It isn't. In *The Language of the Law* (1963), I documented the case against the claim of precision, and documented the case in favor of law using "the common speech, unless there are reasons for a difference." The remaining reasons for a difference are few, and apply only to the tiniest part of the language of the law.

Some lawyers, and many more people, have become convinced that it is possible and also important to write law pretty much in English, understandable English. Some of the language of the law needs translation. Some of it needs explaining. Law need not read like a novel, nor be reduced to grunts. It need not end up "plain" to everyone; few things are. But legal writing can do better than *lawsick*. *Lawsick* is on its way out.

This book will help you to understand legal writing, and how it can be improved and shortened without hurt to the law. Legal writing can be made more intelligible to people generally, not least to the lawyers.

This book gives some rules and examples to show how it can be done. This book will show you how you can end up "writing like a lawyer"—unless you are very careful.

***

lawsick n: a peculiar, English-like language commonly used in writing about law; peculiar in habitual indifference to ordinary usage of English words, grammar, and punctuation; and in preferring the archaic, wordy, pompous, and confusing over the clear, brief, and simple; persists chiefly through a belief of its writers that these peculiarities lead to precision. (written in *lawsick* unclear even to its author).

lawsick adj: characterized by one or more of the peculiarities of lawsick, *n,* as a *lawsick* statute.

lawsick v -ed/ -ing/ -s: to transform ordinary English into *lawsick,* n. (the notice we prepared was *lawsicked* beyond recognition).

Read This Before Using

This book calls for a break with the tradition of bad legal writing. Whether it's your legal writing or someone else's, THE QUESTION is always in order: *"Does it have to be like this?"*

If you are writing, The Question will keep you from becoming another piece of office equipment, unconcerned with consequences or the possibilities of improvement.

If you are reading, vary the emphasis. First, softly: "Does it *have* to be like this?" Then louder: "Does it have to be like *this*?" Annoy the writer into explaining. Occasionally, the explanation will be convincing. More often, it won't satisfy you—or the writer. And you may end up with something closer to human understanding.

You will find one *Rule,* or one *Blunder and Cure,* more useful than any other. But before you start skipping around to find what touches you closest, get a sense of the whole. Read all the Rules over once lightly, in *Short Form* and the two pages of *The Rules Stated.*

The order of Rules is not a gauge of importance nor a schedule of writing mechanics. Still, the order is not by guess.

Before any improvement is possible, the old claim to precision must be recognized as myth, overawing good writers and giving bad writers the contentment of the halter. *Rule 1 (Peculiar)* is aimed at convincing you that peculiarity is not the royal road to precision. Lest you be oversold, *Rule 2 (Precise)* will spare you the debilitating belief that all attempts at precision are doomed.

English (Rule 3) is the way out of the mess legal writers have tolerated for too long. They must come to think the unthinkable: their writing is mainly English; and unless it is good English, it isn't worth writing. Besides, today more than ever before, the idea of *Clarity (Rule 4)* is tied closely to the persistent urging on all sides that legal writers speak to people in language they can understand.

But don't be carried away by *Rule 4,* not *Clear* at any cost, even forgetting the law. That's why *Law* is *Rule 5,* a reminder that this kind of writing has a special mission.

Like each of the others, *Rule 6 (Plan)* has a special claim to first rank. Planning must precede writing. In the order here, planning takes cognizance of the materials the planner must work with. But without *Plan,* only rubble.

For many writers *Cut! (Rule 7)* ought to be number one, as verbosity is the most ancient sin of legal writing. *Cut!* ends the list: no matter how well done the job to this point, your legal writing will be better if leaner.

Some grace notes.

Documentation, historical and practical, in *The Language of the Law* is not repeated here, but is certainly available.

Most examples of *lawsick* are bad for a number of reasons. Editorial focus on one crime against the language should alert you to the likely presence of others.

Most examples of *lawsick* are not made-up. They are undocumented because not unique, and because their authors—for all I know—may even repent.

PART ONE

The Seven Rules

THE SEVEN RULES:

Short Form

RULE 1.

Peculiar

THE LANGUAGE OF THE LAW IS MORE PECULIAR THAN PRECISE.
DON'T CONFUSE PECULIARITY WITH PRECISION.

RULE 2.

Precise

DON'T IGNORE EVEN THE LIMITED POSSIBILITIES OF PRECISION. THE PRICE OF SLOPPY WRITING IS MISUNDERSTANDING AND CREATIVE MISINTERPRETATION.

RULE 3.

English

FOLLOW THE RULES OF ENGLISH COMPOSITION.

RULE 4.

Clear

USUALLY YOU HAVE A CHOICE OF HOW TO SAY IT. CHOOSE CLARITY.

RULE 5.

Law

WRITE LAW SIMPLY.
DO NOT PUFF, MANGLE, OR HIDE.

RULE 6.

Plan

BEFORE YOU WRITE, PLAN.

RULE 7.

Cut!

CUT IT IN HALF!

THE SEVEN RULES:

The Rules Stated

RULE 1.
Peculiar

THE LANGUAGE OF THE LAW IS MORE PECULIAR
THAN PRECISE.
DON'T CONFUSE PECULIARITY WITH PRECISION.

Precision is sometimes peculiarly expressed,
but don't be taken in by the
peculiar expression of nonsense.

RULE 2.
Precise

DON'T IGNORE EVEN THE LIMITED POSSIBILITIES
OF PRECISION. THE PRICE OF SLOPPY
WRITING IS MISUNDERSTANDING
AND CREATIVE MISINTERPRETATION.

Some day someone will read what you have written,
trying to find something wrong with it. This is
the special burden of legal writing, and the
special incentive to be as precise as you can.

RULE 3.
English

FOLLOW THE RULES OF ENGLISH COMPOSITION.

If it's bad writing by the standards of ordinary English,
it is bad legal writing.
If it's good writing by the standards of ordinary English,
it is more likely to be good legal writing.

RULE 4.

Clear

USUALLY YOU HAVE A CHOICE OF HOW TO SAY IT.
CHOOSE CLARITY.

Lack of clarity is a common but not necessary
feature of legal writing. It is not an inevitable by-product
of precision. Clarity depends more on how you say it
than on what you have to say.
As you write, keep asking, "Clear to whom?"

RULE 5.

Law

WRITE LAW SIMPLY.
DO NOT PUFF, MANGLE, OR HIDE.

The only thing about legal writing that is both unique
and necessary is law. To simplify legal writing, first
get the law right. You can't simplify by omitting what
the law requires or including what the law forbids. The
better you know the law the easier to decide what law
ought to go in, and what is overkill or window dressing.

RULE 6.

Plan

BEFORE YOU WRITE, PLAN.

In the quiet time before you become excited with your
own words-on-paper, plan. Talk over the goals with
those who know more facts than you do, and maybe
even more law. Mull, jot, fret, read, outline. Then write. If
you start from a plan, the writing will help your thinking
and writing. Unplanned, the flow of words becomes a
distraction.

RULE 7.

Cut!

CUT IT IN HALF!

Repeat the operation until you run out of time
or material. Don't say the same thing twice inadvertently. Rewrite. Rewrite. Rewrite.

THE SEVEN RULES:

The Rules Outlined

RULE 1. THE LANGUAGE OF THE LAW IS MORE PECULIAR

Peculiar THAN PRECISE.

DON'T CONFUSE PECULIARITY WITH PRECISION.

Precision is sometimes peculiarly expressed,
but don't be taken in by the
peculiar expression of nonsense.   **1**

RULE 2.

Precise

DON'T IGNORE EVEN THE LIMITED POSSIBILITIES
OF PRECISION. THE PRICE OF SLOPPY
WRITING IS MISUNDERSTANDING
AND CREATIVE MISINTERPRETATION.

Some day someone will read what you have written,
trying to find something wrong with it. This is
the special burden of legal writing, and the
special incentive to be as precise as you can. **15**

RULE 4.

Clear

USUALLY YOU HAVE A CHOICE OF HOW TO SAY IT. CHOOSE CLARITY.

Lack of clarity is a common but not necessary feature of legal writing. It is not an inevitable by-product of precision. Clarity depends more on how you say it than on what you have to say.

RULE 5.
Law

WRITE LAW SIMPLY.
DO NOT PUFF, MANGLE, OR HIDE.

The only thing about legal writing that is both unique and necessary is law. To simplify legal writing, first get the law right. You can't simplify by omitting what the law requires or including what the law forbids. The better you know the law the easier to decide what law ought to go in, and what is overkill or window dressing. **100**

RULE 6.

BEFORE YOU WRITE, PLAN.

Plan

In the quiet time before you become excited with your own words-on-paper, plan. Talk over the goals with those who know more facts than you do, and maybe even more law. Mull, jot, fret, read, outline. Then write. If you start from a plan, the writing will help your thinking and writing. Unplanned, the flow of words becomes a distraction.   **114**

RULE 7.   CUT IT IN HALF!

Cut!   Repeat the operation until you run out of time or material. Don't say the same thing twice inadvertently. Rewrite. Rewrite. Rewrite.   **126**

THE SEVEN RULES:

The Rules Explained

RULE 1.

Peculiar

THE LANGUAGE OF THE LAW IS MORE PECULIAR
THAN PRECISE.
DON'T CONFUSE PECULIARITY WITH PRECISION.

Precision is sometimes peculiarly expressed,
but don't be taken in by the
peculiar expression of nonsense.

The first quick exposure to the language used by lawyers is enough to convince anyone that something is wrong, or at least peculiar. Lawsick.

Two ordinary people sit down to write out a simple contract. They get off to a good, precise start with two words:

We agree. . .

Soon the good start stumbles. They get help. They start over. The contract now says nothing more than it said before, but there is more of it:

In consideration of the agreements herein contained, the parties hereto agree . . .

An aroma as distinctive as stale cigar fills the room. A lawyer has been here. Or someone trying to imitate one. Somebody stumbled on a form. It is made to look different. So that people will know this is legal. Peculiar sells it. Like lawyers write. It's supposed to be peculiar.

Agreement about the language of the law usually goes one step farther. With a charity born of ignorance, most people believe that there must be a good reason why lawyers write like they were trying to reach spirits long departed. The lawyers say so. The difference between ordinary people and lawyers is that ordinary people take all of this on faith, and lawyers should know better.

Ordinary people buy the reason the lawyers have sold them. *Law has to be written in this peculiar way in order to be precise.* Fortunately, that statement is not true.

Give 100 competent lawyers the same facts and the same law, and tell them to write the contract the facts and law require. Turn off the telephones, and lock them in separate rooms. You will end up with 100 different contracts, some more precise than others. Almost all of them peculiar, but not peculiar in the same way. A few will be written in common garden-variety English, and right on the button. With the rarest of exceptions, there is no single right way to express law with precision. The judges prove this with every new opinion. Most often, the law may be expressed most precisely without being peculiar at all.

How the language of the law became lawsick makes a fascinating tale. Full of vice, virtue, chance, habit. No single reason explains it all.

This is no tale of conspiracy of the profession against the people. Most lawyers are as ignorant as their clients of the history of the language of the law. They believe that in their language everything is precise, especially if it's peculiar. Generations of lawyers have accepted the easy rationalization passed on to them. In the language of the law little bits of precise and peculiar mingle freely with the great mass of just peculiar. The peculiar also mingles freely with ordinary English, badly mangled. The forms that give the illusion of safety are full of indiscriminate peculiarity. Lawyers are born into the profession learning to follow or be damned. Or worse—disbarred. Or worse—never admitted.

So the first thing to know about legal writing is that the peculiarity of the language of the law has nothing to do with precision. Legal writing doesn't have to be lawsick. What a relief! Relax, and read on.

Point 1

Precision Rare

Do not count on automatic precision by the use of special law words. Some of the most peculiar words in the law are the least precise. Most law words are not precise. Neither antiquity nor origin (Latin, French, Old or Middle English) is a reliable index to current precision.

a. Junk antiques of the legal vocabulary

Many of the words that we now identify as law words never were precise, and were not originally peculiar. Lawyers started using them because they were the common currency of people able to write, not because they were either precise or distinctive. The fashion in words changed, but the formbooks didn't. In surviving, these words have not become what they never pretended to be—precise. These are the junk antiques of the legal vocabulary.

[1] Ordinary Old and Middle English words

Appendix A is a representative sampling of law words that were ordinary words in the English of 400 years ago, with no claim to precision then or now. They range from *aforesaid* through *witnesseth*.
The list includes along the way legal favorites like:

> *said*—as an adjective;
> *same*—as a noun (used for comic effect in *Destry Rides Again*,
>   "and tell them I'm having the same");
> *therefor*—note the absence of a final *e*.

Today, these words are just peculiar. There are current, better substitutes for all of them in ordinary English language dictionaries. To
use the old words in the unthinking belief that they are somehow precise because they are old is looking for trouble. Some of them have
disappointed generations of lawyers searching for precision, words litigated and found lacking, e.g., *aforesaid, forthwith, hereafter, hereby,
herein, hereinafter, heretofore, said, whereas*. Even that has been insufficient to overcome habit.

□ **For example:**
In the United States Archives is a White House letterhead signed by Richard Nixon on August 9, 1974. It is addressed to Secretary of State Kissin-
ger, and says:

> I hereby resign the Office of President of the United States.

It is a sad, short letter. It could have been shorter and just as effectively
ended the Presidency of Mr. Nixon. Some might have been satisfied with

> I resign,

but something less equivocal was called for. It could have said

> I resign as President of the United States.

"The office" is excess description; the Constitution describes that office as
"President of the United States of America." The extra flourish on such a
formal occasion does no harm. But the *hereby* is pure legal kneejerk. It is
definitely not precise. It adds nothing to "I resign," except to tell us that a
lawyer had a hand in the writing. We all knew that already. The saddest
and truest words of Watergate are from the "Nixon Transcript," the President to Mr. Dean: "Hell, I don't need a lawyer."

[2] Coupled synonyms

Appendix B is a representative sampling of law words that take the form of coupled synonyms. This was once a vogue of writers in English generally, not just lawyers. Lawyers followed the language fashions of ordinary English, because it was the fashion, but not for that reason precise.

In ordinary English the fashion has changed. *Wrack (rack) and ruin, safe and sound, might and main, part and parcel,* when they occasionally surface, are clichés. The formbooks and papers prepared by lawyers never stopped following the old, still unprecise fashion. Some of these doubled words are bilingual, picturesquely (but nothing more than that) reflecting the mixture of languages that have come to be considered English. Like:

> *acknowledge and confess*—Old English and Old French
> *act and deed*—French or Latin and Old English
> *goods and chattels*—Old English and Old French
> *made and provided*—Old English and Latin.

Some of them are simply Old English repeating itself, like:

> *each and all*
> *from and after*
> *have and hold.*

Some are repetitions from French, like:

> *authorize and empower*
> *fraud and deceit*
> *null and void.*

Occasionally, coupled synonyms have acquired a special sense for lawyers, e.g., *aid and comfort, by and with, cease and desist, full faith and credit, had and received.*

□ **For example:**
Ordinary English dismisses the coupled bilingual synonym *leaps and bounds* (Middle Eng. & Fr.) as a cliché. The law's coupled French synonyms *metes and bounds* (boundary, boundary) have some utility in designating a surveyor's description of land.

Most of these repetitions add nothing but words and the sound of law. Some of them do offer opportunity, the opportunity to argue that special senses were intended, e.g., as with *fit and proper; force and ef-*

*fect; give, devise, and bequeath; null and void; rest, residue, and re-
mainder.*

Best to stay away from any repetitions, especially old ones. Even
good lawyers become confused; as in this description of an increasing
membership:

> We are almost 60,000 strong and we are growing by metes and
> bounds.

[3] Old formalisms

Appendix C is a representative sampling of law words that bespeak
the politesse of the world in which the law grew up. They never had
anything to do with precision, in the sense of exact meaning. In another age, their absence would simply have been unthinkable for anyone who wanted to remain a member of the profession. *Be it remembered, comes now the plaintiff, from the beginning of the world,
strangers to the blood,* on and on. Today, some lawyers continue to
use these formalisms. Many of them fortunately are reserved for talking not writing, e.g., *may it please the court, plaintiff rests, your honor.*
None of them adds to precision. One oddball, *ss,* is still so peculiar
that no one knows for sure what it means.

b. The Latin habit

Appendix D is a representative sampling of legal Latin terms, with
English equivalents that today are at least as precise and far more intelligible.

Centuries ago Latin was the required language of the writs, i.e.,
court orders requiring that something be done. It was once the principal language of statutes. It was the language of the formbooks. English was a wild, loose language, growing, absorbing grammar from
Latin and absorbing words from every language it touched. English
was not a language to be depended on. By comparison with unfixed
English, Latin generally was more precise. An educated person, especially a lawyer, was thoroughly grounded in Latin. No wonder that
lawyers acquired the Latin habit. The wonder is that they have kept it,
when the old reasons for it have disappeared.

Some of the law's Latin has been used for so long by so many
people that it is no longer looked upon as being Latin. It has been absorbed into ordinary English, e.g., *habeas corpus, affidavit, quorum.*

A number of Latin expressions have become terms of art, e.g.,
quo warranto, supersedeas.

Most of the Latin in the law no longer has the old competitive
advantage over English in any search for precision. Most of it de-

serves to be in the junk antique category (Point 1.a., p. 2); it was the fashion of a day that has passed. For lawyers at one time to say that the right to administer an estate had been granted *cum testamento annexo (c.t.a.)* was as ordinary and no more or less precise than to-day's English translation, *with the will annexed*. Some courts and some lawyers still use the Latin. So too with a court overturning the result of trial by jury, and giving judgment *non obstante veredicto (n.o.v.)*. Some courts and some lawyers still say it that way, but it is no more precise than today's English translation, *notwithstanding the verdict*. Some law professors delight in impressing a captive audience with the oral roll of the never precise legal maxims, e.g., *cessante ratione legis cessat ipse lex*. The thunder is lost in print, but the sense is not lost in translation, *when the reason for the rule ceases, the rule itself ceases*.

The lack of precision of some Latin has been giving lawyers headaches for centuries.

☐ **For example:**
Bona fide translates readily as *good faith*. But there is nothing precise about what lawyers mean by either *bona fide* or *good faith*.

Mens rea is often translated in legal usage as *guilty mind* or *criminal intent*. But whether Latin or English, the expression lives in constant controversy.

Except for limited service as terms of art, the chief function of Latin in the law today is to add confusion, not precision. Lawyers and their clients, even judges, suffer with it. Sometimes it shows.

☐ **For example:**

terminus a quo = *the end* [limit] *from which;* freely, *the starting point*.

Why use the Latin to come up with this:

"It is the *terminus a quo* from and after which . . ."?

c. Law French

Appendix E is a representative sampling of law French terms, with English equivalents that today are at least as precise, far more intelligible to lawyers as well as non-lawyers, and usually much easier to pronounce.

It is part of the history of the legal profession in this country that for centuries lawyers in England did not speak English in court. They used a variety of French, now generally referred to as *law French*. Englishmen, trained in the law, brought their vocabulary to America.

Some of what was once law French has become commonplace, accepted as part of ordinary English, e.g., *appeal, contract, evidence*.

A number of law French terms have become terms of art, e.g., *estoppel, laches, voir dire*.

Most of what is still distinctively law French serves no useful purpose in the language of the law.

☐ **For example:**

The term *cestui que trust* (pronounced SET-A-KUH *trust*) is no more precise than *beneficiary of a trust*. Some lawyers still use a nickname, *cetty*.

See also law French *demise* (Rule 2.3, p. 21), and *alien* and *assigns* (Rule 4.1, p. 64).

d. Flexible words

Appendix F is a representative sampling of flexible words associated with the law and lawyers.

These law words, a very large group, don't look like law words at all. They don't look peculiar. The only thing peculiar about them is that anyone could possibly think them precise. These are the flexible words, deliberately flexible, the lawyer's *reasonable (reasonable care, reasonable doubt, reasonable man, reasonable speed, reasonable time)*, and *due* and *undue*, *adequate* and *inadequate*, etc. These are useful words. They are "legal." The law could not get along without them. But the one thing they are not is precise.

e. Terms of art

What lawyers really mean to be talking about when they speak with pride of the precision of the language of the law is the legal term of art. Where lawyers mislead themselves, and everyone else, is in believing that most of the words they use are terms of art. They tend to forget the very limited scope of the expression itself. *A legal term of art is a technical word with a specific meaning.* It is important to keep in mind what the definition includes and what it excludes.

[1] "Tradition" not enough

Though used for centuries, many law words either are not technical or have no specific meaning, and so are not terms of art. That removes from the charmed circle of terms of art a substantial chunk of the legal vocabulary.

Right off it excludes *all* of the words described above as Ordinary Old and Middle English, Old formalisms, and Flexible words. It also excludes *most* of the words described above as Coupled synonyms, the Latin habit, and Law French.

[2] "Precedent" not enough

You can't rely on precedent alone to make a term of art. There is more precedent for the use of law words than there is for law itself. That's the trouble with precedent to establish meaning. There is too much of it. And it keeps changing.

Every time an appellate judge drops a written word, some sort of precedent has been born. It's not a genuine, honest-to-Coke precedent unless what the judge says about this particular word was necessary to the decision. But lawyers cannot always be certain which of the too many words about words in an opinion were necessary, and which were only incidental, *dictum* (Latin for *something said*). No lawyer and no judge can possibly keep up with the millions of words that pour from the appellate courts. Even if it's a precedent in Alabama, it's not a precedent in Wyoming (though it is something you can talk about). Even if it's a precedent from the Supreme Court of the United States, that gives little assurance that new justices would follow the usage. Above all, as with all precedent in the law and especially with precedent about the meaning of words, a precedent is only a precedent if the circumstances of the earlier cases are substantially repeated. Change the context, and precedent evaporates like the morning dew.

As a result you have hundreds of precedents for the usage of hundreds of law words. And the yield of precision is close to a good clear zero. The now massive *Words and Phrases* (70 volumes in Spring, 1962, 90 in Spring, 1979) demonstrates the impossibility of finding precision by precedent. Precedent points in too many directions.

☐ For example:

Precedent says that *cause of action* refers to facts, and precedent says that *cause of action* refers to rights. Precedent says that *cancellation* means *termination,* and does not mean *termination.* It says that *accident* can refer to something done intentionally, and that it can't; that *proximate cause* means only a *direct cause,* and that it may also mean an *indirect cause.*

Don't bank on the precedents to give you terms of art. Look further.

[3] "Requirement" not enough

Sometimes a statute or a court order or a government regulation will require that specific words be used. That requirement does not turn the word into a term of art.

□ **For example:**

A statute may require that a witness be sworn to tell *the truth, the whole truth, and nothing but the truth.* It has to be done that way. It is also traditional; some think it impressive. But none of that makes the oath more precise, for having three truths instead of one.

The exact wording of jury instructions is prescribed in some states. If you say it that way you have complied with the law, but that does not mean that the jury instruction or its language is precise. You may repeat the words required by a government regulation till you run out of ink, but that won't give the words of that regulation the sharpness of edge required to make them terms of art. Requirement and precision sometimes join, but don't count on it.

[4] "Argot" not enough

Appendix G is a representative sampling of legal argot, with equivalents in ordinary English.

Precisely or not, lawyers spend a lot of time talking to each other. As with any other group (police, plumbers, soldiers, street people, teachers) who repeat common tasks, and have much in common to discuss, lawyers have shorthand ways of talking with each other. The words of that talking are called argot. Often quite useful, some of it carries fairly specific, if untechnical, meaning, but falls short of the sharpness of terms of art.

□ **For example:**

For centuries lawyers have been talking and writing about *Blackacre* as a hypothetical piece of real estate. They have never been certain why they chose it or why they keep it, except that it's traditional and useful. It is learned in law school and carries into the practice. It serves a purpose of quick communication, but it is not technical nor are its edges sharp. So with a *horse case,* one *on all fours,* i.e., an earlier case just like this one.

The variety of lawyer's argot is endless, some of it no more than slang. Fortunately, most argot is used in speaking about the law, not writing about it, and so is subject to quick correction if anyone is confused.

9

[5] The McCoy

Appendix H is a representative sampling of legal terms of art, together with short explanations in ordinary English.

The legal term of art is the nearest lawyers have come to tying down the meaning of words. If it is really *a technical word with a specific meaning* it can only be used in a carefully restricted setting. Variety is out. It is not flexible. It is not *reasonable.* The sharper the technicality and the more specific the meaning, the more closely limited are the circumstances that justify its use. Tradition, precedent, requirement, even argot may reinforce the making of a term of art. But ultimately it earns the title by persistent professional use in only one way to achieve a specific legal end.

Where do you find words like that?

[a] Adjective law

The technicalities that hold the law together and keep it running make up the largest single category of legal terms of art. They describe the working mechanisms of the legal process. The words are the names of the legal remedies to redress specific grievances, and of the procedural details that make those remedies work. This whole topic is sometimes described as *adjective law,* as distinguished from *substantive law.*

Lawyers who practice in court become acutely aware of a whole technical vocabulary that helps them get things done. Their professional lives depend on repeated use of the procedures of the law. They learn the details through repeated, practical testing. Repeated experience teaches as nothing else can that using one procedure unlocks the doors and using another does not.

At its simplest level, some of the technical words become familiar to the public through the press, and to a lesser extent through jury service and personal litigation. A lawsuit usually begins with a *plaintiff* suing a *defendant.* The plaintiff's *complaint* is met by the defendant's *answer.* Or the defendant *demurs* or *moves to dismiss:* Even if what you say were true, you don't have a legal leg to stand on.

From that beginning, the lawsuit goes in a hundred different directions. Each calls into service special language of procedure and evidence, increasingly technical, yet conveying definite ideas to others in the profession. *Fictitious defendants, garnishment, quo warranto* (Latin, by what warrant), *mandamus* (Latin, we command) *subpoena duces tecum* (Latin, under a penalty bring with you), *voir dire* (Old French, speak the truth), etc. Soon the non-lawyer is lost. And when the lawyer *moves* that the judge *recuse* himself, i.e., formally requests that the judge disqualify himself from hearing the case, a newspaper reporter would have it that the lawyer *motioned* and the judge was *rescued.*

Terms of art here are the names for the details of a lawsuit and how to run it. Lawyers who have anything to do with lawsuits have to know the details and their names, as auto mechanics know pistons and camshafts, and doctors know systolic and diastolic blood pressure. These terms of art are addressed to lawyers and judges in papers filed in court, and the judges hand them back in opinions. Lawyers write treatises about these details, but again, the writing is for lawyers. Outside of this tight circle, few people need these terms of art. Lawyers themselves have no need for them except for the working details of the legal machine. And then, you had better know that it's a Phillips screwdriver that you need, and not a monkey wrench.

[b] Legal specialities

Technical, specialized words within a specialized branch of the law make up another large category of legal terms of art. These words are often so technical that a lawyer in general practice, or a lawyer in a different legal specialty, cannot cope with them at all.

[i] **Land law**   The land law, what lawyers call the law of *real property*, supplies the greatest number of specialty terms of art. These are the specialty terms of art with the widest recognition within the profession. This is an old area of legal technicality; technicality established here has been used by analogy to develop technicality in other fields of law, e.g., *personal property*. In a society centered on private ownership of property, techniques of acquiring property, holding on to it, and disposing of it are a continuing preoccupation of lawyers. Terms of art are the building blocks. All lawyers call them out as familiars, even when their handling of the technical operations of acquiring, holding, and disposing is less than expert. All lawyers recognize the names: *fee simple*, the basic absolute ownership of property; *covenants running with the land*, agreements about land that bind and benefit whoever owns it; *words of purchase*, that tell who takes an estate, and *words of limitation*, that describe its duration; the *rule against perpetuities*, that limits an owner's power to designate the future owners of the property; etc.

[ii] **Other specialities**   The law, like medicine, has numerous specialities, each with its own terms of art. Few lawyers outside the specialist group use them at all. One of the older specialities is the law of the sea, *admiralty law*, with its *libellant* (for plaintiff), *libelee* (for defendant), and *libel* (for complaint), etc. Another specialty, old but still growing like crab grass, is *tax law*, its terms of art occurring with such profuse repetition that many outside the speciality recognize them. *Capital gain, loss carryback, boot*, etc. The list of specialities goes on and on, *anti-trust, commercial, patent law*, etc. In each the

pattern is similar: repeated use by practitioners, constant refinement, accepted restriction to a peculiar, severely limited context. A term of art is born.

[c] Miscellany

Apart from recognized specialities in the practice, there are many readily identifiable, distinct areas of the law, e.g., conflicts, constitutional law, contracts, criminal law, torts, etc. In each of these fields also, repeated technical use in a special way has hardened some words into terms of art. In contracts, *novation, third party beneficiary,* etc. In constitutional law, *search and seizure, double jeopardy, self-incrimination,* etc.

As with terms of art in the adjective law and the specialities, terms of art in miscellaneous areas of the law find their place in very limited contexts. You may draw countless contracts, statutes, regulations, without ever being called upon to use a term of art. You may discuss the constitution endlessly, focusing on a single term of art, but most of the discussion will use ordinary English, or terms of art from the adjective law or the specialties. Terms of art are self-limiting. They are an important, but small part of the language of the law.

f. Constant change

Understanding law words, with their peculiarity, comes only with long struggle. After even partial mastery, lawyers tend to regard change in the language of the law as a dead historical phenomenon. It isn't. Any estimate of the precision of law words must take into account that they don't stay put. As with language generally, especially English, the language of the law has a history of constantly changing usage. The process continues, in the direction of more precision, and less.

Continuous use in a constricted context has given a limited precision to some old tautologies, e.g., *aid and comfort, cease and desist, full faith and credit.* More dramatic has been the decline and fall of some of the law's most technical and precise terms of art. Some of them have simply fallen into disuse; nobody needs them anymore. Less than a handful of states still countenance a *fee tail.* It is a shriveled survivor, finding ancient companionship of the *fee tail male* and *fee tail female* in law school texts. Other terms of art, like the stalwarts *feoffment* and *seisin,* have been swept aside by the currents of change in both law and language; using them today on the assumption of precision, you risk disaster.

As it must to all words, a time comes in the history even of a term of art when something else says it just as well, or even better. When that day arrives, the term of art is on its way out. If that sounds gloomy, proceed to Point 2.

Point 2.

When In Doubt

When in doubt, err on the side of assuming that law words are not precise, and explain yourself.

The language of the law has not overcome the basic imprecision of language generally. Like the common speech, it relies on words, not numbers, and like the commonest speech, it is concerned more with people than with abstractions. In the quiet of your library you can swallow large doses of abstraction; no one ever died of a dictionary definition. Law words in action are another matter. They can kill you (a *death warrant*), take away your property (a *writ of execution*), or put you in the catbird seat (holding *irrevocable proxies*). With that much at stake, few words that tangle with the law are tough enough to come out unbruised. Lawyers ought to know that, but they have spent so much time learning law words that the temptation to use them, as learned, becomes irresistible.

Contrary to the ancient maxim, familiarity with law words breeds respect among lawyers, and among those who follow the lawyer made trails. Yet as Point 1 shows, the odds on a law word being precise make it a poor bet. Continuous change in society and the law, changing decisions, changing legal routines, changing language habits of lawyers and of ordinary people with whom they deal and whose lives they share—all reduce the possibilities of fixing the meaning of law words.

Is this a term of art, old nonsense, or the language of the legal marketplace—slangy, more or less precise? Sometimes it is difficult if not impossible to be sure of the words you use.

☐ **For example:**
Law dictionaries, statutes, regulations, opinions give you a definition:

> *fair market value* = the price that would be paid by a willing buyer to a willing seller, neither under compulsion, and both reasonably informed.

Other expressions are often said to be synonymous, *actual cash value, fair cash value, reasonable market value,* etc. Does *fair market value* mean the same thing in tax cases that it means in condemnation cases? Does it

13

mean the same thing in all kinds of tax cases? What if there is no market? What if the sales are few? Does the definition vary with the kind of property? With the kind of buyer and seller? What is compulsion? etc. Is *fair market value* a legal term of art? Or something the accountants have to answer for? Is it precise?

☐ **For example:**
Dictionaries, including law dictionaries, say that when used as a noun,

prior = the head of a convent, ranking next to an abbot.

Lawyers, with more knowledge of criminal law than of convents, make a different connection.

prior = an earlier conviction; and
no priors = no earlier convictions.

Trial judges use it. Appellate judges use it. Non-lawyers familiar with the criminal courts understand it that way.

What precisely is it that they understand? The shorthand for *earlier conviction* does not specify conviction of what, nor whether felony or misdemeanor. *No priors* does not really mean what it seems to say; there might have been a *prior* that the law will not permit in evidence. Lawyers argue about what kind of conviction that might be. Yet to an habitué of the criminal courts, *prior* and *no priors* refer to an earlier conviction (a) that might bring a steeper (*enhanced* is the expression) sentence for a second conviction, or (b) that can be used to impeach a witness. The stage of litigation reveals which. *Prior* and *no priors* lean heavily on context. What would the words mean in an application for employment? Or for a license?

Are *prior* and *no priors* terms of art? Argot? Precise?

If you assume precision, and use a law word as though it were precise, you risk all the evils of interpretation. If you assume lack of precision, and spell out what you are talking about, you risk being thought an ignoramus by some lawyers. What you stand to gain is accomplishing your purpose. That's a pretty good tradeoff.

RULE 2.

Precise

DON'T IGNORE EVEN THE LIMITED POSSIBILITIES OF
PRECISION. THE PRICE OF SLOPPY WRITING IS
MISUNDERSTANDING AND CREATIVE MISINTERPRETATION.

Some day someone will read what you have written,
trying to find something wrong with it. This is
the special burden of legal writing, and the
special incentive to be as precise as you can.

When you have acquired a healthy skepticism about the precision of law words and are beset with doubts about the possibility of ever attaining precision, then what?

Point 1.

Precise-As-You-Can

Precision-as-myth is not a license to carelessness.
Precise-as-you-can takes longer, and is well worth it.
You can be a little bit precise.

"Precise" is not an absolute; it's not all or nothing. Legal writing at its best tries to be as precise as can be, using everything at the writer's command. That includes a discriminating use of terms of art; spelling things out when explanation helps to remove uncertainty; correct use of English, punctuation, and typography; and a planned sequence of ideas.

Abandoning even the striving for precision yields mush, mud, slush, fuzz; call it what you will; it takes many forms, none a credit to the writer, nor a help to the reader.

☐ For example:
A "plain language" bill, passed by one house of a state legislature (not enacted), required "understandable terms." It said in part (but without the italics):

"Written agreements covered under this act *shall only permit* the following terms:
    a. *Terms* whose meaning is generally *understandable to persons other than persons with more than* a twelfth grade reading level. . ."

Did they mean to eliminate language understandable to those who had gone beyond the twelfth grade? Or did they mean to say this?

> a. *Terms* whose meaning is generally *understandable even to persons with no more than* a twelfth grade reading level. . .

The ambiguity of daily speech, like lawyer's courtroom argot, is subject to quick correction if it matters. What doesn't matter in over-the-fence conversation, or even in casual writing, may matter in court.

☐ **For example:**

> Over-the-fence gossip: "To my knowledge, A hit B."
> Neighbor: "He had it coming."
> *or*
> Neighbor: "You mean you saw A hit B?"
> Gossip: "Oh no, but that's what I heard."
>
> No harm done.
>
> In court papers: "The testimony was
>
> 'To my knowledge, A hit B.' "
> *to my knowledge* = 1. *I know* (of my own knowledge)
> = 2. *As far as I know* (to the best of my knowledge).

The distinction is critical.

Point 2.

The Interpretation of Sloppy Writing

Sloppy writing requires special attention, and usually gets it, in court.

All writing requires some interpretation. If you write as precisely as possible, there is always the chance that a reader might not understand it exactly as you did. The market price might change since the contract was signed, and someone is looking for a way out. The pressure on courts to be "fair," to do justice, sometimes results in interpretations of language that no competent writer could have anticipated. These are ordinary hazards of legal writing.

Sloppy writing multiplies the hazards of interpretation. Even a normal, honest reader has to spend much more time and effort just to figure out what it's all about. And to the natural stimulus of self-interest, sloppy writing adds the spark that kindles creative misinterpretation. It is the direct route to misunderstanding and lawsuits. To the harassed middler between writer and reader, the judge, sloppy writing provides the occasion for trotting out the clichés of construction, also known as the "rules" for the interpretation of writings.

a. The plain meaning rule

Like the other "rules" of interpretation, *plain meaning* is a label the judge stamps on a writing. "Plain meaning" is a stamp of approval. The judge is saying:

> The place to begin is the words of the writing. I understand them. They have been used with such care that any normal person (like me) should understand them. I accept their plain meaning.

No one says it quite as well as A.P. Herbert's Lord Mildew:

> "If Parliament does not mean what it says, it must say so."

That is the simplest and recurrent sense of the plain meaning rule. Beyond that, the going is sticky.

"Plain meaning" does not necessarily mean literal meaning. "Husband and wife are one." ("If the law supposes that," said Dickens's Mr. Bumble, "the law is a ass, a idiot.")

"Plain meaning" that results in an absurdity will not be accepted. In one of the judiciary's favorite clichés, to follow "plain meaning" down that rat hole would be "to exalt form over substance." "I promise to pay you everything you owe me."

"Plain meaning" may be shown to be ambiguous by evidence outside the writing. "I give my property to Roxy Russell." It turns out there are two Roxy Russells, both airedales, one dead.

The upshot of all this is that if you have written well, as precisely as can be, the opportunities for misunderstanding and creative misinterpretation are restricted. Precise writing is a discouragement to fault finders. You too may hit the jackpot—"plain meaning."

b. Interpretation favoring intent

One "well-established rule" is the rule favoring an interpretation that carries out intent—of the testator, the legislature, etc. (See the good discussion on legislative "intent" vs. legislative "purpose," in Dickerson, *The Interpretation and Application of Statutes* [1975], Chapters 7 and 8.)

The argument is endless. How do you find "intent"? Especially "intent" on a topic never considered? The "rule" is not a "rule," but a practical notion. If you can, try to make sense out of a writing. But if the writing is clear without "interpretation," usually no one starts looking for "intent." Don't invite the search.

c. Everything means something

Smile when you call this a "rule": that interpretation is favored that gives meaning to all the words in a writing. Of course.

☐ For example:

"I agree to deliver a horse and a mare." Is the agreement satisfied if I deliver two mares?

The agreement is ambiguous. In one sense *horse* is a general description that includes a mare. In another sense it means only geldings and stallions, not mares. If "horse" here means "mare," why did the writer say "a horse and a mare" rather than "two mares"?

The "rule" is not a rule that you can count on. It is rather the expression of an old hope that people will use words to say something. It is discussed in Point 3 (p. 20), Beware the Twofer.

d. Interpretation by context

Several of the "rules" give resounding Latin restatement to the old saw that we understand what we read in the context of other words, other ideas, other things.

[1] Words are known by the company they keep

The Latin is *noscitur a sociis* (pronounced KNOW-SA-TER AH SOSH-E-EES), loosely, one is known by the company he keeps. Words are interpreted in the light of other words in the writing. *Draw a draft* is at home in a saloon or a bank. *Draw a light draft* resolves ambiguity in favor of beer.

[2] Writings on same topics similarly interpreted

The Latin is *in pari materia*, loosely, on the same topic. This is a specialized application of being known by one's company. Writings, especially statutes, dealing with the same topic should ordinarily be given the same interpretation. In similar contexts, the meaning of words should ordinarily be uniformly interpreted.

[3] Specific listing reveals the general category

The Latin is *ejusdem generis* (pronounced YOU-SSS-DEM-GENEROUS), of the same kind. This is another specialized application of being known by one's company. General words following a listing of specific words are construed to be limited to the same sort specifically listed. "Bring a shovel, a rake, a hoe, and other things for the garden" should not include a 10-ton tractor. Why give anyone the opportunity to suggest it?

[4] Inclusion of one excludes the other

The Latin is *inclusio unius est exclusio alterius*. The "rule" says that if you specify something, but not everything of the same category, the reader may infer that unspecified items have been deliberately omitted.

☐ For example:

"This agreement may be changed by another written agreement."

Is the natural sense of that sentence that the agreement cannot be changed by an *oral* agreement? Maybe. If the agreement "may be changed *only* by another written agreement," why didn't it say so? Careful writing can eliminate the questions and the maxim, in Latin or English.

e. If you made it uncertain, suffer

The "rule" says that uncertainties will be resolved against the one who caused the uncertainties. The "rule" is sometimes called by the Latin *contra proferentem* (against the offeror), and has also been called "the preparer principle." It is neither a rule nor a principle, for it all depends on a preliminary determination of uncertainty, with the writer insisting that there is a "plain meaning" and no uncertainty. When the writer loses that battle, he loses everything. The "rule" rubs salt in the wounds of the beaten writer: You have yourself to thank for what I am doing to you. The "rule" is commonly called down on the heads of insurers. If the writer had another writer looking over his shoulder (like opposing lawyers), who is the writer?

f. The rule of "rules"

The discussion here is not an exhaustive listing or description of the "rules" of interpretation. Sometimes they rationalize results, but they do not decide cases. And they give little guidance to the legal writer, except as a warning against sin. The best rule that a legal writer can derive from the "rules" of interpretation is part prayer, part resolution: Don't let them happen to me. Sloppy writing begets excessive interpretation. Avoid both.

Point 3.

Beware the Twofer

Do not use one word to convey more than
one of your meanings (A = *gawk;* and A = *squawk*).
And do not use more than one word to convey
your same meaning (A = *gawk;* and B = *gawk*).
Context affects these efforts, but you can affect the context.

One practical way to be more precise is to avoid the twofer—two meanings for one word and two words for one meaning. This is the old virtue of consistency, and applies to all parts of your writing, not only individual words but also the construction of phrases, sentences, and paragraphs. Easier to keep track of that way, which is a more casual way of saying it is more precise.

Some say you can't avoid the twofer. It is an old story that words are nervous. They won't stand still for anyone, for very long. Sometimes this old truth goes by the name of the "one-word-one-meaning-only-fallacy." The counsel of despair is don't attempt the impossible.

What this really means is that context, and "interpretation" used as scalpel or sledgehammer, may destroy the best of single-meaning intentions. When Swift had Gulliver explain that lawyers are bred to prove that *"White is Black, and Black is White,"* he thought he was writing satire. With a little bit of context, satire has blossomed into court interpretation.

All of this is telling you what someone else might do to you. You don't have to do it to yourself. You may not be able to foresee all possible contexts, but at least don't intentionally risk confusion.

Sticking to one word for *your* meaning, you avoid the "rule" preferring an interpretation that makes sense of all words. Different words raise at least a healthy suspicion that different meanings are intended. The "rule" reflects a polite regard (often unwarranted) for the capabilities of other writers. It also assumes (often erroneously) that a writer (especially a lawyer) is not changing words simply out of boredom. At least for legal writing, it is better to bore the reader than to confuse him, much worse to do both, not necessary to do either.

Taking care to hold the line at one word, one meaning, you increase your chances of achieving precision. Here are a number of common opportunities for slipping.

a. Words with several meanings

Dictionary fresh, most words have more than one meaning. That doesn't make them taboo. Some are very useful. Just handle with care.

[1] Single use

Even a single use of a word with several distinct meanings can create ambiguity.

☐ For example:

> *demise* = 1. death
> = 2. lease (noun and verb)
> = 3. convey
> = 4. conveyance

"The date of the demise" is ambiguous. Even if context can make the particular meaning clear, here there is no good reason to give the reader even a moment's pause. Don't use *demise* at all. Use ordinary English—*death, lease, convey, conveyance.*

☐ For example:

> *lease* (verb) = 1. to give someone the use of property under a lease (noun). [This speaks of what the lessor is giving.]
> = 2. to obtain use of property under a lease (noun). [This speaks of what the lessee is getting.]

In a statute, *"anyone leasing property"* is ambiguous. It could mean (and could have said) *"a lessor," "a lessee," "a lessor or lessee,"* etc.

Hire presents the same problem (see Rule 6, p. 115).

[2] Use repeated

A single, simple use of a word with several distinct meanings is trouble enough. Used more than once, confusion is inevitable, unless meaning is made overwhelmingly clear from context.

□ **For example:**

Sanction is a strange word that has found a permanent home in the law even though it has completely opposite meanings. As an added complication, *sanction* functions with equal maladroitness as verb or noun.

> *sanction* [noun] = approval
> = a penalty
> *sanction* [verb]   = approve
> = penalize.

Used only once, *sanction* can be tricky: *His conduct is sanctioned by Canon 5.* That can mean (and you had better say which):

(1) His conduct is approved by Canon 5, or
(2) Canon 5 imposes discipline for his conduct.

Used twice, with a *not* thrown in to liven things up, *sanction* has a field day: *The Board sanctioned his conduct. We will leave matters as they are. The Code does not sanction his conduct.* That can mean so many things you had best forget about *sanction.* Here are six of the possibilities:

(1) The Board approved his conduct, though the Code is silent.
(2) The Board approved his conduct, though the Code disapproves it.
(3) The Board approved his conduct, though the Code, while not approving it, does not impose discipline.
(4) The Board imposed discipline for his conduct, though the Code is silent.
(5) The Board imposed discipline, and the Code disapproves his conduct.
(6) The Board imposed discipline for his conduct, though the Code does not.

[3] What to do

[a] If you don't have to use words with several meanings, don't.
[b] If you feel a need to use a word, you don't have to use all its meanings at the same time: "Are you now in a state to state the state of the title in this state?"
[c] If you feel a need to use a word with several meanings, make *your* meaning crystal clear from the context.

b. Synonyms

In addition to the coupled synonyms of the law that are only relics, *null and void,* etc., legal writing is full of synonyms and near synonyms, some distinctly legal, some not. In one piece of legal writing, choose one word to express your meanings, and don't switch to a synonym or a near synonym.

☐ **For example:**
What do you say when you want to say that a contract says something? You can say, "The contract *says*."

You can also say, it *contains, describes, designates, discloses, expresses, fixes, identifies, lists, names, provides, sets forth, sets out, shows, specifies, states*, etc. Unless you have a reason, a distinction to be made, a deliberate and different shade of meaning in mind, don't hop from one to another for the sake of variation—or through inadvertence.

A contract says: "We have agreed to deliver the goods *indicated* in paragraph 1." Later on, it says: "You have agreed to accept the goods *specified* in paragraph 1." If you prefer *indicated* use that in both places; if you prefer *specified*, use that in both places.

If the context is the same, in the same writing, pick one word, and stay with it. Otherwise someone might come to the conclusion that the variation was intended to convey a different meaning, or at least could convey a different meaning. *Indicates* could be weaker than *specifies*. But how do I know for sure that you are drawing nice distinctions on word usage here, especially when I can't help but observe a certain tendency to sloppy writing elsewhere? If you have a nuance in mind, spoon feed it.

The policy of avoiding synonyms applies, all the more, to doubled and redoubled synonyms. Bad enough to use *null and void*, without any improvement over *void*. Worse yet to use *null and void* in line 10, topped by *null, void and of no further force or effect* in line 20.

A waste. A torment. Trouble.

c. Word alone, plus word with modifier

Your writing uses the word *necessary*, a word with a long history of flexibility, not an absolute. You use *necessary* repeatedly. Do you nod? Do you yearn for "elegant variation"? Do you want it to sound more "legal"? Or are you making a distinction when you suddenly throw in *reasonably necessary?* You have now joined to a flexible word the equally flexible modifier, *reasonably*. In a long writing you now begin to wobble between *necessary* and *reasonably necessary*. Do both say the same thing? Do you intend to toughen up plain *necessary* by the contrast with *reasonably necessary?* Do you intend to water down *necessary* by pointing out that it really means *reasonably necessary?* Are you deliberately leaving it for someone else to decide? Or don't you know what you are doing? The variations on this theme are endless.

☐ For example:

realization	*—effective realization*
demand	*—due demand* (or *duly demand*)
right of set-off	*—valid right of set-off*
obtain possession	*—lawfully obtain possession*
inoperative	*—wholly inoperative*

You are the one to make the decision. If it's one meaning you intend, stick to what says it best, either the one word or the word with modifier, but not both.

d. Definitions of convenience or confusion

Definitions are frequently useful in legal writing—contracts, statutes, regulations. They avoid repetition of details. They can make things more precise by tying down meaning. But definitions should be used with the greatest restraint, and only when they will really help. They can result in less rather than greater precision if you forget the twofer point. Here are some of the hazards.

[1] Forgetting your own definitions

In a writing of any length, one of the most difficult jobs is to remember and follow your own defintions.

☐ For example:

"As used in this statute, *automobile* means a vehicle with four wheels."

Ten paragraphs later, the statute speaks of "a six-wheeled automobile." If you apply the definition, the statute is now talking about "a six-wheeled vehicle with four wheels" or "a four-wheeled vehicle with six wheels." *Automobile* means one thing as defined and something else as used. Do the other provisions of the statute regulating automobiles apply to this six-wheeled contraption? Has the definition been revised or ignored or abandoned?

[2] "Unless the context otherwise requires"

One of the devices frequently used to avoid the embarrassment of the "six-wheeled vehicle with four wheels" is to preface a whole series of definitions with the cop-out "unless the context otherwise requires." That gets rid of the difficulty of following your own definitions.

But the price is not right. The formula abandons the client for whom the writing was prepared and the reader to whom it was addressed. It leaves them to the tender interpretation of strangers. If you define, you create an important part of the context. It is your responsibility to adjust your definition to fit your context, or your context to fit your definition, or to forget about definition as a route to precision.

☐ **For example:**

The Uniform Commercial Code says that unless the context otherwise requires:

> "*Banking day* means that part of any day on which a bank is open to the public for carrying on substantially all of its banking functions."

Five paragraphs later, the Uniform Commercial Code says that unless the context otherwise requires:

> "*Midnight deadline* with respect to a bank is midnight on its next banking day following the banking day on which it receives the relevant item. . ."

What an unusual bank whose *banking day* ends at midnight, open to the public for overdrafts. Or does the context require something else, like "the *date* of its next banking day"? Or maybe what is needed is new definition or new context. If your object is precision, your work is not complete when you have created a monster definition with a short life, or an environment in which your monster cannot survive. A definition prefaced by "unless the context otherwise requires" violates the twofer point. A = *gawk*, "unless the context otherwise requires," that A = *squawk*. Who is to decide?

[3] Mind benders

With or without the phony life preserver "unless the context otherwise requires," a *banking day* with a *midnight deadline* offends the sense of reality. Such definitions violate the twofer point, for the reader is unable to get off the world. The reader will continue to think and read in terms of two meanings for the same word: "It says that A = *gawk*, but I know that A really = *squawk*.

To serve the goal of precision in legal writing, a definition (if you find it desirable) ought to conform to language that people are famil-
i with. An alternative is a complete break with past experience, an
a straction that alerts the reader to be on guard.

[4] "This includes"

Many statements in contracts, statutes, and regulations that are passed off as definitions, complete with a reserved seat in the "definition section," are not definitions at all. They do not say this word means something, or *is* something; rather, this word *includes* something.

That doesn't mean it is improper to say that one word includes another. Maybe it does, as *animal* includes a *cow*, and *litigant* includes a *plaintiff*. But you must constantly be aware that you haven't defined *animal* or *litigant*. As pseudo-definition, the formula violates the twofer point.

☐ **For example:**

> "Definition. In this statute, *will* includes *codicil*."

This violates the twofer point coming and going. First, consider the fate of *will*.

The statute does not outlaw use of the word *will* in its ordinary sense, a will as distinct from the addition ordinarily called a *codicil*. So under the statute, *will* has two meanings. When the statute says *will* it might be talking about a *codicil* (A = *gawk*), or it might be talking about an ordinary will *will* (A = *squawk*).

> Second, consider the fate of *codicil*.

The statute does not outlaw use of the word *codicil*. So under the statute, there are now two ways of saying *codicil*. *Will*=*codicil* (A = *gawk*) and *codicial* = *codicil* (B=*gawk*). And sure enough, under a statute that says "*will* includes *codicil*," the formula is ignored, and the statute goes on to talk about *wills* and *codicils*.

e. Labels of convenience or confusion

Labels can be useful in legal writing to avoid repetition. In some instances they make for clarity. Labels are similar to definitions, and the hazards of definition are present here too. Labels of convenience should not be used unless there is clear gain. The serious risk is that they become labels of confusion.

[1] Worthless labels

Here is the opening of a Court of Appeal opinion:

> "This is a petition for a writ of prohibition to restrain the respondent superior court . . . from taking any action, except dismissal thereof in a writ of mandate proceeding pending in that court, wherein the real

parties in interest seek to set aside a decision of petitioner. . . For convenience the term 'petitioners' will be used to refer to petitioners in the present proceeding, who are the real parties in interest in the superior court proceedings; the term 'respondent' will refer to the superior court; and the term 'real parties in interest' or 'real parties' will be used to refer to real parties in interest, who are the petitioners in the superior court proceedings."

The confusion is of the writer's own making. No labels at all are required.

The opinion refers to two lawsuits; each has a name. The first one (in the Superior Court) is *Jones v. Board*. The second (in the Court of Appeal) is *Board v. Superior Court and Jones*.

Even if you don't want to tell a stranger any more about the case than the Court of Appeal has, you can make it clearer—and shorter.

Introduce a stranger to the case by using the ordinary names that have remained constant throughout:

Jones sued the Board in a writ of mandate proceeding to set aside a Board decision. The Board now asks us for a writ of prohibition to stop the Superior Court from going ahead with Jones' suit.

[2] Keep the label intact

A complaint deals with two businesses with closely similar names, The Marshall Jones Corporation and a partnership The Marshall Jones Company. You decide to label one "the Corporation" and the other "the Partnership," which could make it easier for anyone to follow the story line.

Once having made that decision, if the label is to serve its purpose, it must be used consistently throughout. If you oscillate between official name and label, you violate the twofer point. For the stranger (like a jury) you have multiplied the number of litigants to keep track of.

The same vice is inherent in the label with the escape hatch, "The Marshall Jones Corporation, *sometimes* called 'the Corporation.' "(This is similar to the definition good "unless the context otherwise requires.") The "sometimes" label gives the writer a freedom to slip freely from name to label without warning, leaving the reader with the burden of identification, and destroying whatever claim to precision or clarity the label was to achieve.

Label or don't label. If you do use a label, keep it intact.

Point 4.

Thou Shalt Not Never

A large part of the law consists of saying "No."
Too much of "No"-saying fosters ingenuity and rebellion.
Say "No" only when you have to.
And make sure your "No" means "No."

Legal writing has no monopoly on trouble with negatives. But what may be only an infelicity in ordinary writing can become a disaster in legal writing.

For years, the good English people have been touting the virtues of accentuating the positive, and warning of the perils of the negative. Still the blurb for an Agatha Christie mystery tells (or warns) prospective readers: "Cannot be too highly recommended." And George Orwell met with only limited success with his cure for "not un-": "A not unblack dog was chasing a not unsmall rabbit across a not un-green field."

My father knew the value of the right amount of negative coupled with lots of positive. When he was through with someone, he made sure you knew it. He said, "That man is a crook, a liar, and a thief, and what's more, he's no damn good."

A positive statement is easier to understand. Negatives have a habit of doubling and redoubling. They need close watching, or they will run away with meanings. Negatives can hedge a statement with nuance, at the same time making it difficult to fasten upon meaning with precision or clarity (which is why some people like them).

A large part of the law tells people what they can't do. "Thou shalt not kill" is a more widespread pattern than "Honor thy father and mother." When it isn't actually *prohibiting* (a popular way of saying "No"), the law spends a lot of time telling you what will happen if you *fail* to come up to a fixed standard (i.e., do not comply). In addition to these basic negative concepts, our system of law—criminal and civil—is an "adversary system," at least two distinct sides to almost everything: charge and *denial*, right and *limitation*. Negatives all over the place.

Our law is at its positive best with an affirmation of personal rights. But these rights too are cluttered with negative expression. The safeguards in the Bill of Rights are mostly framed in negatives —"Congress shall make no law. . ." etc. The presumption of innocence is customarily expressed in terms of proof *beyond a reasonable doubt.* Are you sure he's guilty? Maybe he's not.

Little wonder that people who work closely with the law (lawyers, judges, legislators, bureaucrats) become attuned to the sound of the negative. Negatives are commonplace. Affirmation is suspect. The law people become cautious about affirmative or positive assertion. Someone might even think you meant what you said. You could be sued. Make it tentative. Hesitate. Express doubt. Hedge. Wiggle, On the one hand "Yes," but on the other hand "No." "This shall not be construed to mean. . ." The negative becomes so deeply ingrained it is thrown in without much thought. When you really meant to say "Yes," what sometimes comes out is only half there ("maybe"), or ends up as "No," or in hopeless confusion.

Negatives cannot always be eliminated. They can be made respectable. The only respectable negatives for general legal use are those that are deliberately and unmistakably negative. You have to work at it, for negatives can sneak up on you. They come in so many varieties.

a. Negatives plain

No, not, never have a plainspeaking bluntness that ought to recommend them.

If the witness answers "No," why weaken and stretch it into "She answered in the negative"? I once read a transcript of courtroom testimony that reported the answer "No," when the witness had remained silent. To those in the courtroom the witness' hands, shoulders, and whole body gave an emphatically eloquent "No." As with many circumlocutions, "She answered in the negative" would have had a technical accuracy, but that's all. Vague, and no force.

But plain negatives have other problems.

No, not, never, and none are perilously absolute. Judges and lawyers, like ordinary people, will strain to beat the inevitable. If there is any possible alternative, someone is sure to find it. In the name of "commonsense," or being "practical," or "extraordinary circumstances," someone will discover an exception to the apparent harsh absolutism of the plain negative. Are you really sure that "lips that touch liquor must never touch mine"?

A nagging doubt of the effectiveness of the plain negative as an absolute suggests to some writers that they might do better by piling absolute on absolute, with even more equivocal results.

☐ **For example:**
The sign on the college campus:

"Motorbikes Not Permitted Beyond This Point At All Times."

29

Does that mean they are permitted "sometimes"? Stop when you've said enough:

"Motorbikes Not Permitted Beyond This Point."

☐ **For example:**
The report of delay in a court's ruling on retroactive pay for government employees:

"As a consequence, all eligible employees will not find the bonus reflected in their August 1 paychecks."

What did they intend to say?

"As a consequence, some eligible employees will find the bonus reflected in their August 1 paychecks, and some won't."

OR

"As a consequence, even though eligible, employees will not find the bonus reflected in their August 1 paychecks."

The law's more serious problem with the plain negative is the difficulty of tying it down. It is so small. And unless securely tied down it can easily wander about or disappear entirely.

☐ **For example:**
The newspaper report of a bureaucrat's memo:

"No clothing-optional beaches will be designated within the California state parks system at this time."

What does the wandering "no" attach itself to? Or is it surplus?
Is it:

"No . . . beaches will be designated where clothing is optional";

OR

"Beaches will be designated . . . where clothing is optional";

OR

"Beaches will be designated . . . where no clothing is optional"?

The last one could be a redundancy, or the shadow of a nuance—a slight preference for "no clothing."
Better make it:

"At this time, the California state parks system will not designate any clothing-optional beaches."

Better yet, drop the euphemism "clothing-optional":

> "At this time, the California state parks system will not designate any beaches where nude bathing is permitted."

☐ **For example:**
A banker claims a saving of $100,000 by not sending customers their cancelled checks:

> "One new clerk must be hired for every 1,000 new checking accounts, according to the bank's formula. But no clerk has been hired in the last year and a half. 'We have not hired 17 people,' he said."

"Not" has become a comedian. Why only 17? It calls for a different sort of negative. "We have avoided hiring 17 people." Better yet, a direct, affirmative statement. "In this way, we have saved the cost of hiring 17 more clerks."

Worst of all is the ever present possibility of the small goof: a failure of hearing, a failure of typing, a scanning failure to pick up the absence of two letters in a mountain of letters, an error of transmission. "No" is left out and there is a complete change of sense. The military learned long ago that too much might hang on too little. "No retreat" can turn into "Retreat." When unavoidable in field orders, the formula is "NO REPEAT NO." Better yet; eliminate the risk of error with the classic positive: "I am here: and here I stay."

It is the same with contracts. "Costs in excess of $50,000 shall not be paid by the owner." If the ringing telephone interrupts concentration, the three letters are omitted, and the whole scheme of the building contract is changed. Better make it positive: The Contractor shall pay costs in excess of $50,000.

b. Negative prefixes and suffixes

One legacy of the language mixture that is English is a rich variety of affixes (prefixes and suffixes) that often make a negative of what they are hitched to. In legal use the common ones are *dis-, ex-, il-, im-, in-, -less, mis-, non-, -out,* and *un-*. Meanings have got to be carefully sorted out. Sometimes the affixes are interchangeable; sometimes they aren't. Sometimes they make a negative; sometimes they make some other change. Sometimes they make no change at all.

☐ **For example:**
One of the most versatile of the lot is the *in-* prefix.
Incorporeal is negative, *no body* (like a copyright rather than a

house). *Incorporate* means to form *into a body* (become a corporation). *Inchoate* is a curiosity, not originally a negative, but now understood as a negative, opposed to the made-up *choate. Inflammable* is the same as *flammable;* the *in-* means *into* rather than *not. In-* is sometimes interchangeable with *un-.* Something *undisputable* is *indisputable.* With small changes that bear watching, *undisputed* reverses itself and becomes *in dispute.*

☐ For example:
Observe the nuances of *il-* and *un-.*

    It is *unlawful* or *illegal* to park in a red zone. If you don't mind repeating yourself, you can say than an *unlawful assembly* (first cousin to a riot) is *illegal.* But people may be *illegally* assembled (gathered together in violation of some law) without being guilty of *unlawful assembly.* When a tenant overstays his welcome, you sue for *unlawful* (not illegal) *detainer.*

☐ Final example.
An *unconstitutional violation* is the same as a *constitutional violation.* But you should be used to that. Perhaps you *could care less,* by which I will understand that you *couldn't care less.* Still, watch it. *Payless* is cheaper than *pay less.*

c. Negative sense

Some English words do not bear the obvious brand of the negative. They are not plain negatives, not overdressed plain negatives (like *notwithstanding*), and are not formed with the popularly recognized prefixes and suffixes. Yet the sense is distinctively negative. Some common ones used in the law are: *absent, ambiguous, avoid, contrary, delinquent, deny, fail, forbid, minimum, null, obnoxious, overdue, prevent, prohibit, remote, shun, void.* Like the more obvious negatives, they require discriminate use to avoid an excess of "No."

d. Negatives incognito

Some legal expressions are negatives only if you are aware of the reference hidden beneath a bland verbalization.

☐ For example:
The *"testimonial privilege"* speaks of a right to remain silent, i.e., *not* to testify. *"Negligence"* consists of the *absence* of due care. *"Constructive"* something or other means that it is *not* the same as reality, but will be treated as if it were: *constructive possession, constructive notice,* etc. *"Le-*

gally blind" means *not* really blind, but for some purposes considered as if blind.

These are useful negatives. The call is simply for their recognition as negatives, again—to avoid an excess of "No."

e. Negatives that may be affirmatives

[1] Negatives doubled and redoubled

The most famous species of negative is the *double negative*. It may, but does not inevitably produce an affirmative.

[a] Double negative or affirmative?

☐ For example:

> Not absent = present.

Even as simple as that, the writer may intend a shade of meaning. But most often in legal use, the double negative springs from bad habit rather than a desire for nuance. If nuance is intended, its subtlety escapes the busy reader. The simple affirmative is neater, swifter, and clearer.

☐ For example:

When an appellate court reverses, the too habitual formula sends the case back to the trial court for "proceedings *not inconsistent* with this opinion." Neither legal necessity nor good manners dictate the circumlocution. Many equally polite and learned judges give it the simple affirmative treatment, "proceedings *consistent* with this opinion."

☐ For example:

One judge says that the time taken to deliver the goods was *"not a commercially unreasonable time."* Another translates that to mean *"a commercially reasonable time."* Why not?

☐ For example:

When the judge writes, "But the holding of the case is *not unambiguous,"* is it nuance or Orwell again? Ambiguous?

[b] Double or single negative?

Sometimes a double negative is used deliberately, for emphasis. "No. I did not say that." But the law's experience with the emphatic negative has been dismal. *Void* becomes *null and void* becomes *totally null and void* becomes *totally null and void and of no further force or effect.* This is habit, to no useful legal purpose. A good plain *void* has lost its vigor. It has become confusing rather than emphatic.

The simple affirmative turns on the green light for the reader: *reasonable.* The single negative *unreasonable* turns green off and red on. When the negative is doubled—*not unreasonable*—greens and reds flash at the same time. Is the red even brighter for two negatives, or does the green outshine two now dimmed reds? As the negatives multiply, more lights blink on and off, grow brighter or dimmer; the decision for the reader becomes more difficult.

☐ **For example:**

An element of the crime of kidnapping is *asportation,* the still used Latin, meaning that the victim must be *carried away.* Defendants took their victim to a deserted beach, forced him to strip, and swim out to sea. A jury convicted the defendants of kidnapping. An appellate judge considers the issue of "carrying away." He writes:

> "Whether the defendants 'carried away' Morales at the beach, so as to satisfy the asportation requirement of the statute is more debatable. However, viewing the evidence in the light most favorable to the Government, *I cannot say* that the *jury could not have found* that when the defendants forced Morales to swim *against his will,* that *this was insufficient* to establish that Morales was 'carried away' by the defendants."

Does the judge think the evidence justified a finding of 'carrying away' or did not justify it? Is he saying "I cannot say this was insufficient," or "I cannot say this was sufficient"? If that single involved sentence, with its multiple negatives, is all you have to go on, the answer is completely muddled. With the negatives stripped away, he probably meant, "I think a reasonable jury could have found that Morales was 'carried away.'"

Even where it is possible to figure out a meaning, the reader has to keep very alert to make certain that the blinking lights are bright or dim, or turned off completely.

☐ **For example:**

Here is a discussion of an insurance policy.

> "However, it does not appear from the *Sheppard* and *Coombe* cases that injuries not attributed to a single event are not covered by part 2."

Even with temptations to negate, think of the reader who does not know what you do. Make his life simpler. State it with one negative:

> "*Sheppard* and *Coombe* do not limit coverage of part 2 to injuries attributed to a single event."

Or state it affirmatively:

"For all that appears in *Sheppard* and *Coombe,* injuries attributed to more than one event may still be covered by part 2."

[2] Middling or dubious negatives

Once you depart from the simple expression of uncertainty, *I doubt that,* the shadings of negative-mixed-with-affirmative in the varied forms of doubting come by the bushel. This is true in the common speech, where "*Doubtless,* you have attended to that" (or, I have *no doubt*) is understood as the affirmation of a skeptical negative: "You've goofed again, haven't you?" When *doubt, doubtful, no doubt, doubtless, without a doubt, indubitably,* etc. are used in the law, and coupled with other negatives and a bagful of modifiers, you can anticipate trouble.

☐ **For example:**
In mild form:

"There can be *no doubt,* and indeed it is *not even suggested,* that she *lacked notice* or in any manner found it temporarily *inconvenient* to present herself at that particular time and place."

That one eventually rights itself. The writer got wound up in trying to talk at one time (in one long sentence) about the negative states of three different people—the judge (*no doubt*), the lawyer (*not even suggested*), and the client (*lacked notice, found it . . . inconvenient*). It could have made a simple affirmative, "It is clear that she had notice and could have been there." It could have been chopped up: "I have no doubts about this one. It is not even suggested. . ." There are other possibilities, but the quickly dictating "writer" forgot that he was dealing with troublemakers.

☐ **For example:**
A more difficult case:

"It is *very doubtful* that the court *would not have* the power to control release of information by these individuals in appropriate cases . . . and to impose suitable *limitations* whose *transgressions* could result in disciplinary proceedings.

What nuance is the writer after? Does it say, "The court *has* the power"? Or is there a question about the power that might be better conveyed in other ways?

"There can be *little doubt* of the court's power. . ." Or, "I think it *likely* that. . ." Or, "I think it *probable*. . ." Or, perhaps straightforward true confession would be best of all: "I think the court has the power, but I am not sure."

If you are in doubt, say so, if you aren't, forget the word, forget the wanderings by which you arrived at your conclusion, and state it positively.

The middling or dubious negative can be achieved without actually using the word *doubt*. Here is a brilliant example:

> "At the bare minimum, one cannot say with even the slightest degree of confidence that the judge's ruling—which the commission unreservedly adopted—was not bottomed on that predicate."

No doubt that rich medley of negatives was intentional. But it is more difficult to cope with than Mr. Justice Harlan's tentative "No," which amounts to a gentle "Yes":

> "In these circumstances I am unable to say that the case bears no reasonable chance of review in this Court."

[3] Negatives of measurement

Negatives of measurement present a special aspect of the difficulty of putting number concepts into words. Words are not only less exact than numbers, they have an unmatched versatility. The same measurement can be expressed in a variety of ways. With a flick of the wrist a plain negative may become an affirmative, without change of sense. Or the sense may be altered ever so slightly. The plain negative may also be swapped for a word of negative sense, which context may turn into an affirmative sense.

☐ For example:

> *no less than 3* = at least 3
> = 3 or more
> = a minimum of 3.
> *no less than I have* = as much as I have
> = at least as much as I have.
> *no smaller than* = as large as
> = at least as large as
> = the smallest
> *no more than* = the maximum
> = the most.

Depending on context, *maximum* and *most* may be thought of, not as limiting negatives, but as an affirmative expression, the *best*.

If the writer dozes over negatives of measurement, the reader is obliged to dissect and diagram to discover the sense.

☐ **For example:**

Statutes require a notice about calls made on a party telephone line. The notice, fouled up for more than two decades, still frequently says:

> "In every telephone directory. . . there shall be printed in type *not smaller than any other* type appearing on the same page, a notice preceded by the word 'warning' printed in type *at least as large as the largest* type on the same page. . ."

The cure is to stop sooner. Put a period after 'warning.'

[4] Negative pregnant

Lawyers continue to use this old expression, *negative pregnant,* i.e., a negative pregnant with a fatal affirmative. This describes a denial in the very words of the charge. It is a quibble over triviality, without denying substance.

☐ **For example:**

> Plaintiff: "Defendant owes me $100."
> Defendant: "I deny that I owe you $100."

The denial is insufficient, because it implies that something is owing, though not exactly $100. Avoid the *negative pregnant* by saying: "I deny that I owe you $100; I don't owe you anything."

[5] Affirmative pregnant

Less frequently, lawyers use the expression, *affirmative pregnant,* i.e., an affirmative pregnant with a fatal negative. This describes an assertion that sidesteps the charge.

☐ **For example:**

> Plaintiff: "Defendant owes me $100."
> Defendant: "I paid him $50."

The denial is insufficient, because it implies either that none of this particular debt has been paid, or that $50 is still owing. Avoid the *affirmative pregnant* by saying: "I paid him $50; I don't owe him anything."

f. Negatives unlimited

There are so many opportunities for legal writing to burst out with negatives that any natural inclination to say something directly is quickly suppressed. The cumulative effect of unlimited negatives of every variety is to bend the reader's mind back and forth till it is massaged into stupor.

☐ For example:

"But on the record now before us it is *not clear* that further publicity, *unchecked,* would so *distort* the views of potential jurors that 12 *could not be found* who would, under proper instructions, fulfill their sworn duty to render a just verdict *exclusively* on the evidence presented in open court. We *cannot say* on this record that alternatives to a prior *restraint* on petitioners *would not have* sufficiently *mitigated* the adverse effects of pretrial publicity so as to make prior *restraint unnecessary. Nor can we conclude* that the *restraining* order actually entered would serve its intended purpose. Reasonable minds can have *few doubts* about the gravity of the evil pretrial publicity can work, but the probability that it would do so here was *not demonstrated* with the degree of certainty our cases on prior *restraint* require."

I think that says this:

"Prior *restraint* of a free press is a last resort. Under our cases it requires a demonstrated probability that pretrial publicity will *prevent* a trial by 12 fair minded jurors. The order made is itself only *possibly* adequate to its intended purpose. The court could have tried alternatives that might have proved sufficient to the evil feared. On the record before us, we are convinced that prior *restraint* was *not justified.*"

It is worth experimenting with cutting down on negatives. They multiply. They confuse. They cause the reader trouble.

Point 5.

On Time

Don't trust time to a "rule" unless you have to. And never trust a preposition to fix time exactly. If exact time is important, spell it out.

Some of its archaic language makes the law seem a land where time has stopped. The impression is not accurate. Time enmeshes the law in metaphysics, mathematics, astronomy, and geography. Mere lawyers are concerned about the spinning of the earth, the calendar, time zones, the International Date Line, and much more. Ordinary people can play with the problems of time. Skillfully or not, lawyers are forced to resolve the practical problems of time, and resolve them with words. It is too readily assumed that because problems of time have been around for a long time that the job has been done, that "the law" takes care of time, and that all a writer need do is mention it. But time changes the law and the meanings of words. Yesterday's "solutions" cannot be taken for granted.

a. The "rules" of time

There is so much of it around that people tend to treat time casually, like air. It is not easy to make time certain, and the legal "rules" of time have tried to do that. Don't take them literally. There are exceptions to them all. Be aware of them as you write, because some day someone might try to interpret your writing in terms of the "rules" of time. The "rules" deal with clock-time as well as calendar-time. Special statutes affect these "rules," but the statutes tend to follow the old "rules."

[1] Time is indivisible, usually

Time is "indivisible," cannot be "fractioned." By this the old books meant that if you speak of a "day," you must mean the whole day.

But the law changes the "rule" when it doesn't make sense. It will even split a second when that makes better sense, as in the case of simultaneous death. (Other rules say it really doesn't happen simultaneously.) So time is indivisible, except when it is divisible. But the memory lingers on, and occasionally matters.

[2] A day is 24 hours, usually

A "day" means a 24-hour day, the time between one midnight and the next. The length of a day can be critical in deciding *effective date* or *expiration date*, e.g., the day a law changes, when coverage of an insurance policy begins or ends, time remaining to file a lawsuit (*statute of limitations*).

But the length of the day can change by custom.

☐ For example:
The day may end at the end of the usual *business day,* without two businessmen explicitly saying so, if that is the well understood custom of the business.

Similarly, a statute or an agreement can change the time in which to do something.

☐ **For example:**
The time (calendar-time or clock-time) specified to do something may be extended by holidays, or by *acts of God* or *force majeure,* i.e., some specified conditions beyond your control.

[3] A month is a calendar month, usually

A "month" usually means a month as named in the calendar, January, February, etc. As a result, you are not writing about a uniformly fixed number of days, but of a period (as shown by the calendar) that may be anything from 28 to 31 days. If the exact number of days is important, you should be writing in terms of days, not months.

☐ **For example:**
Sometimes interest is computed according to a *30-day month.*

[4] A year is a calendar year, usually

A "year" usually means a "calendar" year, the 12 calendar months January through December.
But that can change too. Here are two common ways.

☐ **For example:**
Some taxes are assessed according to a *fiscal year,* e.g., July 1 through June 30. Some taxes are paid according to the taxpayer's own special "fiscal year."

☐ **For example:**
A lease for one year *starting* May 10 means a lease for 365 days (366 in leap years) counting May 10 as the first day.

[5] Time to do something excludes the first day and includes the last, usually

If the time in which to do something runs from a fixed day (e.g., the day an order is made, the end of the month, the day you receive a "notice"), you start counting time the next day.

☐ **For example:**
If May 10, a judge says you have 10 days to file a paper in court, you don't start counting with May 10; that would make your last day to file May 19. The first day is May 11; the last day is May 20.

This rule "exclude the first, include the last," can affect not only lawyers filing papers in court, but ordinary people deciding how much time they have to pay taxes, or exercise an option in a lease, etc.

But the rule does not apply if it is clear that the first day is included—like the one year lease *starting* May 10. Then you count the first day *and* the last. Sometimes lawyers speak of so many *clear days* to do something; that means they don't count either the first or the last day of a period, but only the days in between.

[6] What to do about the "rules" of time

Don't depend on the "rules" of time unless you have to (as when it is controlled by law). If you can control the "rules" and time needs pinning down exactly, do it yourself in your writing. Don't leave to later interpretation what you can say better now. The "rules" are too flexible for comfort. There are too many variables for fixed "rules" to cope with. If clock-time is to be decisive, spell it out, e.g., *Eastern Standard Time*. If a day deadline is to be decisive, spell it out. Where practical, convert the day to a date, e.g., *the last day to exercise this option is May 10, 1990.* If you can't change a day to a date (as when the date is variable, depending on some other uncertain event), you will have to work with the prepositions of time. That calls for special handling.

b. Never trust a preposition

Never trust a preposition to fix time precisely, except when there is no other way to do it.

That goes for all the common prepositions of time: *about, after, at, before, between, by, during, from, in, on, since, till, to, until, within.* It also goes for their medieval counterparts, *thereafter, thereat,* etc. And the usual lawsick antidote for an inadequate word—double it —only makes matters worse. That tried and untrue formula yields such chestnuts as *at and after, at or before, from and after, on and after, on or before, up until.* They make you talk to yourself and count on your fingers to figure out what they are trying to tell you. Like their first cousin *and/or.*

You have to use some prepositions, but don't lie down with a preposition casually, or with any sense of security. They have been used and misused for so long in so many places that they have acquired a tricky ambiguity. Like plain negatives, they hide easily in a pageful of words. They switch place with each other. They travel alone and in pairs. The riddle of the preposition of time is this: Do I lead you just up to a point, onto it, or past it?

☐ For example:

Look at your tax bill. It tells you taxes are *"Delinquent* Dec. 10"; that sounds like pay Dec. 9. It also says "6% penalty *after* Dec. 10"; that sounds like pay Dec. 10. It also says 6% penalty if not paid *by* Dec. 10"; that sounds like maybe Dec. 9, maybe Dec. 10. Better pay Dec. 9.

41

Tax bills are for ordinary people, only some of them lawyers, some of them inexperienced property owners paying taxes for the first time. What the tax bill might have said once and for all in big red print, and *with* the italics:

TAXBILL: TO AVOID PENALTY, PAY THIS TAX *BEFORE* 5 P.M., DECEM-
BER 10. STARTING *AT* 5 P.M., DECEMBER 10, YOU WILL HAVE TO
PAY THE TAX PLUS 6%.
TAXPAYER: WOW! GOTTA GET IN LINE BY NOON DECEMBER 10.

The message is loud and clear. The prepositions have not been eliminated, but the message does not depend on them alone. *Payment* of tax *before* is tied together with *penalty starting at* a fixed dividing line.

☐ For example:

On and after December 10 can be converted into the simpler *after* December 9. But if you want to fix the date in the reader's mind as well as in the law, you can do it best by avoiding the prepositions entirely. If you want to stress the new date, say *Starting* December 10. If you want to stress the old and the new, spell it out: *The last day* to buy at par ($100) *is December 9. Starting December 10 . . .*

☐ For example:

A lease for one year starts May 1 and ends April 30, with an option to extend the lease "for another year on 30 days notice *before* the end of the lease." Problems arise in the interpretation of this simplest of lease forms.

(1) How does the rule "exclude the first, include the last" work here, in computing 30 days?

(a) Where do you start counting? The only fixed point is the "end of the lease," April 30, so you ought to start there. Exclude April 30. Count back in time to find the last day to exercise the option. That means April 29 is day 1, and you arrive at March 31 as the last of the 30 days.

(b) The difficulty with that computation is that while the lease ends April 30, it does not end till midnight April 30. The end of the lease is not a day but a moment. Wouldn't April 1 be 30 days "before the end of the lease"?

(2) If the deadline is important, and it often is, it ought to be fixed by the calendar. "The last day to exercise the option is March 31." Often the lease is a form lease, where starting date and number of options are not filled in until last moment. The time taken to compute the calendar dates for exercise of option will still pay off.

Sometimes a calendar date cannot be fixed in advance. If the date is important, be as explicit as possible, stating your own "rules" of time.

☐ **For example:**

Notice of protest must be mailed not later than the deadline fixed in the next sentence. The last day to mail is the 90th day *after* the date of the meeting (not counting that date as one of the 90 days).

c. Some other time words

The law uses many time words that sound like ticking precision chronometers. The sounds please the legal ear, but they don't turn words into some kind of stopwatch. *Forthwith, immediate, eo instante* (at the very instant), *instanter* (instantly), *imminent* are all subject to interpretation according to circumstance. Moments are turned into hours, and days, weeks, and months. No one seriously believes that something is going to happen before you can say "Jack Robinson." If it has to happen that fast, the time ought to be fixed by the numbers on a clock; words alone won't do it.

When a contract says that *time is of the essence,* it's an old fashioned way of saying, "Look, I mean this; this time." But it's not a term of art, and it still won't make things go like clockwork. The law, like people, is more comfortable with a *reasonable time,* the time usually taken for such things, taking everything into consideration. You can season your language *with all deliberate speed,* but *in due course* someone will find that it isn't going that way. The clock and the calendar are the ultimate resort for precision. And sometimes you can't depend even on them.

RULE 3.

English

If it's bad writing by the standards of ordinary English,
it is bad legal writing.
If it's good writing by the standards of ordinary English,
it is more likely to be good legal writing.

The overwhelming bulk of legal writing is ordinary English. The junk antiques, the Latin, the law French, the terms of art are the seasoning —a bit of it essential, most of it not. It does not account for the discouraging gloom that settles over legal writing. You can look up the peculiar words or hire a translator. What oppresses the ordinary intelligent reader, lawyer or not, is a feeling that something has gone awry. Someone scraped up a pile of words off the floor, and didn't know how to put them together; or didn't give a damn. No feel for the language, for English composition—subjects, predicates, and all that sort of thing—the basic patterns of talking and writing to each other.

☐ **For example:**
A note says:

> "If the time of sale of land for which this note is given is prepaid in full by cash before the final instalment date, the Buyer shall receive a rebate."

It's a sort of English, not complicated by peculiar words at all. A judge called it "gibberish." Perhaps the writer switched forms in midstream. Perhaps the writer meant to say this:

> "This note is given for the purchase price of land. If the note is prepaid in full by cash before the final instalment date, the Buyer shall receive a rebate."

Like everyone else, lawyers spend more time with ordinary English and ordinary English composition than with special usages of the law. The "everyone else" in the twentieth century is a readership multiplied a thousand fold over the select group that was directly concerned with legal writings when the language of the law was in its infancy. Today, as never before, the broad road to understandable legal writing is ordinary English composition. Depart from that road, and you risk being misunderstood by the people you want to reach —lawyers as well as non-lawyers.

On the basics you can't pass the buck to a secretary. Even a good legal secretary grows careless if the in-charge doesn't bounce sloppy work. And the secretary might be a whiz on the typewriter but a functional illiterate, just like the boss. The same relationship of reciprocal ineptitude too often exists between law clerk and judge, junior associate and partner, law student and professor, "drafting" clerk and top bureaucrat. Language no longer flows. It squirts, and bubbles, and drizzles, and stops.

☐ **For example:**
Disregard of the basics results in *error,* readily *corrected.*

error	corrected
PETITION TO HAVE TUBAL LIGATION PERFORMED ON MINOR AND INDEMNITY AGREEMENT	TUBAL LIGATION FOR MINOR: PETITION AND INDEMNITY AGREEMENT
. . . it is to the best interest of said child that a Tubal Ligation be performed on said minor daughter to prevent unfortunate circumstances to occur.	. . . it is in the best interests of the minor daughter that she have a tubal ligation to prevent unfortunate occurrences . . .
* * *	* * *
Attached is a corrected copy of page 1 . . . Please replace this page with the earlier one. Sorry for any inconvenience.	Attached is a corrected copy of page 1 . . . Please substitute this page for the old one. Sorry for any inconvenience.

Point 1.
There Is No Special Legal Syntax

The first requisite of ordinary English composition is also the first requisite of good legal writing— grammatical construction of a sentence.

a. English grammar

[1] Past imperfect

The language of the law grew up using mostly Latin and law French. For centuries there was little or no guidance to a modern English grammar. The lawyers got along without it, and many of them have been getting along without it ever since.

45

With highly inflected Latin, the endings of words told you what modified what. The sense did not, as in modern English, depend on word order. You could save a verb till the end of the sentence, and no one minded. When English overwhelmed the law, and, by statute, the lawyers were dragged, kicking and protesting, into the era of grammatical modern English, they dragged with them their Latinate indifference to word order.

☐ **For example:**

Disregard of word order results in *error,* readily *corrected.*

error	corrected
And the said land in the quiet possession of the Grantee, his heirs and assigns, against all persons lawfully claiming the whole or any part thereof, the Grantor will warrant and defend.	The Grantor will warrant and defend the quiet possession of the [said] land by the Grantee, his heirs and assigns, against all persons lawfully claiming the whole or any part [thereof].

* * *

As grounds for an injunction the buyer urged a statutory provision against the solicitation of legal employment which by its terms had been violated by the defendants.	As grounds for an injunction the buyer urged that defendants had violated the terms of a statutory provision against solicitation of legal employment.

English has improved since the early days of the law. A large part of legal writing has not. It has no standard pattern, whether a bastard, neglected Latin or an unlearned English.

[2] Back to the basics

The rules of grammar you once learned in school are designed to put words together in ways that will make sense even to a reader who was not the writer. Whether legal writing is using ordinary words or special law words, the way the words are put together must follow ordinary grammatical usage. There is no other way. There is no special legal syntax.

☐ **For example:**

Disregard of the rules of grammar results in *error,* readily *corrected.*

error	corrected
McGee encouraged the Hawkinses to allow him to operate on the hand for three years.	For three years McGee encouraged the Hawkinses to allow him to operate on the hand.

* * *

This is independent to admission to the bar.	This is independent of admission to the bar.

* * *

This Court has recently reaffirmed with regards to attorney disqualification that a former client need only to show . . .	With regard to attorney disqualification this Court has recently reaffirmed that a former client need only show . . .
* * *	* * *
This is precisely the type decision which has given the exclusionary rule a bad name.	This is precisely the type of decision which has given the exclusionary rule a bad name.
* * *	* * *
Since the essential power of government resided and emanated from the people . . .	Since the essential power of government resided in and emanated from the people . . .

The more complex the legal writing, the greater need for the traffic rules of ordinary English grammar. If you don't know the basics of English grammar, review the basics before trying to write for the law. (For references on grammar, see Appendix J.)

b. Special case: grammar v. sexism

Discrimination by a male-dominated society has met with grand protest, typified by the pending Equal Rights Amendment. A smaller aspect of that protest has sparked a conflict between what is accepted English usage and what is offensive to a growing number of people of both sexes.

As with any emotional controversy, language takes its knocks. No one, not even the Supreme Court of the United States, consistently tells us what to call the controversy. Is it about *sex* or *gender?* Without change of pace the courts speak of *sex discrimination* and *gender discrimination, sex neutral* and *gender neutral.* They talk of what tends to "exacerbate *gender consciousness,*" and inevitably retreat to lawsick's double-up—*gender or sex. Gender and/or sex* cannot be far behind. Confused usage begets misunderstanding. Already some judges say they are concerned with *sexual discrimination,* and with a rule that is "*sexually neutral* on its face."

One longstanding aspect of the problem is the use of appropriate nouns. A male oriented culture gave male names to historically male jobholders—*fireman, mailman, chairman,* etc. With some other names, e.g., *innkeeper, housekeeper, storekeeper, lawyer,* the original identification of the *-er* with maleness has passed into the mists, and bothers no one. So *fireman* becomes *firefighter,* and *mailman* a *mail carrier. Chairman* becomes *chair* or *chairperson,* the tepid *-person* suffix now ubiquitous. Professors are even experimenting with *remainderperson* for the law's revered *remainderman* (the person, male or female, who gets the property after someone else); others would like to try *remainderer, remainderor,* or *remainor.*

47

Like the ending -er, the ending -or also originally spelled maleness. To the extent that words formed with that suffix have been identified as typically male, some eyebrows are raised. The law still uses
testator, distinguished from the female *testatrix*. Once defined as "a
man who leaves a wi¹i" (Webster's Second), *testator* is now defined as
"a person who leaves a will" (Webster's Third), or "one who . . ."
(Black's). The law also uses *administrator, executor,* and *prosecutor,*
and the female versions *administratrix, executrix,* and *prosecutrix*.
Those female versions have become suspect, and are headed for ex-
tinction. The once male forms may eventually become as sex neutral
as the once equally male *juror*.

While the battle over suitable non-sexist noun substitutes burbles
on, the more serious everyday problem for legal writers is the pronoun. Despite long use for general reference to both sexes, *he, his,
him* have an undoubted flavor of maleness that some now sense as
perpetuating attitudes of female inferiority. Traditionally, the law has
made explicit that the concentration on the masculine is not to be
taken seriously. Statutes and other writings repeat—"Words used in
the masculine gender include the feminine and neuter." But whatever that ritual cliché may mean legally, it is a poor sop to sensitivity.

The language people have been unable to come up with a bland
new set of pronouns that might promise anything approaching consensus. A few are doodling with *s/he*. The suggestion of plain *E* (or
similar grunts) as a substitute for *he* and *she* has not been hailed as a
breakthrough. In this crisis of conscience and grammar, the lawyers
have been reduced to reliance on their own pragmatic illiteracy. The
word juggling is fierce.

[1] Some possibilities

Here are some (certainly not all) of the formulas lawyers are using to
avoid the taint of sexism.

[a] Substitute nouns for pronouns

□ For example:

    A lawyer shall not, on behalf of himself *[the lawyer]* . . .

□ For example:

    A lawyer shall not, on behalf of himself *[such person]* . . .

Comment:
In a long passage, this can end up with a confusing profusion of *lawyers* or
persons.

[b] Substitute plural for singular pronouns

☐ For example:

> If a client wants his *[their]* lawyer to . . .

☐ For example:

> If client*[s]* want [their] lawyer to . . .

Comment:
The first example is ungrammatical, plural pronoun for singular noun. The second example will not be available if the passage goes on to distinguish between a single and several clients.

[c] Substitute sex neutral pronouns

☐ For example:

> The duties which counsel *[one]* must fulfill to meet his *[one's]* obligations as a competent advocate . . .

☐ For example:

> The duties which counsel *[you]* must fulfill to meet his *[your]* obligations as a competent advocate . . .

Comment:
Not always available.

[d] Double the pronouns

☐ For example:

> The lawyer must have a reasonable opportunity to make a living for himself *[himself or herself]* and his *[his or her respective]* family.

☐ For example:

> The lawyer must have a reasonable opportunity to make a living for himself *[himself/herself]* and his *[his/her]* family.

Comment:
In either case, length increased. The "respective" helps to clarify the first example. The meaning of the doubled pronouns joined only by "or" or by a virgule is not entirely clear, and burdens the reader with the task of deciphering as with *and/or.*

49

[e] Alternate the single pronouns

☐ For example:

> A client goes to see her lawyer but has not brought with her *[him]* the papers the lawyer needs.

Comment:
This is the equal time doctrine. Sexist madness.

[f] Rewrite to avoid the problem

☐ For example:
A statute required that on registering to vote, a woman label herself as "Miss" or "Mrs." The statute was amended to permit any name to be preceded by "Miss, Ms., Mrs. or Mr." It went on to say:

> "No person shall be denied the right to register because of *his* failure to mark a prefix to *his* given name . . ."

The next year, that was amended to read:

> "No person shall be denied the right to register because of *his or her* failure to mark a prefix to such given name . . ."

Comment:
Delete the three words—*his or her.* Delete "such"; insert "a".

[2] What to do

If the now controversial *he, his, him* (and other sex-scented language) can be eliminated without making legal writing even more difficult to understand, the sensibilities of those affected ought to be respected. At the same time, the legal writer (more than others) has an obligation to write as clearly as possible, which also means grammatically. If you can't find a way out of *he, his, him* other than illiteracy or bad grammar, you had better stick with what you've got; but . . . Literacy and grammar are neither acceptable sacrifices nor necessary sacrifices to the cause of non-sexist language usage. Illiteracy and ungrammatical writing result from the slapdash grab for a mechanical solution. With care, non-sexist writing can be completely consistent with literacy, grammatical usage, and clarity.

Enthusiasm for ending sexism should not warp the critical judgment. Some writing would need correction whether or not deliberately "sexist." Some of it is just plain bad use of the language.

☐ **For example:**
An indecent exposure statute prohibits "an act of exposing *his genitals.*"
That gets close enough to the basics of sex to make it unclear whether or
not the statute applies to females. If it applies to both sexes, make it *"the*
genitals" or *"one's* genitals."
Neither male chauvinism nor anti-sexism ought to tolerate nonsense.

Point 2.

Correct Use of Ordinary Words Is Just As Important As the Correct Use of Law Words

Any square foot of legal writing uses more ordinary words
than law words. Sloppy use of the English language can destroy
what would otherwise be good legal writing.

One horrible result of the myth of precision is smugness. Look to the
law words, and the ordinary words will take care of themselves. They
don't. They need lots of attention, for there are more of them. They
form the context for law words, and if the context is garbled the sharp-
est term of art will not accomplish its mission. Any approach to precise usage requires at a minimum the correct use of law words and
the correct use of the ordinary language. (For references on word usage, *see* Appendix J.)

a. Misuse of ordinary words

An oral gaffe may be excused as a momentary twist of the tongue.

☐ **For example:**
A judge's *error,* readily *corrected,* once you know what he meant to say.

error	corrected
"Mr. Nixon seems rather at-tenuated from this lawsuit."	Mr. Nixon seems rather removed from this lawsuit.
	or
	Mr. Nixon seems to have a rather attenuated connection with this lawsuit.
	or
	Mr. Nixon seems to have lost weight as a result of this lawsuit.

51

But writing is a more deliberate process. Those who care bemoan a growing illiteracy from top to bottom of our society. Congress is asked to authorize billions "to complete the essential gaps" in the interstate highway system. It is reported that "the blue vehicle encountered a flat tire," and "this may be just the top of the iceberg." Bad enough for hurried journalists, harried politicians, and the uneducated to abuse the ordinary language. Yet every such gaucherie is easily matched by the lawyers, the learned profession that is paid to say it right.

[1] Makes lawyers look silly

It would be nice if, like "the top of the iceberg," one might dismiss the profession's goofs as misprints: "writing a contract in sanscript"; this was "redoubtably a labor cost." But don't shoot the printer. He's doing the best he can. The message that bore "redoubtably" also said that it was "volitive of several recognized fundamental rules of contract interpretation." Would you buy a used contract from someone who wrote like that? Those are not isolated instances. Here is a sampling.

☐ **For example:**
Some lawyers misuse the italicized word, an *error*, readily *corrected*.

error	corrected
The prisoners should be *appraised* of their rights.	*apprised*
He was a *literal* missionary.	*literally* a missionary; or *virtually* a missionary. (This was to be a compliment.)
This would *accomplish* the need for more police protection.	*satisfy*
Otherwise it would *rent* the very fabric of the judicial system.	*rend*
He *carried* the laboring oar at the trial.	*had* (If you carry an oar, you're not paddling.)
He appeared *regaled* in 'mod' clothes.	He appeared in 'mod' *regalia; or* He *regaled* us by appearing in 'mod' clothes.
With *regards to* what we were discussing . . .	*regard*

error	corrected
He stated the police are permitted to *flaunt,* defy and violate the law.	*flout*
This does not *effect* us one way or another.	*affect*
This *affects* a complete change in our relationship.	*effects*
We will, instead, *defer* this matter back to you.	*refer;* or *defer* to you in this matter.
Chemical *dependents.*	*dependence*

[2] Distorts through redundancy

For legal writers, redundancy is a special evil. Redundancy does more than increase length; it takes a good word and casts doubt on its integrity. You are more apt to approach precision if you follow the old injunction to leave well enough alone.

☐ For example:

In this short sampling of lawsick redundancy, omit the words in italics. What's left says the same thing better in ordinary English.

> *surviving* widow
> *true* facts
> Unless counsel *by agreement* otherwise agree . . .
> The defendant has a *prior* criminal record.
> He did not premeditate *before* the killing.

And the best of all—

> *unnecessary* redundancy

[3] Affects the sense of law words

A lack of respect for the common vocabulary has a deadly side effect. It weakens the sense of law words that make special uses of ordinary English.

☐ For example:

Taking the common English *adhesion* (the act of joining), the law has fashioned the expression, a *contract of adhesion* (a take-it-or-leave-it contract, with one side having all the bargaining power). An opinion refers to such a

53

contract, but calls it instead an *adhesive contract,* twisting the mind to thoughts of a contract that sticks to you, as distinguished from one that you are stuck with. The new expression is reported in the law's meticulous accumulation of verbal trash; it acquires a limited following. The law now has another unneeded twofer.

☐ **For example:**
Putative (reputed) is a Latin based word that made it into common English. The law put it to use with *putative marriage, -father, -wife.* Without warning, an opinion uses the expression *putative clients,* referring not to people who are reputed to be clients, but to those who might become clients. The new expression is much reported and will be long remembered. Another writer follows that authoritative lead with *putative lawyers,* referring not to people who are reputed to be lawyers, but to those who might become lawyers. The fate of *putative marriages, -fathers,* and *-wives* is made uncertain.

Language, especially English, thrives on innovation, and changes with repeated error. But those who want the law written with precision ought to be more deliberate in their moments of creativity, explaining to readers the excitement of the moment. Otherwise they leave a legacy of puzzlement: Is is nuance or inadvertence? Lawyers and judges argue over such distinctions; and the arguments are long and costly.

b. Pomp without circumstance

One of the simple rules of ordinary English composition is to keep the language simple. If it's clear that *he is against it,* don't turn it into a blob—*he is taking a negative posture.* Don't use language to conceal thought or its absence.

With legal writing, there are occasions enough when a legalism must be used *(writ of certiorari),* when words serve a ceremonial function *(Your Honor).* When no reason exists for either technicality or ceremony, and yet you continue to puff up the words, the result is pomp without circumstance. It's lawsick—a pompous, wordy, confusing corruption of the ordinary language.

☐ **For example:**
Here is some *inflated* usage, readily *corrected.*

inflated	corrected
negotiative interaction	bargaining
an upward price modification	a price increase
adversely affected plaintiff's cost position	cost plaintiff more money

inflated	corrected
de-escalated the royalty	reduced the royalty
sustained prejudice	was prejudiced (or *damaged*)
interstate nexus	interstate connection (or *tie* or *link*)
terminations per judgeship	cases finished by each judge
Subsequent to that time and prior to the gubernatorial signing of the bill . . .	After that date and before the Governor signed the bill . . .
one John Smith	John Smith
contractual relations subsisting	contractual relations

In the ordinary language, people call that sort of talk gobbledygook. With the tradition of legal writing, gobbledygook comes too easily —old formalisms, euphemism, and pompous expression. All of this is out of place today in ordinary good English. It is especially out of place in English that aims at precision and clarity.

c. Special case: and/or

The high failure rate of legal papers that depend on *and/or* for anything of importance should have long since eliminated it from the legal vocabulary. Yet it persists, and is widely used in legal and ordinary writings. For the writer in a hurry, for the writer content to let others solve the problems created by the writer, *and/or* is such a short, quick, and easy way out. It has a special currency in academia, where the lure of the scientific (*interface, parameter*) gulls some into confusing the compact form of *and/or* with the precision of a lopsided fraction.

One book on usage says its popularity even in "respectable places" means that it "is therefore acceptable current English." Most of the English usage people condemn it as ugly, unnecessary, and confusing. They usually end up blaming it on the law, saying (in charitable ignorance), "Maybe it's all right for them, but let them keep it."

This reverse smugness should give lawyers pause. Instances of non-legal *and/or* do not encourage imitation. They demonstrate its mindlessness ("Rape: The Hidden Crime.' Also shown is how other women can prevent *and/or* survive rape."), and its complicated silliness. (We look forward to seeing *and/or* hearing from you.)

55

Despite the relative simplicity of *A or B or both* (when such specification is necessary), legal writings continue to spew contradictions joined by an habitual *and/or*.

☐ **For example:**

> . . . the order was not made *and/or* was kept in abeyance.
> [Make it *or*.]
> . . . might be discharged *and/or* paroled at any time.
> [Make it *or*.]
> . . . it was uniformly specified *and/or* implied.
> [Make it *or*.]

Like a tic, *and/or* intrudes without effort, even when the writer has already covered all the possibilities.

☐ **For example:**

> . . . the application of one or more of doctrines of A, B, C, *and/or* D.
> [Make it *and*.]

If the lawyers did invent *and/or*, they owe it to the common language to atone, by now eliminating *and/or* from the legal vocabulary, and hope that the common language will follow. It is still confusing readers and costing litigants money. Anything *and/or* can do, ordinary English can do better.

Point 3.

Punctuation Usage of Ordinary English Applies to Legal Writing

Punctuation can drastically change the meaning of words.
Deliberate lack of punctuation is the cause of the
worst disasters of legal writing—the long, long sentence,
and the one sentence paragraph.

An old and recurrent bit of lawsick nonsense tells us that "punctuation is no part of the English language." Variation makes it "punctuation is no part of the statute," and "instruments are to be construed without regard to the punctuation." In whatever form, the notion is still nonsense. Use as much punctuation as the reader needs. (For references on punctuation, see Appendix J.)

a. Misunderstanding

[1] Readers will punctuate

Judges and lawyers and everyone else are accustomed to reading punctuated writing. If you don't punctuate, a reader will do it for you, in places you never wanted it. Sense can be reversed by punctuation or the lack of it, especially where words may carry more than one meaning.

☐ For example:
Did you mean

	this	*or*	*this?*
	The defect in my opinion is the lack of any mention of *Jones v. Smith.*		The defect, in my opinion, is the lack of any mention of *Jones v. Smith.*

[2] Limit your reliance on punctuation

[a] It may disappear

Punctuation is rarely dictated, which means that for a large part of legal writing punctuation depends on the typist's understanding of the "writer's" meaning. Sometimes punctuation is inadvertently omitted or misplaced in typing or typesetting. Sometimes it is overlooked by hasty readers. Try not to rely on punctuation alone to give meaning to what you are writing. The marks are too precarious, as in "Sams' Fresh Fish." You can resolve all doubts by a few extra words, or by a combination of word change and punctuation.

☐ For example:
Do you mean

	this	*or*	*this?*
	The defect in my opinion for the majority in *Doe v. Roe* is the lack of any mention of *Jones v. Smith.*		In my view, the defect in the majority opinion in *Doe v. Roe* is the lack of any mention of *Jones v. Smith.*

[b] Some writing incurable

Punctuation is not a universal cure for bad writing. Some writing needs rewriting, not more or different punctuation.

☐ For example:

"At Carter's suggestion, the family grouped around Humphrey, who was wearing a gray tweed jacket that seemed too large, and Mrs. Humphrey."

There's more there than the last comma can bear. Left uncorrected, it became the model for another press dispatch:

> "Beside him were Sen. Alan Cranston (D.-Calif.) wearing an eye-catching yellow sun hat, and an elaborately costumed young festival queen."

b. The long, long sentence

Senator Humphrey's jacket and Senator Cranston's yellow hat are mild lay examples of lawsick's oldest curse— the long, long sentence. Those examples set no records for word count or extra syllables. But you don't have to count either to decide that a sentence is too long. It's too long when too many ideas are squeezed into the open space between the first capital letter and the final period.

The long, long sentence has a lesser offspring—the long, long clause, and a terminal state—the one sentence paragraph. All originated in ancient times when punctuation was intended as a guide to proper breathing for oral delivery, and had nothing to do with today's punctuation for written meaning. The sense of written Latin did not depend on punctuation any more than it did on word order.

The tradition of the long, long sentence has been perpetuated in the law by habit, the forms, and the seductive ease of getting everything tied together, without bothering to consider whether it makes your kind of sense that way. The habit is so strong that it prevails over reason. It intrudes itself into every kind of legal writing, even when there is not an iota of legal compulsion.

☐ For example:
Here is a single sentence from a telephone company's notice of application for a rate increase. It is directed to people who use telephones.

> "The requested increase is made necessary by the company's sharply increasing construction program undertaken to improve levels of telephone service, double digit inflation and interest rates which increase the cost of providing service, and the necessity to attract investment capital at reasonable rates to finance the service improvement program when needed."

This semi-literate ramble at first seems to suggest that the company's construction "program" is going to "improve" not only telephone service but double digit inflation and interest rates. That bright picture fades rapidly. A separate thought tags along at the end. The increase "is made *necessary* by . . . the *necessity to* attract investment capital . . . when *needed*." The panic cry of "Necessity!" is watered down, and you begin to wonder about all those wrong numbers.

Perhaps they were trying to say something like this:

> "This is why the company needs the rate increase. The company is sharply increasing construction to improve telephone service. In today's money market, it costs more to attract investment capital to finance improved service. Double digit inflation and higher interest rates have also increased the day-to-day cost of providing [even bad] telephone service."

The bracketed true confession is optional; clarity isn't.

The long, long sentence is even more confusing in more technical legal writing.

☐ **For example:**
Here is a relatively short, long, long sentence from the Uniform Commercial Code. That Code is a collection of law used not only by lawyers, but by ordinary people in business, and by that vast assortment of clerks, administrators, and executives who work in banks. This is a definition, in the article on "Commercial Paper."

> "Presentment is a demand for acceptance or payment made upon the maker, acceptor, drawee or other payor by or on behalf of the holder."

As I pointed out some years ago, the sentence is grammatical gibberish. It is first cousin to "A mouse is what is eaten or caught by a trap or a cat." In each case, words are thrown into a black bag that looks like a sentence, but you have to know how the words are to be paired off to make sense of them. You have to know what it intended to say before you can know what it is saying; which is a slight weakness in a definition.

Without knowing any law, you might think it strange that anyone would make "demand for acceptance" upon an "acceptor," which sounds like someone who has already accepted. Your hunch would be right. And you would be much better off if you knew in advance that you present to "makers" and "acceptors" for payment, but not for acceptance.

The thoughts are all there, crowded into a single sentence, but the reader is left the considerable task of sorting them out. This is what it means.

> Presentment is a demand for acceptance or payment, made by or on behalf of the holder. Demand for acceptance is made upon the draw-

59

ee. Demand for payment is made upon the maker, acceptor, drawee, or other payor.

The technicality of the other words you can find elsewhere in the bowels of commercial law. But at least you now know what *presentment* is, in three short sentences.

The long, long sentence is a bad hangover. It is not necessary. It can be avoided. Other examples are in Part II.

RULE 4.

Clear

USUALLY YOU HAVE A CHOICE OF HOW TO SAY IT.
CHOOSE CLARITY.

Lack of clarity is a common but not necessary
feature of legal writing. It is not an inevitable by-product
of precision. Clarity depends more on how you say it
than on what you have to say.
As you write, keep asking, "Clear to whom?"

Clear, intelligible, understandable, plain language. They are all talking about the same thing—language that is easier to understand. Whatever the sense, make it easier to find. Sometimes, *simple* is used in the same way.

"Clear as crystal" means that even I can understand it. "Loud and clear" means that I'm getting the message; no static. When people talk about legal language and legal writing, they seldom use those expressions. More often it is "Could you clear that up a bit?" "Maybe it's clear to you, but not to me." "It's clear as mud."

Unclear writing is one of the oldest causes of litigation. It is also the oldest cause of popular complaint about legal writing. Today the old complaint has more substance than ever. The law directly touches (or hits) more people. More people are expected to understand some legal writing. More people are trying to understand some legal writing. Yet lawsick has changed very little.

The collision has heated up the old complaint into a national frenzy over "plain language," "plain English," "simplified language." Dozens of bills have been introduced requiring "plain English" in consumer contracts. Typically, the bills are written in the style that they condemn. Some of them are horrors. Some have become law. They represent a frustration with lawsick. "If someone else doesn't do something about it, we will, for better or for worse." (For a discussion of plain language laws, see Appendix I.)

You are that "someone else." You can do something about it in your own legal writing, without the threat of the guillotine, if you know what you are trying to accomplish, and how to go about it.

Most legal writers simply fall into a habit of writing mud. It is not difficult to write law unintelligibly; if you can copy a form, you can do it easily. What you are trying to accomplish is to change a whole pattern of legal writing—the words, the grammar, the composition of sentences. Above all you are going to end the nasty trick of losing your reader in the long, long sentence. You are going to be as precise as possible, and you are going to be as clear as possible, without making it a choice of one or the other.

Writing law clearly is not easy. It encompasses the whole business of how to write. Rule 3 (English), Rule 5 (Law), Rule 6 (Plan), and Rule 7 (Cut) are of special importance. But the first thing to do is to take away the roadblock to ready understanding—law words that aren't necessary.

Point 1.

Choose Ordinary Words
Over Law Words

Make it your practice to use ordinary words
of the English language unless there is a good reason not to.
Test a law word before using it.

The habit of thinking in English is not permanently subverted even by three years of law school or many years in the practice. Lawyers ordinarily even speak to each other in English. But the moment that "words-on-paper" darts through the lawyer's consciousness, the old bewitchment starts to work. The myth of precision casts its spell, and the lawyer starts "writing like a lawyer," unintelligibly. Non-lawyers follow the leader.

The belief among writing lawyers that the ordinary English language is somehow inferior is an inheritance from the infancy of the common law and the infancy of modern English as a well organized language. Things have changed.

English is better now. "English" here means the English language, not necessarily words of English, as opposed to Latin or French, origin. Using "pure" English words gives no assurance of being better understood; most people would think French *consider* easier to understand than Old English *deem*. Some foreign words in today's English also have some of the crisp brevity that we sometimes think of as distinctively English, e.g., *cheat, clear, peace*. From a variety of languages, the English language and the language of the law have taken some of the worst (e.g., *criminal conversation, executrices, testament*) and some of the best (e.g., *judge, jury, legal, verdict*). Clarity is too precious a commodity to be fussy about the national origin of words.

Sticking with ordinary words of the English language simplifies existence for writer and reader. It comes easily to lawyer and non-lawyer, including first of all a secretary, paralegal, clerk, or printer, with less chance of error all around.

The temptation to flash a vocabulary that you have spent years learning is sometimes almost irresistible. Resist it, before it does you in. In this tail-end of the twentieth century, it is a departure from ordinary English that is suspect. Make a law word justify itself before you run the risk of becoming unintelligible. Here are two quick tests, spelled out in the following paragraphs:

a. Does it have to be this word?
b. Is this better than ordinary English?

a. Does it have to be this word?

If the law (e.g., a statute, a regulation, a decision) says that you must use this specific word, of course use it. Use it because you have to, clear or not. Use it whether it is a law word or an ordinary word.

☐ **For example:**
A Federal Trade Commission regulation requires these very words:

"This warranty gives you specific legal rights, and you may also have other rights which vary from state to state."

With the exception of *warranty*, the words are ordinary English. Both the law word and the ordinary words are specifically required.

Even if a word is required, take these precautions.

[1] Specific

Make sure that the word is specifically required. More often, regulation of wording sets standards, without requiring specific words. With that sort of regulation, scrutinize the standards with an eye to the people affected by the regulation. This is discussed in Point 2 (p. 75).

[2] Now

Make sure that the word is required now. It might be an old turkey like *ss* that sneaked in years ago, and stayed in, without anyone knowing why it's there or what it does.

[3] Explain

And if it is specifically required now, you may still want to add an explanation. This is discussed in Point 2.

b. Is this better than ordinary English?

If a law word is neither required nor barred, a final challenge remains. Is there anything worth doing that this law word can do better than ordinary English? If there isn't, it flunks the basic fitness test, and should be discarded.

Some law words, with nothing to recommend them but habit, make it fairly certain that non-lawyers and some lawyers will not understand. This is true of some of the archaic usages described in Rule 1. Some law words are even worse than archaic. They are recognizable as ordinary English words; the form is the same but the legal meaning is different from the common meaning. There you have a good beginning for misunderstanding. A law word like that is a hazard. If is can be easily translated, get rid of it fast.

☐ For example:

alien (verb) means *to transfer*. That says it just as well, and eliminates the persistent recollection of *alien* as a noun and a foreigner.

assigns (noun) means *assignees*. That says it just as well, and eliminates the nagging impression that *assigns* might masquerade as a plural noun, but at heart it's a verb. Lawyers cling to the noun as a matter of habit in *heirs and assigns,* but the expression has no special virtue. And read to a lay audience, it is a real puzzler. Both words sound like verbs—*errs and assigns.*

Not all law words can be as easily dismissed.

[1] Is it more precise?

If the odds are even, choose the ordinary.

In some cases, ordinary English beats lawsick on its own turf. Some ordinary English is more precise.

☐ For example:

will, by itself, is more precise than the traditional *last will and testament.*

give, by itself, is more precise than the traditional *give, devise, and bequeath.*

all other property says what you mean. It strips away the phoney technicality of *rest, residue, and remainder.*

In a small number of cases, the law word is more precise. (See Rule 1.1, p. 10). When that is settled, it should give you pause, but not overwhelm you. Think it over. For your present purposes, does an edge by the criterion of precision outweigh the virtue of clarity?

[2] Does it get the message across quicker?

Sometimes, with terms of art and legal argot, the answer is "Yes, but . . ." Sometimes these law words can get the message across quicker, but only if they are used in the right place at the right time. Move to Point 2.

Point 2.

Write Selectively.
Explain When Useful

Don't waste your time tailoring words to an audience
that isn't there. But don't make things difficult
for those who do want to read you.
Some law requires technical words.
Hardly any law forbids explaining them.

If you want readers to understand, you can't simply throw words at paper; you've got to aim them at someone. The main reason why so many people find legal writing unclear is that it wasn't written for them. Most legal writing isn't written for anybody at all. Most legal writing is written to get it written. There. I've done it!

☐ **For example:**

"On February 13, 1976, appellants filed an application for a stay of the judgment of the Supreme Court of Illinois entered on January 19, 1976, reversing an order entered by the Circuit Court of the Seventh Judicial Circuit, Sangamon County, Illinois, on January 12, 1976 enjoining the defendant officers of the Illinois State Board of Election Commissioners from conducting a lottery for the purpose of assigning ballot positions in accordance with Regulation 1975-2 adopted by the State Board of Elections on November 21, 1975."

That is not complete gibberish, but it comes close enough for purposes of illustration. That is the whole first sentence (as well as the whole first paragraph) of a short opinion. All those words, and you still don't have the foggiest notion of what people are scrapping about. You begin to get a glimmer at the start of the next paragraph:

"Regulation 1975-2 prescribes a lottery system for breaking ties resulting from the simultaneous filing of petitions for nomination to elective office."

65

Yet even two sentences into the message, you have the uneasy feeling that no one really cares whether you get this right or not. The writing hinders rather than helps understanding.

What overwhelms the reader is not the modest bundle of technicality but the massive lawsick onslaught. Everything run together and topsy-turvy—in reverse chronological order. That is the easy way for the writer to copy from a thick legal manila folder, with the latest filing on the top of the pile. But the writer knows what went before; the reader doesn't.

You have to take out pencil and paper to sort it out. Then you could put it together like this.

> When candidates tie in filing nominating petitions, the Illinois State Board of Election Commissioners assign ballot positions by lottery. A state court enjoined the defendant Board officers from holding such a lottery. The Illinois Supreme Court reversed, and appellants ask us to stay that judgment.

If the writer considered the information essential for some readers, references to the regulation, state court, and dates could be inserted parenthetically or by footnote. But at least now the reader has some idea of what this opinion is about, and can decide whether to go on, or pass it up.

Nothing in the law required the original to be written the way it was. But it did not strike the writer (or dictat[e]r) as at all strange. It is not an isolated formula. It has a legal sound. The writer was satisfied to get it down in print.

The critical question was never asked, "Clear to whom?" If it had been asked, the answer would have been an embarrassment.

"Clear to whom?"

"Only to me, God, and the litigants."

And all of them already knew.

Perhaps the writer figured that they were also the only audience. Even though it ends up in the reports of the Supreme Court of the United States, it was an unimportant procedural step.

That is one of the legal writer's special difficulties—knowing for sure who is in the audience. There is so much law. It gets around, turning up where least expected. And excites so many peculiar interests.

When in doubt, write for the broadest audience.

When the particular reader is clearly identified, write straight to the reader.

Here are some bases worth touching.

a. Lawyer to lawyer

If you are certain that this one isn't going anywhere—just for us lawyers, use some shortcuts. In a memorandum of law for another lawyer, in a letter about law to another lawyer, use some terms of art and argot.

☐ For example:

> I am willing to *stipulate* that this memorandum will be *without prejudice* to your defense of *mootness*.

Explanation is not called for, any more than one farmer explains to another which is Adam's *off* ox.
 But if it's not just for lawyers' eyes, take the time to spell it out like this:

> I am willing to agree that despite anything in this memorandum, you will still have the right to defend on the ground that the whole controversy has been rendered academic by the recent decision in *Smith v. Jones.*

In any event, keep the special words within bounds. Use them when precision requires it, or when they serve the purpose of quick communication within the in-group. Take special pains to see that argot doesn't degenerate into idiosyncratic slang.

☐ For example:

Not all lawyers speak of *res ipsa loquitur* as a *resipsey* case. Some don't even quickly realize that *a horse case* is the same as one *on all fours.*

b. Lawyer to judge

Writing to a judge, you work with the same lawyer-to-lawyer assumptions of familiarity with terms of art and argot. But it is no longer a closed circle of intimacy. Even if you know the judge, you write for the record. The difference of position calls for restraint.

☐ For example:

You could say it like this, but don't!

> Dear Charlie:
> Here's a copy of a really hot one from your pals (ha, ha) on the Court of Appeal. I think this *Elmer v. Jones* wraps it up for me. Sorry but nobody told me about it till after the gab fest yesterday. I'll send a copy of the opinion and this letter to Pete.

67

This says it too; and says it better. More formal; duller; longer; appropriate.

Re: *John v. Elwood*
Civ. #1234567

Dear Judge Rogers:
At the hearing on this matter on January 10th, I regret to say that I (and apparently opposing counsel as well) was unaware of the Court of Appeal decision in *Elmer v. Jones*, published Jan. 9.

The facts in *Elmer* on long-arm jurisdiction are so strikingly similar to those in the case at bar, that—in my view—the decision in *Elmer* is controlling in favor of plaintiff here on the very issue argued before you.

I am taking the liberty of enclosing a copy of the full opinion in *Elmer,* with a copy of the opinion (and this letter) to opposing counsel. If you deem it desirable, I shall be happy to brief the point further or argue it orally at your convenience.

c. The judge's opinion

When an appellate judge writes an opinion agreeing or disagreeing with a trial judge, that opinion becomes part of the largest concentrated mass of single purpose writing in the western world. (On the details of opinion writing, see the excellent discussion in Witkin, *Manual on Appellate Court Opinions,* 1977.)

For whom is the opinion written?

If only for the litigants and their lawyers, most opinions could be reduced to a few lines, sometimes to a few words:

Affirmed [or, reversed] for the reasons stated in *Smith v. Jones.*

Those connected with the case know the facts; they want to know who wins, and why. The judge can talk directly to informed people, especially to the lawyers who have fought the case. They will tell their clients about it very quickly. Recitation of facts the litigants have lived with for too long is unnecessary. The lawyers are familiar with most of the law. They want to know what impressed the judge, and why. Is there anything here making it worthwhile to challenge the result by further appeal?

The theory of our law is that the opinion serves a broader purpose.

The opinion becomes part of the law that binds us. It instructs other lawyers and judges in other cases, law students, scholars. Some opinions create public controversy. "Turn over the tapes." "De-segregate." "Obscene." Some are continuing education in democracy:

> "In this case we hold that the publication of a letter, which, in substance, charges a candidate for public office with engaging in political chicanery is protected by the First Amendment. . . . It is an essential part of our national heritage that an irresponsible slob can stand on a street corner and, with impunity, heap invective on all of us in public office."
>
> (Gardner, P.J., in *Desert Sun Pub. Co. v. Superior Court,* 97 Cal App 3d 49, 51, 158 Cal. Rptr 519, 520 (1979)).

With some opinions, the ripples of interest are more concentrated, but numbers of people other than the litigants are still immediately concerned. Will it cut my taxes? Can I buy out that corporation? Can they put a road through my land? What does the warranty cover?

The circle may contract even more, and still something more than "Yes" or "No" is called for.

☐ **For example:**

Are you interested in leotards? Not just looking at them or wearing them, but making them? If you are, you will take special note of this:

> "The Plaintiff surrendered by amendment all rights to patent claims which could include any garment with a crotch opening having inter-engaging means on opposite sides of the split unless the garments specifically have non-aligned primary and supplementary fastening means."

If you are into leotards that might mean something to you. If you aren't, do you really care about it? It can be written for the leotard people. If it helps them, that's probably enough.

In most cases, there are so many possibilities of interest that the individual judge is hard pressed to fix the limits of the audience. Better to over-explain than to leave someone out. Keep technicality to a minimum. Make the English as ordinary as possible, with a determined effort at clarity.

☐ **For example:**

On *dissolution of marriage* (some still call it *divorce*), Arnold is ordered to pay June *spousal support* (some still call it *alimony*). Before the ink is dry, June is living *(cohabiting)* with Leonard.

A new statute creates a "rebuttable presumption . . . of decreased need for support if the supported party is cohabiting with a person of the opposite sex."

Arnold wants to stop paying money to June. The trial court refuses his request, and Arnold appeals. It is an old and an ever-new story. Arnold, June, and Leonard are not the only ones interested in what the judge has to say about this statute. One sentence (one paragraph) says this:

> "Legal analysis would indicate that the Legislature created the presumption against a cohabiting former spouse supported by a divorced husband or wife based on thinking that cohabitation establishes a status for the benefit of the supported spouse and such status therefore creates a change of circumstances so tied in with the payment of spousal support as to be significant enough by itself to require a re-examination of whether such need for support continues in such a way that it should be charged to the prior spouse."

This would have done it:

> "On the facts here, the Legislature presumes that cohabitation with Leonard benefits June, and so changes the circumstances that dictated the order that Arnold support her. Accordingly, we must re-examine June's need for support from Arnold."

There is a further and special reason for care in writing opinions. The way opinions are written—form, language, style—has its widest and most enduring influence on one segment of the judge's audience —the law students. After three years of forced reading of opinions, law students respond automatically to words by judges. Good writing or bad writing, it is a judge's writing. This is the language of those who decide the cases. This is how it is done. The recollection of how it was said often outlasts the recollection of what was said. For better or worse, the opinion affects the basic writing pattern of the profession. And that pattern is inseparable from "the law" itself.

d. Statutes and lesser legislation

Even though "ignorance of law is no excuse," many people are content to stay that way. The Internal Revenue Code (IRC) is not an impulse item snatched up eagerly at supermarkets and airports.

Part of the reason is IRC writing style. But no matter the style, IRC's load of intricately connected detail discourages browsing. So much law builds on other law, minutia that depends on minutia, that few people, other than professionals, want anything to do with it.

Many statutes are of a similar character. Though they touch thousands of lives, most people would rather wait till the moment of violent collision, and then let a professional work things out. It is a continuing gamble we all take, betting against catastrophe in favor of intervening tranquillity. Such statutes need not be meticulously rewritten for those who prefer not to read them.

That does not mean that we ought to resign ourselves to IRC style. Even if it need not be rewritten for a casual readership, the very way the IRC is written helps make it unclear even to those to love her.

☐ **For example:**

Take this excerpt from the IRC on "Amount of carrybacks and carryovers," §172(b)(2):

> ". . . The portion of such loss which shall be carried to each of the other taxable years shall be the excess, if any, of the amount of such loss over the sum of the taxable income for each of the prior taxable years to which such loss may be carried."

Legions of lawyers, dozens of judges have gone down with all guns blazing in that treacherous snatch of long, long sentence construction. As one of the judges states the problem, "the issue in this case is whether the last phrase of section 172(b)(2) 'to which such loss may be carried,' modifies 'taxable income' as well as the words 'prior taxable years.'" In his opinion:

> "As one should probably expect in a case involving the IRC, it is impossible to find any plain meaning in the statutory language that would dispose of this controversy. Given the typically tortured wording of the Code, we feel that each of the parties' interpretations presents a plausible reading of section 172(b)(2) on its face."

> (Mehaffy, C.J., in *Foster Lumber Company, Inc., v. U.S.*, 500 F2d. 1230, 1232, 8 cir., 1974)

Resolution of the controversy by the United States Supreme Court falls very short of a recommendation of the writing. A majority reversed, finding a "natural reading" contrary to the Circuit's "strained reading" of the statute. A dissent (one short of a majority) remained stridently unconvinced:

> "The Court today accepts the Government's contention that the meaning of the critical §172(b)(2) is clearly and unambiguously against the taxpayer. It is said that the phrase 'to which such loss may be carried' obviously modified 'each of the prior taxable years,' rather than 'taxable income.' That the language of the statute is *not* clearly in favor of the government is demonstrated, if by no other means, by the existing

conflict among the Circuits and by the decisions of the District Courts and of the Tax Court, cited above . . . , that have run so uniformly against the Government. If the language were as clear and unambiguous in the Government's favor as is contended, it hardly could have been read otherwise by so many capable and experienced judges. And the clear meaning which the Court now perceives does not, and cannot, comport with the underlying purpose of the carryback and carryover provisions."

(Blackmun, J., dissenting, in *U.S. v. Foster Lumber Co., Inc.,* 429 U.S. 32, 49, 56–58, 50 L.Ed. 2d 199, 212, 216–217, 1976)

The majority's reply is an old reliable. "If Congress had intended to allow a loss deduction to offset only ordinary income when the alternative tax calculation method is used, it could easily have said so."

Why not plainer English, even for tax lawyers? I leave that task to the specialists who know tax law backwards and forwards, what is there, how it got there, and what might be there but isn't. Some of them must be fed up with lawsick.

The character of some legislation precludes the smug IRC assumption that only experts need take notice.

☐ For example:
A city ordinance about sex.

"No person shall, while in or in view of a public or private place, perform:
(1) An act of sexual intercourse.
(2) An act of deviate sexual intercourse.
(3) An act of exposing his genitals with the intent of arousing the sexual desire of himself or another.
(4) An act of urination or defecation, except in toilets provided for that purpose."

The press gleefully reported that a law intended to forbid "lovemaking in public" had been turned into "a ban on sexual intercourse." The ordinance also had the effect of approving a toilet on the front lawn, while forbidding quick relief behind a very private backyard tree. These results cannot be laid at the door of complex legal technicality.

This sort of law generally forbids some acts in *public places* (whether or not viewed by the public), and also forbids those acts in *private places* if *viewable* by the public. Other law (subject to constitutional challenge) defines "deviate" sexual conduct. No law required "*his* genitals" or "desire of *himself*" (Rule 3.1.b.[2], p. 51). No law required the long, long sentence (Rule 3.3.b, p. 58). No law required the writer to forget what modifies what under ordinary rules of English grammar (Rule 3.1, p. 45), nor to abandon any effort at clarity. It is easy to conclude that all of this was the result of too little care rather than too much zeal.

For the books, the ordinance might have said this:

(1) Each of these acts is illegal in public view, or in a public place:
   (a) Sexual intercourse.
   (b) Deviate sexual intercourse.
   (c) Exposure of the genitals, with intent to sexually excite oneself or someone else.
(2) Each of these acts is illegal in public view, or in a public place other than a toilet:
   (a) Urination.
   (b) Defecation.

That makes the ordinance clear enough, while keeping legislative language a cut above baby talk and vulgarism. For posting in a city part, "Clear to whom?" requires another level of language and less detail. This would get enough of the message across:

NOTICE

You are in a public park. Under penalty of the law, these things are not permitted here.
1. To have sex of any sort.
2. To expose your sex organs, trying to excite yourself or someone else.
3. To urinate or move your bowels, except in a public toilet.

Prohibitions that can land someone in jail demand something more than a casual or cavalier approach. Is the writing sloppy because no one thinks you are going to consult an ordinance before pursuing your whims, and so it doesn't really matter? Or that only "bad" people will be arrested anyhow? Whatever the social policy of a criminal statute or ordinance, the theory of our legal system is that you tell 'em before you hit 'em. In the background is a notion of fairness, a right to know; but little is done to see that that right becomes a possibility, let alone a reality. Clearer writing would help.

Many other statutes fall somewhere between the weird complexities of IRC and the broad based prohibitions of the criminal law. There are statutes, for example, that affect people in their daily lives —health, housing, family, the basic buying and selling of household goods. It is lawsick writing rather than legal necessity or conspiratorial design which succeeds in eliminating a substantial audience.

☐ **For example:**
Here is a Uniform Commercial Code (UCC) definition that affects all sorts of people in business, buyers and sellers of goods, as well as ordinary people who buy for their own use.

> "'Buyer in ordinary course of business' means a person who in good faith and without knowledge that the sale to him is in violation of the ownership rights or security interest of a third party in the goods buys in ordinary course from a person in the business of selling goods of that kind but does not include a pawnbroker. . . ."

There is so much stuffing between the head and tail of this turkey that the meat is hard to find. Not until 28 words later do you learn that the "person who" actually "buys." And the unpunctuated rush of words succeeds in creating a doubt whether the tag end "pawnbroker" is a buyer or a seller. Even without disturbing the general pattern of UCC definition, it is possible to make life a bit easier for the reader.

> "Buyer in ordinary course of business" means a person buying: (a) in good faith, (b) without knowledge that the sale violates a third party's ownership rights or security interest in the goods, (c) in ordinary course, (d) from a seller in the business of selling goods of the kind sold. A pawnbroker is not a "buyer in ordinary course of business."

Statutes like these need not be rewritten in basic English to be read by millions. But what of those who could be readily included?

First, the lawyers. It would have been useful, for example, if the UCC could be read and understood by lawyers generally, not only by those few who have made a detailed study of the commercial law. Many lawyers (including many who become judges) do not have daily contact with the buying and selling of goods, nor with the intricacies of checks and promissory notes. Constant litigation proves plainer than anything else that lawyers and judges are overwhelmed by the needlessly technical and obscure jargon of the UCC, and by the long, long sentences that have been used to slap it together.

Non-lawyers are even worse off, until self-educated by bitter necessity. Those who have daily contact with buying and selling, paying and being paid, ought to be able to get some help from such statutes, without consulting a lawyer, or searching to find the right one. Your banker, your broker, your candlestick maker need not be excluded from the basic law they meet every moment of the working day. (For a detailed analysis of UCC talk, see Mellinkoff, "The Language of the Uniform Commercial Code," 77 *Yale Law Journal* 185, 1967.)

e. Regulations and guidelines

Government regulations and guidelines address audiences even more varied than the audiences of the statutes they are designed to give life to. They should not all follow the same pattern.

Where the statute may speak to broad policy, regulations and guidelines get down to the working details.

Sometimes these details are for technicians.

☐ For example:

Here is a regulation about "Position light system dihedral angles" of rotorcraft.

> "If the rear position light, when mounted as far aft as practicable in accordance with §25.1385(c), cannot show unbroken light within dihedral angle A (as defined in paragraph (d) of this section), a solid angle or angles of obstructed visibility totaling not more than 0.04 steradians is allowable within that dihedral angle, if such solid angle is within a cone whose apex is at the rear position light and whose elements make an angle of 30° with a vertical line passing through the rear position light."

Is that clear to you? It's not to me, but it tells me as much about the subject as I care to know. I just hope that before I fly in a *rotorcraft* (you can look it up as I did), somebody will have figured out that regulation. It would take more time and space than its worth to spell it out for me. Most of us wouldn't read it even then, any more than the rotorcraft people are itching to be informed of the "Requirements for certification" of streptomycin sulfate powder oral, covered in another portion of the Code of Federal Regulations.

Sometimes the details are for ordinary people, who may not give a hoot about policy, but are very interested in practice. This audience has been discriminated against by being given equal treatment, i.e., subjected to the same language thrust upon experts.

☐ For example:

Citizens Band Radio (CB) freaks constitute a popular cult in the millions, complete with its own argot. Until recently they were plagued with Federal Communications Commission (FCC) rules written in gobbledygook. They were told (in old rule §95.421(d)):

"Applications, amendments, and related statements of the fact need not be signed under oath. Willful false statements made therein, however, are punishable by fine and imprisonment, U.S. Code, Title 18, section 1001, and by appropriate administrative sanctions including revocation of station license pursuant to section 312(a)(1) of the Communications Act of 1934, as amended."

A lawyer speaks there—to other lawyers, but it tells the guy who wants a two-way radio in his car more about the law than he cares to know.

Two intelligent people (Gregory Jones and Erika Ziebarth) were given the job of rewriting the CB Rules. They reduced it all to a little booklet of CB Rules, in the form of questions and answers. Look at the boldface type of **CB Rule 11   How do I sign my CB license application?** Part of the answer is a rewrite of the old rule §95.421(d). It now says this:

"If you willfully make a false statement on your application, you may be punished by fine, imprisonment and revocation of your station license."

Enough! We get the point.

FCC Commissioner Fogarty gave the new rules an appropriate send-off (March 15, 1978):

"The instant Order, to which this statement is hereby appended, promulgates the subject CB rules, metamorphosed into "plain English" (i.e., visual stimuli more readily perceived and assimilated by median human cognitive faculties and processes). This endeavor has proven to be a salutary and laudatory exercise in efficacious re-regulation designed to bring government into a more symbiotic and empathetic interrelationship with its mass democratic constituency. In a word, this item marks the ascendancy of semantic simplicity over obfuscatory verbiage inimical to the common weal. I am gratified that this collegial body today gives approbation to the felicitous regulatory enterprise concluded herein."

"10-4 Good Buddy!"

President Carter encouraged federal executive agencies to make regulations "as simple and clear as possible." A regulation was to be "written in plain English . . . understandable to those who must comply with it." (Executive Orders #12044—March 3, 1978, and #12221 —June 27, 1980, both revoked by #12291—February 17, 1981.)

The constitution of Hawaii was amended in 1978 to say (Article XVI, Section 13):

"Insofar as practicable, all governmental writing meant for the public, in whatever language, should be plainly worded, avoiding the use of technical terms."

In California, a new law, effective July, 1980, (Govt. Code §§11349–11349.9) calls for a review of the clarity of regulations to see that they are "written or displayed so that the meaning of regulations will be easily understood by those persons directly affected by them."

In New York, a new executive order (No. 100, April 8, 1980, effective June 10, 1980, Par. 2) requires rules, regulations and forms to be "understandable" to those who must comply, "and to the public." It requires "plain language, except where technical terms or terms of art must be used."

These are large orders, only as effective as the degree of informed and insistent guidance at the top. The underlying message is clearer than most regulations: there is no one way to write a regulation. "Clear to whom?"

f. Business contracts

Contracts written by lawyers draw upon the law, but most of those contracts are completely unregulated by the law as to form or language. They are not usually required to be clear, or even legible, and too many of them are neither. They are prepared to be signed. If there is any negotiation at all, the writing lawyer's focus is on another carping lawyer. The writer easily falls into the pattern of the forms and the language he has been taught to rely on.

Sometimes it works. It works best when the contract is signed and forgotten, the job is done, and everyone loves everyone else. This happens oftener than many people suppose. If it didn't, the whole system would collapse. If everyone who could, sued, the catastrophe would be somewhat worse than if everyone who could, divorced.

Systematic indifference to the way contracts are put together also works when the same people repeatedly use the same involved form in the same circumstances, so that no one really bothers to read them to know what they say.

These instances do not prove that clear writing is unimportant, but that the labored contract itself—as it turned out—was unnecessary. A handshake would have done as well, and frequently does. Clarity counts when the contract counts, especially when there is controversy.

Typically, business deals vetted by two sets of lawyers entail bundles of paper. Everyone expects it. The basic deal is agreed upon, for example, between borrower and lender. Each assumes that the lawyers will take care of the details, and the lawyers set out to fulfill those expectations.

The lender's lawyer, in the catbird seat, draws on the firm's old financing agreements to load in protection for the lender. Page after page of special agreements by the borrower. In the piling up of those pages, the English language, grammar, and punctuation are the first casualties. As the mass increases, objective becomes more and more remote, detail more and more important. Consistency of expression goes by the board. Eventually, the search for precision is abandoned in the comforting warmth generated by rubbing details together, repeatedly.

☐ **For example:**

Here are excerpts from an agreement to finance a business. The heading of this section is *Events of Default.*

(1) It starts like this:

"An event of default under this Loan Agreement and the Notes shall be deemed to have occurred if . . ."

Note that the writer is not talking about a plain old *default,* but about a pumped up *event of default.* Also, it doesn't say straight out, *This is a default,* but that the event *shall be deemed to have occurred,* like learned speculation over an eclipse. This is nothing more than warning of low-hanging fog; more predicted.

(2) The agreement goes on to specify a dozen ways in which the borrower can go wrong, "fails to pay," etc. Some of these failures aren't fatal unless they persist beyond a grace period. But the grace period is haphazardly described as so many *days* or so many *business days.* No reason is given for a difference. And no one can be sure that a difference is intended.

(3) A critical part of the agreement covers representations and warranties by the borrower as to the condition of the business. It says this:

"If Borrower shall have made any representation or warranty herein or in any report, financial or other statement or instrument furnished pursuant thereto which shall be in any material respect *false and/or erroneous and/or incorrect* . . ."

What does that mean?

False has the taint of evil; but sometimes it is no more than a synonym of *erroneous* or *incorrect.* If *erroneous* or *incorrect* is enough to hang you, either would easily include falsity. Any difference between *erroneous* and *incorrect?* Find it if you can. Linking redundancy with a double dose of *and/or* seems to create myriad possibilities; but it is the complexity of pretentiousness rather than substance; and can serve no purpose but to give room for later argument. If it is intended to mean *incorrect, whether intentionally so or not,* easy enough to say so.

Six paragraphs later, the writer has forgotten the fine strands of pseudo distinction. Reverting to the same topic, the agreement continues:

> "If any representation or warranties made, or information furnished by Borrower shall be *false and misleading* in any material respect . . . "

There can be a difference between *false* and *misleading.* But for all the phony complexity of *false and/or erroneous and/or incorrect,* now when it counts, nothing. A fine mess to untangle. Which paragraph governs? There are different grace periods in each.

If any written contract is necessary for a business deal, the contract has a better chance of survival if it is so clear to those who write it that they can keep their bearings as they write; and so clear to the lawyers who have to read it now that they can spot trouble in advance and avoid it. Clarity will eliminate potential sources of friction between lawyers, and so between their clients.

In addition, it will be of some help if the writing makes sense to the clients themselves. When the trouble comes, an old dialogue between lawyer and client goes round and round like this.

Client: I told you what I wanted. Why didn't you say that in the contract?

Lawyer: I had to put it in legal language, so it would hold up in court.

Client: What if it doesn't?

Lawyer: Well, *you* looked at it before you signed it.

Client: Sure, I *looked* at it, but that's all; I didn't understand all that stuff. I was depending on you.

Lawyer: Well, I still think it will hold up.

Client: The lawyer on the other side doesn't think so. Is he a dummy?

Lawyer: Well, I still think it will hold up.

Client: What if it doesn't? I told you what I wanted. Why . . .

Stripped of worthless law words, written according to the rules of English grammar, with sentences unwound and chopped up, the ordinary contract need not so widely separate lawyer and client. In trying to make the contract clear to clients, the lawyers will also make their contracts clearer to each other.

g. Writing for ordinary people

Many of the legal writings discussed in the preceding paragraphs may incidentally come to the attention of ordinary people. Some legal writings, written by lawyers or not, are specifically intended for readers who are not usually lawyers. Public notices, official notices to individuals, some contracts, for example, are addressed to people who need to understand in order to decide whether to move or sit still. They are required at their peril to know what the writing says. When that is the case, the legal writer has a special responsibility. Unless it is crystal clear that the intended readers do not want to know what they are entitled to know (as with some statutes and regulations), the legal writer is derelict in putting words on paper that cannot possibly be understood by those to whom they are directed.

If the non-lawyer who is confronted with such a writing has a lawyer by his side, we are back to the case of lawyer-to-lawyer talk. Good English, good grammar, proper punctuation are always essential, but there is no overriding need to scrupulously avoid technical expression.

Few ordinary people habitually go about armed with lawyers: Have lawyer; will translate. So for people of whatever means there is a preliminary question. Do I need a lawyer for this? And for most people, there is the added worry. Can I afford a lawyer for this?

When the writing must be absorbed without professional guidance, and the writer knows it, legal writing cannot be routine. For people without lawyers, technicality wrapped in lawsick prose ought to be studiously avoided. Legal terms of art should not be used except as a last resort. Use terms of art only when necessary to make the writing effective. (See Rule 5, Law, p. 100.) If the law does require terms of art, or if you find yourself unable to part with some other technical expression, hardly any law forbids explanation. That leaves you with the practical problems of deciding when to explain, and how to explain.

[1] When no explanation is necessary

Not every legal term of art or other technical expression used in a writing for non-lawyers need be explained. Some people don't want to be educated in the law. Some people don't want to take the time to inform themselves, and certainly don't want to pay for the cost of enlightenment, whether it's tax money or strictly their own. Some very sharp legal terms of art are so commonplace that for everyday purposes the non-lawyer is content not to know more than he does.

☐ For example:

A *check* (term of art) is a beautifully simple looking piece of paper. Even delinquent juveniles are familiar with it. It consists of a few ordinary words, some blank spaces, and one legal term of art, *Pay to the order of*. The law that affects these little pieces of paper and that particular phrase fills volumes. The ordinary check-writing bill payer has some general awareness

of a smidgin of the pertinent law. If a name is inserted after PAY TO THE OR-
DER OF, that person (whom lawyers call the *payee*) must usually sign on
the back of the check before the check can be cashed or used by someone else.

How much more of the law does an ordinary check-writing bill payer
need to know? Before checks start bouncing, and people start suing, and
the civil and criminal lawyers are called in, does an ordinary check writer
want to be informed of potential hells? I think not. Check writing is repeated, common, and customarily hurried. And I think that ready commercial use of checks need not be burdened with vast recitals of the law of
negotiable instruments.

☐ **For example:**
The relatively ordinary words *I lease to you and you lease from me* would
be generally understood to mean that an owner was agreeing to let someone else use his property.

What the non-lawyer does not understand is that in that combination,
lease is a term of art, sufficient to create the relationship known to lawyers
as *landlord and tenant*. Suddenly, without bugle calls or the roll of drums,
hundreds of years of law governing that relationship spring to action. Except as changed by statute, most of that law favors landowners. Should all
of that be explained in the ordinary modest lease? I think not. If the implica-
tions of the law are too lopsided and too severe, they should be changed
by statute, as protection for the helpless. A simple lease is probably not the
appropriate place for a lecture on the law of real property. Most tenants
wouldn't want it or read it, until the trouble starts.

Similar problems arise with other words in leases. If *assignment* is forbidden, need that be explained? If *subletting* is forbidden, need that
be explained? If both are forbidden, should the legal distinction between them be explained? Or do people who rent have a general notion that those words are talking about turning over the lease to
someone else? Is that enough, without a mass of verbiage that might
make it more difficult to concentrate on what is really important—like
money and time? I would guess "Yes."

Similar problems arise with other creatures of the law. A *corporation* is one of the most sophisticated concepts of the law—a person
who cannot be seen, can be fined, cannot be jailed, can make a contract. How much of corporation law does an ordinary person need to
know when contracting with a corporation? *Corporation* can be a
term of art, but it is also as commonplace in America as cornflakes
and the Ford. If an ordinary person contracts with a corporation,
need there be an explanation of the rules of limited liability? I think
not.

Some problems of the marketplace call in question not merely the clarity of an explanation, but the utility of any explaining. Does explanation do any good at all? Or will the problem yield only to a change in substantive law? Borrowing money, for instance.

TILA (the *Truth In Lending Act*, 15 United States Code, §1601, et seq.) is best known of the laws intended to give borrowers an informed choice. The loan contract must tell how much the money will cost. But usually it is lack of bargaining power, not more or less explanation, that induces the borrower to sign. Sometime it is possible that explanation may be more confusing than helpful. Sometimes, explanation is forbidden, on the theory that a little ignorance is better than total ignorance.

☐ **For example:**

A contract says that if the loan is paid off early, unearned finance charges will be rebated under the *Rule of 78's* (taking its name from the "sum of the digits" from 1 to 12). If $100 were borrowed for 12 months at 12% interest, the simple interest charge would be $12. If the borrower pays off the loan at the end of 1 month, the charge under the *Rule of 78's* is not 1/12 of $12 ($1), but 12/78 of $12 ($1.85). How do you explain the *Rule of 78's* in the loan contract? You don't.

The Federal Reserve Board details the disclosures that TILA requires, and permits other disclosures if they won't confuse the borrower (Regulation Z, 12 Code of Federal Regulations, Part 226). The Board says an explanation of the *Rule of 78's* is so complicated that explanation would befog the loan contract, making the required disclosures less clear. Accordingly, says the California Supreme Court, "an explanation of the rule is prohibited." If remedy is sought, it lies not in words of explanation but in change of the substantive law. (*Drennan v. Security Pacific National Bank*, 28 Cal. 3d 764, 170 Cal. Rptr. 904, 910, 1981).

The conscientious legal writer has no quick and standard answer to the silent question, "Is an explanation necessary here?" The answer will be gleaned from experience in dealing with law and with people. It will not be the same for each transaction, for every person, for every legal technicality. Here are some points to consider in deciding to explain or not to:

1. Required by law? That could settle it.
2. Forbidden by law? That could settle it.
3. Deception—trivial, or gut?
4. Disappointment—trivial, or gut?
5. An innocent, or an old hand?
6. Doesn't want it. Wants to get this, and get on.
7. A full explanation would be too long; a shorter explanation wouldn't say enough.

8. They know enough to make the whole deal reasonable.
9. If they knew what this meant, would they make the deal?
10. Shorter is better. (See Rule 7.2, p. 128).
11. As with questions of precision (Rule 1.2, p. 13), when in doubt, explain.

[2] When some explanation is necessary

To repeat, if you can completely eliminate terms of art and other technical expression, do it. (How that can be done is described in Rule 5, Law, p. 100.) Sometimes you can't. You conclude that a term of art or other legal word of some technicality serves such an essential purpose that nothing else can do the job quite as well. You also conclude that nothing in the law forbids explanation. Your problem has just begun. You now realize that some grasp of the meaning of those very words is of critical importance to the most elementary understanding of the writing, and that the reader just won't have it. Unless you know that the reader hasn't the slightest interest in what the writing says, your self-respect—if nothing else—requires an explanation.

The problem arises most often with all-purpose writings, addressed to anonymities—the "public," "voters," "customers," "policy-holders," "taxpayers." The reader is someone the writer will never face, and so the writing is addressed not to live people but to the faceless. It takes an effort to fill in the features, to create the face that will respond to the writing. And this the legal writer must do, whether it's a contract of insurance, a form for all seasons, or a notice that we're going to cut off the electricity.

Here is a sampling of several types of writings that test the conscience, the imagination, and the skill of the legal writer: public notices, form contracts, and jury instructions.

[a] Public notices

The critical feature of the public notice is the unpredictable diversity of readership. Here certainly is the place to speak the common language, to eliminate technical words that aren't necessary, and to explain those that are.

Typically, the writer of public notices makes no effort to conceal an indifference to the reader. Indifference (if not contempt) reveals itself in non-legal gobbledygook as well as lawsick prose.

☐ For example:
A notice at the entrance to a parking garage says, "This *facility* . . ." *Facility* is the tip off.

Facility is the bureaucrat's dreamboat. You can't pin a *facility* on anyone. Now you see it; now you don't. Now you have it. Now you're in it. It can be a factory or a two-hole privy. Sometimes it turns into a *structure,* also good and vague, but lacking the pizazz of *facility.*

83

If you start off calling a parking garage a *facility,* you'll never get down to plain speaking. You will end up saying: "This facility is the property of John Doe."

What it means can be said so simply: "John Doe owns this building."

Some notices are directed to ordinary people, and yet must be sufficiently technical to satisfy carping lawyers. Here is a place for some split-level writing. Usually it's all flat. The contest is to the carpers. Token words for people, overwhelmed by lawsick.

☐ **For example:**

A dozen lawsuits against insurance companies claim that the plaintiffs were not paid interest on industrial accident awards. The average claim is for less than $6, and so the plaintiffs sue for themselves and for others with similar claims (a *class action*). In a notice covering a half page of a metropolitan daily, the others are invited to join in a proposed settlement.

The notice is addressed:

"TO ALL PERSONS WHO HAVE RECEIVED WORKERS' COMPENSATION BENEFITS IN CALIFORNIA."

That is pardonable overstatement. First you have to get their attention. It invites them to PLEASE TAKE NOTICE, an untechnical, old fashioned, half-polite, half-threatening lawyer's way of saying READ THIS (with a whispered aside—because you might be stuck if you don't).

In smaller type, the notice shrinks the invitation.

"To all persons who since January 1, 1944, to June 30, 1979, obtained an Order, Decision, or Findings and Award from the California Industrial Accident Commission or Workmen's (Workers') Compensation Appeals Board granting a money award against one or more of the followed named insurance companies:

The Travelers Insurance Company (Case No. 948,112, Sweeney v.)" [The notice continues in this vein for 10 more lines.]

Lawyers will understand all that. *Order, Decision, Finding and Award* are legal names for different routes to an award. But what of the $6 claimant? Does he know what he is being told: *If you won* (whether it was called Order, Decision, or Findings and Award)?

Lawyers will also understand that *Sweeney v.* is talking about a claimant named Sweeney *versus* (Latin for *against*) the Travelers. With *Case No.* and that title, they will be able to locate the official files. But what of the $6 claimant? What is a *Sweeney v.?*

The lawyers will also appreciate being told next:

"Please take notice that the above class action cases have been consolidated for settlement purposes and are now pending in the Superi-
or Court of Los Angeles County."

They needed to know, and now know, that *Sweeney v. Travelers* is a *class
action,* and that several cases have been *consolidated* for settlement (a
term of art for *put together,* for procedural, though not substantive
purposes, in this instance to try to work out a settlement).

But what of the $6 claimant? Never heard of an *action* like this, let
alone a *class action* (thus far unexplained), and the *above class action
cases* only adds to the mystery. Non-lawyers don't call a *lawsuit* an *action.*
Consolidated for settlement is a zero, which probably needs no popular
explanation.

In the next paragraph, the whole mess is called THIS LAWSUIT,
which begins to make some sense to everybody. The only trouble is, it
says:

"THIS NOTICE IS TO INFORM YOU SO THAT YOU MAY DECIDE
WHAT STEPS YOU WISH TO TAKE RE THIS LAWSUIT."

Re (ablative of Latin *res*) is legal shorthand, good lawyer to lawyer, and
among those who often deal with lawyers. It is useful argot, but not a term
of art and not necessary to this notice. To the $6 claimant it means nothing,
a barrier to the understanding that almost came with *lawsuit. Re* can be
dropped in favor of *about, concerning,* or *in regard to.* Lawyers can understand that; so will ordinary people. The rest of the notice wanders on,
without discriminating between what is completely unnecessary legal
mush, and what is necessary and should be explained.

□ **For example:**
The notice uses *inflated* language, readily *corrected.*

inflated	corrected
"The above entitled actions are brought and maintained by plain-tiffs . . ."	Plaintiffs are suing . . .
* * *	* * *
"failed, neglected, and omitted to pay the interest . . ."	did not pay the interest . . .
* * *	* * *

85

And the notice uses *technicality,* that can be readily *explained.*

technicality	explained
"the court lacks jurisdiction"	(has no right to hear this case)
* * *	* * *
"shall administratively pass upon the claim . . ."	(informally, without going to court).

[b] Form contracts

The form disease that infects lawyers is discussed under Rule 5 (Law, p. 101); there's a lot of it going around. Here, the focus is on form contracts prepared for use by those who know more, in contracting with those who know less.

The potential readership of most form contracts—insurance policies, leases, loan agreements, purchase agreements, etc.—is more predictable, more limited than with most public notices. But there will still be a wide variety of readers. Most of them (as the writer of the form contract knows) will not have lawyers, despite the "Hey, rube" pitch on some of the forms: "See Your Lawyer Before You Sign."

When you have decided that a technical expression must be included in the form, you can't just dump it and run. Here is a *minimum make-or-break test:*

When the expressions go to the heart of contract, and it is plain as day that a person who knew what the expression meant would balk at signing, explain.

Explain, whether or not the language is required by statute. Explain, whether or not a statute requires explanation. You are the professional.

☐ For example:
Part of a *subordination* clause in a form lease.

"This lease is subordinate to existing incumbrances and to any future incumbrances lessor places on the property."

If the lease is long enough, the print small enough, or the house hunter eager enough, that time bomb will be passed over without comment. Except where limited by statute or decision, *subordinate* here means more than it does in ordinary English. It isn't just *inferior.* It is a whole complex of inferiorities. Under some circumstances, it means that the lease can be wiped out if the lessor borrows on the security of the leased property, and defaults. A lender may insist on *subordination,* and so if the lessor needs money, he needs the clause. The lessee doesn't. Worse than that. Even if the house hunter knows that an *incumbrance* is a mortgage, or something like it, it will not occur to him that what is being given with one hand may be taken away with the other. *Subordination* is a legal term of art, and the innocent needs warning, as in the handling of any other explosive.

It could be done with *Subordination* and *Subordinate* in scarlet ink, surrounded by flourescent asterisks (for signing in dimly lit rooms) referring to giant capitals just above the signature line:

> * THIS IS A WORD WITH A TECHNICAL MEANING. IF YOU WANT IT EXPLAINED, JUST ASK—BEFORE YOU SIGN.

But that would cause more disagreements than it would avoid. When the trouble comes, no one will agree on what was said in explanation. Better do it now. It could say this.

> "This lease is subordinate to existing incumbrances and to any future incumbrances lessor places on the property. (That means, for example, that if lessor does not keep up payments on existing or future loans secured by this property, a lender could cancel this lease.)"

Lessors won't like a provision like that, even if there is a good possibility that the eager house hunter won't read it anyhow. The lessor may decide to drop *subordination* rather than alarm customers. But if the lessor decides it has to be there, a decent respect for ordinary people calls for explanation. It ought to be voluntary explanation, before the voice of the people becomes strident.

Even though you are determined to resolve doubts in favor of explaining, when to explain still remains a matter of judgment. Here is one way of putting the words of a form contract to the *minimum make-or-break test.* Imagine the reaction of an ordinary person, after an explanation.

☐ **For example:**
When you buy something at a store, the law (the Uniform Commercial Code) gives you a *warranty of merchantability.* This implied warranty sets minimal standards for goods to be considered *merchantable.* One standard is that the goods "are fit for the ordinary purposes for which such goods are used." The warranty may be excluded by express language. (The contract here is made, not by signing but by buying.)

> *Scene* A hardware store [the first scene of many lawsuits].

>> Salesman: You said you wanted some stain. Here's a great little number. [Hands can of stain to customer.]

Customer: [Reads the label, which says in large type:

"THIS IS SOLD WITHOUT WARRANTY OF MERCHANTABILI-

TY OR ANY OTHER WARRANTY, EXPRESS OR IMPLIED.

(FOR EXAMPLE, WE ARE NOT SAYING THAT THIS STAIN IS

FIT FOR THE ORDINARY PURPOSES FOR WHICH STAIN IS

USED.) IF NOT SATISFIED, YOU MAY RETURN FOR A FULL

CASH REFUND."]

I thought you said this was a great little number.
Salesman: I did. It is. Look at the price.
Customer: But if it's not fit for the ordinary purposes of stain, what is it fit for? Killing weeds?
Salesman: If you're not satisfied, come back and get a refund. Says so, right here on the label.
Customer: I don't want to come back. How do you expect to sell stain if you're not willing to say I can stain with it?
Salesman: The marketplace will take care of that.
Customer: [Drops can on the concrete floor.] It just did. So long! [A bubbling, brown ooze spreads over the floor.]
Customer: [looking back] Not to worry. It won't stain. [Exit customer].

[c] Jury instructions

It should be noted right off that most jury instructions are not read *by* jurors, but *to* them. While the instruction usually enters the juror by ear rather than by *eye*, few instructions are designed with that distinction in mind. The jury "instruction" is more "tell 'em" *instruction* than "educate 'em" *instruction*. To do either job, a jury instruction would have to say something that jurors can understand.

Jury "instruction" is really a euphemism for *Instant Law Pill* (ILP). The diagnosis is "ignorance of the law," inexcusable, but curable. Compounded according to the legal pharmacopoeia (usually books of form jury instructions), each ILP contains grains of law held together with legal guck. Among practitioners, it is widely believed that the ritual giving of ILPs (number and type varying with the malaise) will clear the lay mind of non-legal nonsense and induce decision "according to law." The ILPs are administered orally just before the patient retires. The jury produces a verdict, and appellate judges declare the treatment a success, "The jury was correctly instructed." If the legal pharmacopoeia was not followed, "The jury was incorrectly instructed." Sometimes, appellate judges decide that the jury was given not ILPs but placebos, and they worked (or seemed to work) as well as the ILPs. The verdict is all right. "The error was not prejudicial." The whole thing is an efficient piece of dramatic fiction. It disposes of cases, even though it has very little to do with jurors understanding the law.

A jury instruction ought to speak directly to the jurors. It already does as a matter of formal address, "Ladies and gentlemen of the jury, you. . ." But that is not enough. It ought to speak directly to the jurors about the law.

Jurors will not learn in an hour what lawyers take years to learn; they might as well be told something about the essence of the law that can affect their verdict. Tell them something that will help them. That means speaking in language the jurors can understand.

Most of the language that bores and befuddles jurors has never had any claim to precision, and is still imprecise despite years of use. The all-time prize package is the universal bit about *burden* (i.e., job) of proving (or establishing) by a *preponderance* of the evidence. The jury is to decide what evidence *preponderates*. How do you do that? Do you *ponder* or *preponder* to find a *preponderating preponderance*? Get yourself instructed.

☐ For example:

> "By a preponderance of the evidence is meant such evidence as, when weighed with that opposed to it, has more convincing force and the greater probability of truth. In the event that the evidence is evenly balanced so that you are unable to say that the evidence on either side of an issue preponderates, then your finding upon that issue must be against the party who had the burden of proving it."

The English is confusing, equating effect *(preponderance)* with cause *(evidence)*. Worse than that, it is not talking to human beings at all, let alone the human beings on the jury. No one talks like that. "Hey Joe, ponder a bit to see what preponderates, will you? I'm going out for a drink."

It is difficult to know what a juror might glean from that ILP. As much as is necessary would be clearer like this:

> "Rogers says that Andrew stole his car, and it is Rogers' job to satisfy you that Andrew stole it."

That won't fit all cases, but the ILP doesn't fit any of them.

Whether the legalisms in instructions are precise or imprecise, the main trouble is that they aren't clear. Even self-righteous dispensers of ILPs assume that explanation is necessary. But how?

☐ **For example:**
Mr. Smith got hurt when he slipped and fell on an icy driveway. This was the instruction explaining *negligence* and *contributory negligence.*

> "Now if you find that the plaintiff failed to maintain and keep a reasonable and proper lookout and/or failed to make reasonable and proper uses of his senses and his faculties and/or failed to take the necessary and proper precautions to observe the conditions then and there existing and/or failed to be watchful of his surroundings and/or failed to use reasonable care for his own safety commensurate with the existing circumstances and conditions, it is negligence and if this negligence substantially, materially and directly contributed to his fall, it constitutes contributory negligence."

Worthless words on words. Pity the jurors, trying to find a predicate for a subject half a mile away, with *and/or* roadblocks in between. Try it yourself. It's difficult to know what a juror might glean from that ILP. Better like this:

> "If you decide that Mr. Smith wasn't paying attention to what was going on—as a reasonable person should, or that he was just plain careless, the law would say Mr. Smith was *negligent.*
>
> "If you decide that Mr. Smith was negligent, and that one of the real reasons he fell was because of his own negligence, the law would call that *contributory negligence.*"

Some lawyers light a candle for the jury. In arguing the case to the jury, they translate the dark words of the instructions. There is no good reason for creating the darkness in the first place. (See a useful article by Craig Spangenberg, "Basic Values and the Techniques of Persuasion," 3 *Litigation* (No. 4) 13 (Summer, 1977.)

[3] The plain language laws

If you have any second thoughts about the need for clarity in legal writing, take a look at the popular phenomenon known as the "plain language movement," and its "plain language laws." This has been briefly noticed (p. 61), and is discussed in some detail in Appendix I. If you, and others, write in accordance with the teachings of this book, plain language laws won't be needed.

Point 3.

Format Over Substance

Even mud can be organized.
Good form will make clearer whatever is there.
Just be sure that something is there to make clear.

Accustomed to getting their law in its most unpalatable forms, most legal writers (especially lawyers) are suspicious of any device that might make the law a little easier to understand. As a result, too much legal writing looks like it was dropped, not written. There are ways of changing that.

Clear writing is the product of many elements, and good form alone will not suffice. But a change of format can sometimes work wonders.

Warnings, two of them, against too much reliance on format. (These parallel the warnings on punctuation, p. 57.)

(1) Unless you are certain that you will control the final format, don't rely on indentation, spacing, or other elements of a working format to convey your sense. A secretary, a printer, or a designer might have different ideas on sense as well as form.

(2) If changes in format still don't seem to produce results, don't labor it. Chances are you need a complete re-write. (See Rule 7.4, p. 140)

a. Rearrange: outline form

To get your precise message through to a complete stranger, with only cold words to break the barrier of isolation, is a small triumph of creative art. The task is difficult enough without unnecessary obstacles. The typical solid type surface of the long, long sentence and the one sentence paragraph (discussed in Rule 3.3.b, p. 58) is one of those unnecessary obstacles.

A dense arrangement of type is psychologically intimidating. What should be the solution becomes mystery, with no obvious clues to the reader as to where the body is buried. Who is out to get whom, what is important, what is subsidiary, what modifies what—all left to the reader to unravel.

Topical arrangement in outline form has much to recommend it. (This refers to an outline format for the finished product, as distinguished from outlining your thoughts in the planning stages; see

91

Rule 6, p. 122.) Details essential to a legal proposition can be made to stand out, to be picked up at a glance. In long contracts, statutes, regulations, rules—with many topics covered in one writing—outline form is most helpful. Clear writing becomes clearer. But even writing that is badly flawed can be improved by opening it up, moving the pieces into a different pattern, and numbering them.

☐ **For example:**
Here is a relatively short long, long sentence, a one sentence paragraph starved of punctuation, badly in need of rewriting.

Set Solid

"The decisive question in this case is whether Congress has granted customs officials the authority to open and inspect personal letters entering the United States from abroad without the knowledge or consent of the sender or the addressee, and without probable cause to believe the mail contains contraband or dutiable merchandise."

Comment
At first glance, the sentence seems to be talking about authority over letters *entering* "without the knowledge or consent, etc." as distinguished from authority to *open* "without the knowledge or consent, etc."
A change of format can help.

In Outline

"The decisive question in this case is whether the Congress has granted customs officials the authority
   a. to open and inspect personal letters, entering the United States from abroad,
   b. without the knowledge or consent of the sender or the addressee, and
   c. without probable cause to believe the mail contains contraband or dutiable merchandise."

Comment
The change of format makes the message come through faster and clearer. "In Outline" is an improvement over "Set Solid."
But in this instance, "In Outline" also makes clear that the sentence is misshapen by trying to squeeze too much into it. Given the raw materials, the sentence is beyond rescue by punctuation or change of format. It needs to be rewritten.

What authority has Congress granted customs officials over personal letters entering the United States? Decisive here is the authority to open and inspect. May it be done without the knowledge or consent of sender or addressee, and without probable cause to believe the letters contain contraband or dutiable merchandise?

b. Fine print. Who reads it?

"Fine print" has for so long been associated with lawyers and tricky contracts that it has become synonymous with concealed qualification, whether achieved by small print or not. The word usage points up the fact of typographical life that ease of reading depends not only on type size, but also on type face (e.g., Roman or italic), length of line, open spaces ("leading"), color of ink and paper, and general layout or design of a printed or typed page. Good design clarifies; bad design confuses.

☐ For example:

An intended disclaimer of warranty was set in type like this:

". . . and no other warranties, express or implied, including without limitation, the implied warranties of *merchantability and fitness for a particular purpose shall apply.*"

Instead of emphasizing the absence of warranty, the italicized words stand out from the body type to give the impression that those warranties do apply. (A court so construed it. *Dorman v. International Harvester Company,* 46 Cal. App. 3d 11, 15, 18, 120 Cal. Rptr. 516, 519 (1975)).

"Fine print" in its classic sense is print so small that it makes reading difficult. Efforts to make legal writing intelligible are easily frustrated if the writing is illegible. They can't understand it if they can't read it.

The one justification for fine print is that it saves space, that some legal writings would be unbearably long if printed legibly. If you are sufficiently interested, use a magnifying glass. But most of us go about unarmed. And fine print discourages detailed examination. Most of us live with "the comfortable and trusting assumption that if it were important it would be printed more clearly."

As a practical matter no one reads fine print in legal writings except lawyers—sometimes. And it is plain deception to put into fine print anything of substance directed to the laity.

Some laws regulate the use of fine print. For an old yet pertinent introduction to the topic, read Mellinkoff, "How to Make Contracts Illegible," 5 *Stanford Law Review* 418 (1953). (See also Mr. Justice Doe on fine print insurance policies in Appendix I.)

c. Why footnotes?

Legal writers, even more than academic writers generally, have become slaves to the footnote habit. Footnotes are used because they make legal writing look "legal."

Other addicts are impressed by the very mass of footnote "documentation." Taken in by the display, they rarely read the footnote itself, the sources cited, or much of the text, before pronouncing the writer "sincere," and the work "sound." This sort of hokum breeds footnotes by the ton, some footnotes even sprouting footnotes of their own. Footnotes are produced so indiscriminately that readers are not safe in skipping the footnotes, lest they miss something important, or miss out on humor which many legal writers think out of place above, but just the thing below.

The ease of dropping random thoughts into the footnote basement tightens the hold of the footnote habit. It takes time and care to weave those thoughts into the text, or to decide that they really weren't important after all. The writer's burden is sloughed off, but the reader may or may not be willing to assume it.

Often the footnoter is more devious than lazy. The footnote becomes, like its companion fine print, a means of concealment. Law that one hesitates to flaunt above the line sneaks into the footnote. Hedges against forthright statements in the text are squirreled away for a rainy day.

Worst of all is the footnoter's feeling of freedom to ramble at the reader's expense (and—in the case of opinions—at the taxpayer's expense). The writer argues with himself, protests extraneous sins of the body politic, brandishes erudition, on and on and on.

Footnotes are not all bad. But footnotes annoy readers. They are a pain in the neck, like watching a vertical tennis game. Worse; they are set in fine print. Use footnotes sparingly.

[1] Rule of thumb

Nothing essential to understanding the main text should be put in a footnote. (Only an emergency should justify departure from that rule.)

If you choose to follow some crotchety footnote system of your own, give the reader warning in the text.

[2] What footnotes are good for

[a] Emergencies

Footnotes are often a publisher's device to avoid the time and expense of resetting for last minute changes. For example: a late decision changing something said in the text; a response to a dissenting opinion; a newly discovered authority that saves you from making a fool of yourself.

[b] Sources

The prime, and still useful, purpose of footnotes in legal writing is to give sources. "Document" anything of consequence. Don't document the obvious (e.g., negligence is the absence of due care). Giving sources enables an interested reader to pursue the research further, and to check up on the writer. It enables a reader with some knowledge of the topic to tell at a glance whether or not the writer is familiar with important sources. The citation tells you where to find it; it is not a quotation. If a quotation is essential to the understanding of the text, put it in the text.

Even footnotes to sources distract readers, and some good legal writers (e.g., B.E. Witkin) prefer giving sources parenthetically in the text. Others find parenthetical interruption of the text more annoying than a footnote. Certainly if a long list of "authorities" is injected into the text, the sense of the sentence is difficult to follow. A single source in the text, with a footnote for additional citations, would make many appellate opinions easier to understand.

[c] Context

Sometimes text will quote portions of a statute, regulation, article, transcript, etc. Though the text can stand on its own, some readers might want more context, right now. A footnote with a fuller excerpt or the whole serves that purpose. If the expanded quotation becomes overlong (running to another page ought to damn it at once) it should be relegated to an appendix. There it will be available to those who need it, without disturbing the reading ease of those who don't. The appendix is especially appropriate when the expanded quotation is reproduced because it is something not otherwise readily available to the general reader.

[d] Special effects

The writer may use a footnote to create a special effect—dramatic, humorous, a sidelight. Skillfully executed, such footnotes relieve tedium for the unhurried reader, and establish rapport between writer and reader. As long as the rule of thumb is followed, and the special effect remains "special," the art is worth cultivating.

☐ For example:
An opinion affirms conviction of robbery. At gunpoint, the robber tells his victims:

"Don't say a word, don't say a mother-fucking word."

95

The hurried reader can read on, getting everything essential. But below the line, on the same page, a footnote follows that quotation.

> "It is a sad commentary on contemporary culture to compare 'Don't say a word, don't say a mother-fucking word' with 'Stand and deliver,' the famous salutation of Dick Turpin and other early English high-waymen. It is true that both salutations lead to robbery. However, there is a certain rich style to 'Stand and deliver.' On the other hand, 'Don't say a word, don't say a mother-fucking word' conveys only dismal vulgarity.
>
> "The speech of the contemporary criminal culture has always been a rich source of color and vitality to any language. Yet, when one compares the 'bawds,' 'strumpets,' 'trulls,' 'cut-purses,' 'knaves,' and 'rascals' of Fielding and Smollett to the 'hookers,' 'pimps,' 'Narcs,' 'junkies,' and 'snitches' of today's criminal argot, one wonders just which direction we are traveling civilization's ladder. . ."

(Gardner, P.J., in *People v. Benton,* 77 Cal. App. 3d 322, 324, n.1 (1978))

* * *

(For an excellent critique of the spreading pestilence, see Wheeler, "The Bottom Lines: Fifty Years of Legal Footnoting in Review," 77 *Law Library Journal* 245 (Spring, 1979).)

d. Just "you" and "I"

The "plain language movement" has rediscovered the pronouns "you" and "I." Some now hail these born again pronouns as the key to legal simplification. The pronouns are short, easy to read, and give an appearance of intimacy lacking in a third person label. Any normal person would rather be an "I," or even a "you," rather than a "Party of the First Part." (Recall the new Citizens Band Radio regulations, discussed on p. 76.) But don't be carried away by a formula.

[1] The "letter agreement"

Contracts formed by an exchange of personally addressed letters ("offer" and "acceptance") are as old as the hills. So too, with the personalized offer, followed by some act of acceptance—a shipment of goods, or something else called for in the offer.

☐ For example:
The now familiar magazine campaign.

> *"You too can be in a Campari ad!* Just send your "Campari Quip," snapshot, and phone number to P.O. Box . . . If selected, your photo,

name and witticism will appear in a future Campari ad—and you'll receive $100. (Sorry, nothing can be returned.)"

For decades, many lawyers have cast some of their contracts in the form of the softer sounding "letter agreement." They abandon the boilerplate introduction, "This agreement, made and entered . . . Party of the First Part. . . Party of the Second Part." Instead, they write a letter.

☐ **For example:**

> Mr. John Doak
> Los Angeles, Calif.
>
> Dear Mr. Doak:
> You and I agree:
>   1. . . .
>   2. . . .
>   3. . . .
>
> Agreed: Very truly yours,
>   Bill Jones
>
> John Doak

The format eliminates unneeded formalism. Definitions of "You" and "I" aren't necessary, any more than they are in ordinary correspondence. You can tell at a glance who is talking and who is supposed to be listening. When the contract is short and uncomplicated, it works.

The refreshing informality of "you" and "I" disappears in the bowels of the long, long sentence, and the long, complicated contract. All that is left is an auspicious beginning. The good auspices end with the first line salutation; sometimes sooner.

☐ **For example:**

> "Plotz Corp.
> Wilmington, Del.
>
> Gentlemen:
> As an inducement to you to enter into the employment agreement bearing even date and executed concurrently herewith by and between you and me, I hereby grant to you, your successors and assigns the sole and exclusive rights and license to use, depict and portray certain incidents from my life in and in connection with the writing, composing, and preparing of a motion picture screen story by

97

John John and/or such other writer or writers as you may engage
therefor and to use all of the foregoing in and in connection with the
preparation, production, exhibition and/or distribution of a motion picture photoplay to be based upon said screen story in which motion
picture photoplay you have engaged me to appear and render services as aforesaid. . . ."

That's about as informal as a death warrant. No "I" never wrote such a letter. "You" did it. And "you" have now turned it upside down to make it appear that it was all "my" idea. The personal pronouns are smothered.
Pages later, the reader has to flip back to the beginning to figure out who is
inducing whom. On the long ones, the pronouns get lost. They become a
nuisance. "Plotz" and "Anderson," or "the Corporation" and "the Employee," are easier to keep track of. "You" and "I" have no special magic that
will get you out of a mud hole.

[2] Jolly, jolly — BANG!

The "You" and "I" format also has an inherent frailty that dictates
cautious use. The very virtue of conversational informality lends itself
to conveying a sense of camaraderie that may be essentially inconsistent with the adversary relation of the parties. If pronouns get too
friendly, they tend to induce an unwarranted relaxation of attention to
detail.

☐ For example:
A chatty loan agreement that starts out with a real big Broadway "Hello."

"Dear Money Shopper:
We are real glad to have you with us. We think you'll like it here at
Cozy Finance. We'll try to save you money and make some for us too.
Please read all of this very carefully. If you get the shorts at any time,
let us know, and we'll try to help. . . ."

That's only for starters. It is followed by a lot of jolly loan details, cleanly,
conspicuously printed. After paragraphs oozing with goodwill, BANG!

"WHOLE BALANCE DUE. If you fall more than 10 days behind in a payment, we can without notice declare the whole outstanding balance,
including any unpaid FINANCE CHARGE, due and payable at once.
We can also do this if you break any of your promises under this
agreement or fall behind on any other obligation to us. If this happens,
we can without notice take the outstanding balance out of your check-
ing and/or savings accounts."

So much for jolly, jolly. The party is over. Break your word on this or "any other obligation to us," and "without notice" (not in capitals), we move.

Borrowers, of course, should not expect even a jolly lender to laugh away defaults. But the cosmetic friendliness of "you" and "I" may create a feeling of relaxed good humor that discourages careful scrutiny of the tougher provisions of a loan agreement. For you, the legal writer, it is worth remembering that it is clear law and not a banana split you are serving up, and the customer should never have any doubts about what it is that he is eating.

RULE 5.

Law

WRITE LAW SIMPLY. DO NOT PUFF, MANGLE, OR HIDE.

The only thing about legal writing that is both unique and necessary is law. To simplify legal writing, first get the law right. You can't simplify by omitting what the law requires or including what the law forbids. The better you know the law the easier to decide what law ought to go in, and what is overkill or window dressing.

The oldest cure for complexity of the law is simplicity itself. Repeal it. Or, outlaw lawyers. Both cures have been tried. Neither cure outlasts a modest increase in population, a touch of prosperity, or a mild recession.

Most simplifiers sail under less defiant banners. Don't repeal *it,* or outlaw *them;* rewrite it. But once you are reconciled to the necessity of law, you must stick with it until the law is changed. You deceive yourself, or your clients, or the public, if you confuse the process of changing the substance of the law with the mechanics of rewriting it.

At the right moment, the substance of the law should be changed, deliberately. The writers and the decision makers should work together, whether you deal with statutes or with regulations. (On the details of that collaboration, see Dickerson, *Legislative Drafting,* 1954, and Dickerson, ed., *Professionalizing Legislative Drafting,* 1973.)

When writers and decision makers do not work together, the writer is hobbled. "This is our agreement; this is our deal. Write it up!" The temptation is almost irresistible to eliminate substantive garbage in the writing stage, re-legislating, re-regulating, re-negotiating. Resist it. If definite agreement has already been reached, and forthright persuasion won't work, change of substance under the guise of improving the writing is dishonest. Similarly, with the writing of a contract. To change a deal, to omit what the law requires, or include what the law forbids—under the guise of improving or simplifying the writing—is either fraudulent or incompetent.

Within those limits, a lot can still be done.

Point 1.

Omit Unnecessary Law

The best way to simplify the law in legal writing
is to omit unnecessary law.

Legal writing is complicated enough with the law that must be there.
Its subject matter is formidable enough to scare most people and bore
the rest, without overkill or window dressing. For those who do a lot
of legal writing, especially lawyers, the first problem in trying to omit
unnecessary law is what to do about pre-packaged law—the forms.

a. The form disease

The form disease is a substantial obstacle to any simplification of legal
writing. A long history of dealing in words has left lawyers (and
non-lawyers who follow their deep, muddy trails) overstocked with
forms for everything. Agreements to keep sheep free of cockleburs,
how to deal with atomic energy, on the "care, upkeep, and
maintenance of bees and the extraction of honey," how to sell real
estate or form a corporation, how to plead in court, and what to do
before you get there. If you can name it, we've got it. Don't think;
reach. That's the form disease.

[1] The virtue is the vice

For writers, the virtue of the forms is that they save time—thinking
time, learning time, writing time. They also save reading time. For the
reader in a rut—e.g., judges, clerks, lenders—reading the same old
stuff every day, the forms are a blessing. Check the form number (and
date), what's filled in and what's scratched out, and skip the rest;
you're in business. For busy professionals, the attraction is strong.

The virtue of the forms is also their vice. They are a quick, cheap
substitute for knowledge and independent thinking. The trail is
marked (maybe in blood, but that takes time to find out): the illusion
of security. It looks "legal"; lots of law in there. Take it as it is, and
banish the lawyer's nightmare—"You left something out." It may not
fit exactly, but the sham authority of a printed form is impressive,
discouraging detailed examination. So easy to skim, and—in the
welter of law and language—to overlook defects of inclusion or
omission. Formbooks advise users to check carefully to make sure the
form fits. But if they have to be checked out too carefully the forms
lose their value. To save time, they are taken on quick faith by the
ignorant, the timid, and the too busy—law and all; needed or not.

[2] What to do

Despite the vice of the form, its practical virtue must often carry the day. No one who makes frequent use of the law will ever live long enough to live without forms.

Some forms are required (e.g., some pleading forms, notices, instructions). On those you have no choice, until the next time around, when there is opportunity to have them recast, trimmed, eliminating the unnecessary.

Some forms you can create anew; without the old claptrap. For the rest, the fate of the form rests with the discriminating user. As with other species of legal writing, some forms are better than others. Some can be rewritten, simplified, trimmed of the unnecessary. Against the temptation of time saved today weigh the embarrassment of tomorrow. "I found it in a form" won't satisfy anyone.

b. Varieties of unnecessary law

Bad habit, sometimes rooted in fear of changing a form, routinely overloads legal writing with unnecessary law. What is "unnecessary"? If you don't know the law (or get expert advice), you are doomed to suffer someone else's muddle and mush. Though you need not suffer in silence. You can still ask the needling question, "Does it have to be this way?" Often the answer is "No." Law may be unnecessary because (1) irrelevant, (2) inappropriate, or (3) superfluous.

[1] The sound of law

Some sentences talk a lot of law without saying anything that matters a bit. The talk is confusingly irrelevant, and should be left out.

☐ For example:

> "I, Jane Doe, being of sound and disposing mind and memory, and not acting under duress or the undue influence of any person whatsoever, do hereby make, publish, and declare this to be my last will and testament."

That spells out some of the details of will making, albeit redundantly. To make a will, Jane Doe must be of sound mind. If she acted under duress or undue influence, the will may be void. She must "declare" it to be her will. Some of those details might be instructive in a manual on how to make a will.

But under the law at its maddest, the insane do not become sane by saying so, or the victim of the pointed gun free of duress by saying so. Nor does the law require the duplicating and imprecise *mind and memory, last will and testament,* or *make, publish, and declare.* You can make a declaration without saying "I declare."

Read the will aloud.

"I, Jane Doe, being of sound and disposing mind and memory, and not acting under duress or the undue influence of any person whatsoever, do hereby make, publish, and declare this to be my last will and testament."

It has the sound of law; that's all. Despite its detractors, the law is more than tinkle. The only legal substance in the form that counts in the will can be said better in four words:

This is my will.

[2] A cannon to kill a mouse

Some writing has a wealth of legal detail out of all proportion to what is practically called for by the size and nature of the transaction.

Legal devices to protect the lender of $1,000,000 are written into a $100 note. Precautions appropriate to an expensive 20-year lease are written into a modestly priced lease that landlord or tenant can end in 30 days. A 25-page trust is added to the will of a client whose only asset is a delusion of grandeur.

Holy Coke! Maybe I've left something out. I don't want to use a BB gun to kill a moose. Throw in the works. The result is unnecessary law, greater opportunity for error and misunderstanding. Overprotection. A cannon to kill a mouse.

☐ **For example:**
A long term lease of business property usually has detailed provisions to make certain that the tenant remains the tenant, and doesn't turn the property over to someone else. Prohibitions against the tenant's assigning, subletting, mortgaging or pledging the lease, typically "without the written consent of lessor first had and obtained;" special acts that may constitute an assignment, e.g., sale of stock of a corporate tenant, merger or consolidation of a corporate tenant, transfers of interest from one tenant to the other; the effect of doing these things "without the written consent of lessor first had and obtained;" the effect with consent, etc.

In a lease for one month, such detail is overkill. The lease will end before it is understood. The landlord is overprotected. Prospective tenants are frightened off. Instead of all that, this would ordinarily be enough:

Lessee may not assign or sublet.

All the talk about lessor's consent is unnecessary. With the lessor's consent, the tenant can stay there forever, rent free.

☐ **For example:**

A bank loan agreement lists a host of events that permit the lender to "accelerate" the time for payment of a note, i.e., to demand payment in full right now. Only space and the legal imagination limit the number of critical events. Failure to pay an instalment of the note, failure to pay any other debt owing from borrower to lender, death of the borrower, insolvency, an assignment of assets for the benefit of creditors, bankruptcy, a petition filed by someone else asking that the borrower be declared bankrupt or that a business to be placed in receivership, legal proceedings by other creditors to attach the borrower's property, etc.

Felsenfeld and Siegel (the authors of *Simplified Consumer Credit Forms* (1978), in consultation with their banker client, decided that with most small loans most of such detail was overkill. They decided that most of those disasters would show up quickly enough, if not sooner, in one of two ways—late payment or attachment. They rewrote the small loan agreement to list only those two items as events permitting acceleration. The rest was using a cannon to kill a mouse.

It takes time to simplify. It saves using and reading and understanding time, but it is an investment of time in the preparing. A good investment. It means dealing with complexity now—complexity of law, complexity of practical economics. Lawyers and writers and client (or other policy maker) work together to arrive at the joint conclusion that more law is not only unnecessary, but bad—for business, for people, for clear statement of essentials. If the problem is not resolved now, it will come to rest in too many words and too much law, "just in case."

A cannon to kill a mouse is typical not only of agreements, but of all sorts of legal writing. Technical opinions of appellate courts cluttered with law familiar to first year law students, legal articles short on innovation but long on documenting the obvious, regulations written by the timorous with unnecessary law as a cover for ignorance, etc. As with language generally (Rule 4.2, p. 65), law should be dispensed selectively, directed to purpose and persons. Too much law simply gets in the way.

[3] Gilding the lily

Some writings are lengthened and complicated by spelling out in detail law that will be a part of the writing whether or not anything is said about it. It is superfluous, something already "provided by law," by statute, by decision, by regulation, by common law principle. This is what lawyers are supposed to know.

If the spelling out of those details is deliberately designed to inform those who do not know what is "provided by law," it can serve a good purpose. Usually, the details are unplanned. Not design but habit gets them in. And they serve merely to lengthen agreements, beclouding the essentials.

☐ **For example:**
In the detailed provisions against assignment or subletting of a lease (the sort mentioned on p. 103), here is one sentence buried in the mass.

"The lessor's consent to any such assignment, or subletting, shall not relieve the lessee from any obligation under this lease, unless the lessor expressly agrees in writing to relieve the lessee from such obligation."

That sentence states no more than what is "provided by law." It's already in there. Without those 34 words, the lease would be the same. If it were really designed to inform an innocent, it would better serve that function plucked out of the fine print mass. As it is, it gilds the lily, informs no one, and makes it more difficult to know what is really going on.

Point 2.

Change the Words

Whether or not you omit unnecessary law,
you can simplify the law in legal writing
by changing the words that express the law.

Law and lawsick have become so entwined that most people think them inseparable. Lawyers, prepared to condemn every other form of gobbledygook, see their own language as time tested, necessary. Non-lawyers, accustomed to seeing the law couched in the mystifying gibberish of the ages, have been conned into believing that unless the law looks like that it really can't be law. Fortunately little of the meaty substance of the law depends on a peculiar form of expression. (See Rules 1, 2, 3, and 4.) In most cases, it is possible to change the words and still end up with the same old law. That possibility, ignored by most lawyers and bureaucrats and clerks and copyists, holds real opportunity for simplifying the law in legal writing.

Warning To Non-Lawyers

Simplified language alone will not rid you of the substance of the law. What we are talking about here is keeping the law, and changing only its form of expression. Simplified language may make clearer what goes on behind the lines. But do not drop your guard. The law may be in sheep's clothing, but the old wolf with the sharp teeth will still be there.

a. First, a clean sweep

To keep the law, but simplify it by changing the words, the first operation is a clean sweep of accumulated rubbish. As discussed in Rule 1, (p. 2), too much of the language of the law is anachronism, a deservedly endangered species, that needs only a little help to become what befits it—extinct. With the junk antiques of the legal vocabulary, this is a matter of writing in the twentieth century instead of the fifteenth or sixteenth. The written law gets along better today without a single *whereas*, without the coupled synonyms, without the old formalisms that clutter without informing or impressing the modern world. With the Latin habit and law French, it is mostly a matter of translation, as with the translation of any other foreign language; and it is readily done. In and out of the law, today we live with English (Rule 3, p. 44), and—unless there's an awfully good reason to use something else, your best bet for clarity is ordinary English (Rule 4, p. 62). The stumbling block in simplifying legal writing is the term of art (Rule 1.1.e, p. 7), and it deserves special treatment.

b. Dealing with terms of art — guidelines

One of the dangers of learning terms of art is a compulsion to use them. A natural inclination to feel that one's education has not been wasted (Rule 1.2. p. 13, and Rule 4.1, p. 63) harmonizes perfectly with the professional's chronic sense that time is short. Lawyers rarely take the time to consider whether or not a term of art is really called for. A predilection to disgorge congested word mass is reinforced by fear of failure, and by the cliché they have learned from others —"form follows function."

The cliché would have it that since law is complex, the form in which it is expressed must be complex. That becomes a tidy rationalization not only for long sentences with too many modifiers, but also for complicated words. A complicated concept, it says here, cries out for something other than ordinary, simple words; the term of art fills the bill.

The analysis is a distortion. It ignores the underlying idea of the term of art as a relatively short statement of technicality, reducing complexity to precise, shorthand expression. It is simple for those who understand it and know how to use it. Worshippers at the shrine of the term of art go one fatal step further. They believe that because a complicated legal concept *can* be expressed in a term of art it must always be expressed that way.

At the other extreme, some of today's advocates of "plain language" are heirs to the ancient belief that terms of art are at least a conspiracy of the lawyers if not an invention of the devil. They pit themselves sternly against the inevitability of terms of art or any other technicality in the law. In trying to find a way around the term of art stumbling block to plain language, some legislators have proposed outlawing all technical expression. At least one has suggested a compromise—a quota system. The suggestion was not too specific, but it would work something like this: A limit of one term of art per short paragraph, two for long paragraphs, and an overall limit of 10 terms of art per consumer contract. Beyond that, you're drunk.

Centuries ago, the lawyer inventors of terms of art never had any doubts about whom they were addressing: technicians, each other. That assumption, like the companion assumption of the inadequacy of English, no longer stands up. The term of art is not always adequate to tell those who need to know about legal complexity. Complexity in the law is a fact that cannot be soft talked away. But other words can help to explain complexity, if the explainers know something about law and something about language.

Neither forced dosage nor outlawry are adequate methods of dealing with terms of art. No single formula solves all the problems. Here are some guidelines that will help.

[1] Identification

The first problem, how to identify a term of art, is discussed in Rule 1.1.e (p. 7), with samplings and explanations in Appendix H. The definition of a term of art as a technical word with a specific meaning does not work automatically. You have to learn them, or look them up in a law dictionary. Short of that, you can quickly enough get a feel for what they are not.

☐ For example:
You read in a legal publication

> "that the committee was 'considering the possibility of exploring avenues which might give fresh light on the basic problems involved.' "

If you think that's a bad connection, hang up, and dial again.

> "The committee said it expects to present a 'progress report' at the annual meeting . . ."

With half an eye you can see that *progress report* is not a term of art.

Whatever the degree of sharpness, the self-limitation of the term of art as both technical and specific must always be out in front. The blunt instrument doesn't qualify.

[2] How sharp?

Terms of art come in degrees of sharpness, not precisely calibrated. Some are more technical, some more specific. The sharper the technicality, the more specific, the greater the odds that no other words will suffice as a substitute.

☐ **For example:**
Fee simple is an old and sharp term of art describing ownership as absolute as is known to property law. The typical expression is, "It is an estate in fee simple." *Fee simple* is usually shortened to *fee:* "It is owned in fee." No other words quite translate *fee simple* or *fee* in this sense. It can be explained, with details distinguishing *fee simple* from other varieties of ownership.

By contrast, in a completely different area of the law, *holding* or *hold* (in the sense used on p. 69—"In this case we hold that . . .") is a weak term of art. It describes for the profession the precise issue or principle that a case stands for, as distinguished from passing comment—*dictum,* not necessary to decision. Yet the term of art is closely related to the ordinary English—*holding a belief*—"We hold these truths to be self-evident . . ." As much as is essential to a non-lawyer's appreciation can be gathered from the ordinary English sense of the word. Its special, technical sense for lawyers makes it a term of art, but it doesn't have the clout of *fee simple. Holding,* within the profession, is sometimes rendered as *the issue decided, the rule that case stands for,* or *what's decided there is,* and there are few mourners. The flags would fly at half staff at the passing of the *fee.*

☐ **For example:**
Petition is a mild term of art, meaning about the same thing as in ordinary English usage, i.e., *asking.* Usually, a *petition* is written; sometimes lawyers call it an *application,* or a *motion;* it would make the same sense. But *petition* has its special uses. In asking for a *writ of certiorari,* for example, *petition* is the technical way to *ask,* to be sure it's filed in the right basket.

By contrast, look at that *writ of certiorari.* In a limited number of cases there is a constitutional right of appeal to the Supreme Court of the United States. In other cases, the Court has a discretion to hear appeals or reject them out of hand. If enough justices think the questions raised in a request for a hearing are sufficiently important, more important than a crowded calendar, a hearing is granted. There is a special way of asking for that hearing. You file a *petition for a writ of certiorari.* That's a sharp term of art.

The *writ* part is Old English for something *written,* here—a written *order. Certiorari* (legal pronounciation, SIR-SHER-UH-RARE-E) is one of the words of the older Latin form of the writ, directing a lower court *to inform* us about a case, by sending "up" the papers. Some courts have dropped the Latin, using, e.g., a *writ of review* for the same purpose; but not the supremest.

In opinions, *writ of certiotari* is usually shortened to *certiorari.* And one lawyer tells another in legal slang that the Court "granted" or "denied" *cert* (complete without period). The people who have to use it know it as a familiar. It works. In the courts where it has found a home, as in the Supreme Court of the United States, nothing else is quite like *certiorari.*

[3] Controlled environment

The built-in limitations of the term of art (technicality + specific meaning) dictate that it be used sparingly. It requires a highly controlled environment: right word, right time, right place, right people. Out of that environment, the term of art is like a fish out of water. It may flop around a bit, but survival is a poor bet.

[4] Translate or explain

One way or another, a term of art can be rendered in ordinary English, either translated—with a relatively short equivalent, or explained —at greater length. When simplification or explanation is needed (Rule 4.2, p. 65), the most complex ideas in the law can be put into simpler, clearer language—if the choice is made and the effort is made. Though it sometimes sounds like it, no one is born talking lawsick. As it says in the song, "You've got to be taught."

☐ **For example:**
For ordinary people alone, no *certiorari.* Translate: "The Supreme Court has agreed to hear our appeal" would ordinarily suffice. For the curious, a slightly larger dose by way of explanation—a dose that need not be either fully legal or lethal—as in this book.

When ordinary people and professionals are addressed, as in a newspaper report of a Supreme Court decision (perhaps published before the profession gets other word) term of art *and* translation may be in order. This would do it:

"The United States Supreme Court today agreed to hear the appeal (granted certiorari) in . . ."

If the publication is addressed mostly to the profession, but incidentally to others interested, the emphasis can be reversed.

109

"The United States Supreme Court today granted certiorari (agreed to hear the appeal) in . . ."

[5] For professionals

The closer the use of a term of art is restricted to a professional circle, the less occasion there is for abstinence, translation, or explanation. That does not mean "no occasion."

In the technician's workshop (law office, court, court papers, treatise and articles just for lawyers) terms of art are useful and ordinarily need no explaining. Sometimes they do.

As pointed out earlier (Rule 1.1.e, p. 11), some terms of art are so restricted to a particular specialty or area of the law that other lawyers may be as ignorant as non-lawyers. If the term of art is that esoteric, translation or explanation is urgently required if the specialist wants to be understood by lawyers who are members of a different coven.

☐ For example:

Holder is a term of art in the law of commercial transactions. It is defined in the Uniform Commercial Code (UCC §1–201(20)).

> ". . . a person who is in possession of a document of title or an instrument or a certificated investment security drawn, issued, or indorsed to him or his order or to bearer or in blank."

At best, the definition is overlong and ambiguous. For present purposes, note that to qualify as a UCC *holder* it is not enough that you just "hold" something. Smith is "in possession" of a check written "Pay to the order of Jones." If Jones has not indorsed, Smith is not a UCC *holder* of the check, though quite clearly an ordinary English "holder." Non-lawyers are misled, and so are lawyers.

If the specialist addresses someone other than a specialist, *holder* is confusing. *Holder* better be identified—"as defined in UCC §1–201(20)," or, generally, "one who is both in possession of the paper, and directly or indirectly referred to in the paper."

[6] For ordinary people

The closer the use of a term of art comes to touching ordinary people, the greater the desirability of not using terms of art at all, or of translating or explaining those that are used. That does not mean "always." It does not mean outlawing terms of art, nor does it inevitably mean translation or explanation.

As pointed out earlier, some terms of art may be essential to legal validity, and yet the circumstances make explanation unnecessary, undesirable, or even forbidden. (Refer to Rule 4.2.g.[1], p. 80.) Those circumstances are the exception, not the ordinary. Follow the guideline.

[7] When in doubt

If you work your way through all those other guidelines, and are still in doubt about how to deal with a term of art, do not despair. You will have lots of company. Resolution will depend on the nature of your doubt. It is probably one of these.

[a] Is it precise?

As stated before, resolve the doubt in favor of explaining (Rule 1.2, p. 13).

[b] Who is in the audience?

As stated before, write for the widest audience (Rule 4.2, p. 66). With terms of art, that may mean term of art for the professionals, plus translation or explanation for the non-professionals.

[c] Is an explanation necessary?

As stated before, resolve in favor of explaining (Rule 4.2.g.[1], p. 83).

[d] Does the law require these words?

(See Rule 4.1.a, p. 63). The books may resolve the doubt; go to the books. If the doubt won't go away, use the words, *and* translate or explain, according to audience and necessity, as in [b] and [c].

Point 3.

Lay It On The Line

Don't palm off the appearance of simplicity
as simplicity. Don't play hide-the-law.

Practical considerations put a limit on how much law can be spelled out in any particular piece of legal writing. There is so much law on almost any subject you can think of that individual documents can use only a bit of it, with much more always available when there is time, space, and the thirst for more.

Often no one wants legal minutiae spelled out; often there is no need for it. Often opposing sides deliberately put off for tomorrow law that could be spelled out today only at a terrible cost. Other objectives of legal writing are sometimes more important than a full dose of law. (See Rule 6.1, p. 115). Lay it on the line, yes. But, please, not that many lines!

Those considerations to one side, you will want to set out some law in every legal writing. Whatever it is, don't hide it. *Hide-the-law* can become a word game, more fascinating than Scrabble, and twice as deadly. It's bad enough if you are simply carried away by the word game, scattering scraps of law through the paper as the fit strikes you, reckless of how the clues may be put together. It is much worse to plan it that way. As the report out of Washington said, "The errors were primarily unintentional . . ."

Some of the most studied efforts to *hide-the-law* are directed at those most likely to understand, if only they were aware of the legal needle in the haystack. *Hide-the-law* is simply more disgraceful when those who should be helped are deliberately misled.

a. Potpourri

No complete inventory of how to *hide-the-law* is possible. Traditionally, law is hidden in the fine print (Rule 4.3.b, p. 93); footnotes serve the purpose (Rule 4.3.c, p. 94). The boring monotony and the hard-to-follow grammar of the long, long sentence (Rule 3.3.b, p. 58) is an effective hide-away. An excess of words, pages and pages of them, has the special soporific advantage of hiding law that is there, and hiding the fact that some law that ought to be there isn't. A favorite among misleading word combinations is *subject to change by mutual consent* to soften the unpalatable, when nothing at all is given away. The advantages of good format generally as an aid to clarity (Rule 4.3, p. 91) suggest to the devious the reverse. A confused format can drive the reader mad, or a very soothing format can administer a stupefying massage instead of a message. One ploy, common and vicious (sometimes inadvertent), deserves special mention.

b. The shell game

The essence of the shell game is that the pea, obviously under this shell, isn't. It is played out on a dozen fronts in legal writing.

Here is a contract, or lease, or statute. The English is pretty straightforward, plain. The sentences are not too long. The paragraphs are not too long; lots of indentations. The sections are all numbered, and captioned—in type that stands out from the text. The body type is not too small; could have more white space, but you can't ask for everything. This is the kind of legal writing you would like to have every day—most of the trappings of easy-to-read-and-understand, simplicity itself.

Skim it to find what you're looking for. Here's a caption for subject matter that interests me. What I was afraid might be there isn't. If it were included, that's where it would be. Must be left out. Good.

The writing is simple all right, and made simpler by leaving something out. Well, not exactly left out; the pea is under a different shell —far removed from the center of attention. That's the shell game.

☐ **For example:**

Some landlords want to get rid of a rash of annoying local rent control ordinances—18 of them. Their initiative constitutional amendment labeled "FAIR RENT CONTROL STANDARDS" runs to 158 lines, about 1500 words in the ballot pamphlet. Near the beginning, one 8 line section is captioned *"[Local Ordinances]."* That's the guts of the thing; rent control must be by local ordinance, not by the state. What about the 18 local ordinances that caused the brouhaha? *"[Local Ordinances]"* doesn't mention them at all. Left out?

Hey sucker, lookee over here! Seventy-nine lines away from the action is a quick 3 liner—23 words sunk in the 1500 word mass—captioned with 4 words of platitudinous innocence that no one could quarrel with—or even care much about reading— *"[Conformity with State Law]":*

"No local jurisdiction shall continue in force any existing rent control after the next election in that jurisdiction following adoption of this article."

That fixes those 18 nasty local ordinances. It repeals them.

RULE 6.

Plan

BEFORE YOU WRITE, PLAN.

In the quiet time before you become excited with your own
words-on-paper, plan. Talk over the goals with those who know
more facts than you do, and maybe even more law. Mull, jot, fret,
read, outline. Then write. If you start from a plan, the writing will
help your thinking and writing. Unplanned, the flow of words
becomes a distraction.

Before the writing comes the problem, some tougher than others, no
two exactly alike. No problem is self-analyzing except those that need
only a machine for a print-out; no writers. The problems that call for
legal writers need first of all a fixing of general goals, the beginning of
consultation between writer and policy maker. Facts and the law and
more consultation may change the original goal, or at least change
the steps in arriving at it. At some point in the chain of consultation,
the gathering of facts and law and their analysis, the computer may
speed or refine a solution. Codifying scattered pieces of law, organiz-
ing complicated contracts, ferreting out intricate relationships—of
people, ideas, legal restrictions and possibilities: in all these, and
more, computers and computer wise consultants can help in the
planning of some legal writing.

   Planning is itself a complicated and changing movement, as intricate as any dance—with a series of steps, forward, backward, and
side steps. It could be called a process, were that not to invite the snap
conclusion that "What we gotta do here is process your problem,
see." And that would be the end of writing, instead of a beginning. It is
enough that planning is continuous, and never ends till the writing is
over with.

   Your writing will never end up exactly as you first conceived it.
Putting words on paper is a stimulating exercise. Once you start writing, the words will suggest things you never thought of before, and
drive out thoughts you thought you had. But law does not lend itself
to stream of consciousness composition. The words must be chosen
to reach a particular goal. Facts must be accounted for. In the background there is always the law that controls what you write. Even if
you are writing new law, the point of departure is the law as it is. Goal,
facts, and law have to be fitted together in some overall pattern. Ultimately, they will be. Someone will some day discover a pattern in

your completed work. There is a better chance that the pattern will be yours, if you plan it that way before you put words on paper.

☐ **For example:**
A "plain language" bill is intended to protect tenants. It penalizes *persons who hire any dwelling units* for failure to use plain language.

Recall that *hire,* like *lease,* can refer to those who give or to those who receive; it can mean renting *from* or renting *to.* (See Rule 2.3.a., p. 21.) This bill resolves the uncertainty—the wrong way. It uses *persons who hire any dwelling units* "as defined in Section 1940" of an earlier law, forgetting that under that law tenants are *persons who hire any dwelling units.*

So the bill intended to protect tenants could end up punishing them, or at least making nonsense of the law.

When you write, inevitably you write a bit at a time. At line 10, the telephone rings. At page 3, you stop for a drink of water. At page 10, you forgot something; recheck it. At page 50, someone wants a change. A planned pattern can help your creation survive all these shocks. Any fool can improve a single sentence of the Internal Revenue Code. But what you push in here makes something else come out there, unless you know and keep in mind that there is a larger (if more miserable) plan that you are tinkering with piecemeal.

Some troubles with context and interpretation are unavoidable. Planning before writing will help avoid the avoidable troubles.

Point 1.

Ingredients of Decision

Even though the topic is the same,
each time you write your needs for precision,
clarity, law, and brevity are different.
Their relative importance varies
with what you are trying to accomplish.

In any legal writing the Rules discussed to this point are important —Peculiar, Precise, English, Clear, Law. So too with brevity, discussed in Rule 7 (p. 126). The writer's job would be much easier if the degree of importance of each Rule were only fixed. How nice, to have a recipe: "Take equal parts of precision, good English, clarity, and law; trim all verbiage; stir well, and serve cold." It doesn't work that way.

One of the functions of the planning stage is to decide the proportions of each ingredient appropriate to this piece of writing. Granted that you write to your audience ("Clear to whom?"), but to what extent can clarity nudge precision? Or law overwhelm clarity? Or brevity become more urgent than full explanation? Etc. These questions have to be answered anew with each piece of legal writing. With those variables in the background, the weight to be attached to one or the other, the proper blend, depend on other decisions. What are you trying to accomplish?

Are you telling someone, or trying to persuade him? Whether in a trial memorandum or an appellate brief, the need to convince someone to follow you may overwhelm for the moment the Rules of precision, clarity, and all the rest. This is a special art—*the art of advocacy* (itself the title of a fine book by one of America's great trial lawyers, Lloyd Paul Stryker). It is an art as old as the orators of Greece and Rome, and as idiosyncratic as the last jury verdict. The Rules in this book reach advocacy only at a tangent—at the point where someone coldly starts to sort out the kernels.

Each piece of legal writing must accomplish its purpose. Beyond that, the desirables of good legal writing split; often they conflict. What is most important in one piece of legal writing is often least important in another. Apart from the pervasive importance of addressing your audience and keeping your self-respect as a professional, considerations of the moment will shape your writing. Here are two very practical considerations—the rush, and durability.

a. The rush

Sometimes urgency forces precedence over everything else. Get it done. Get something out. We've got to file. This is a "rush." The writer is under pressure to take shortcuts. This has become the normal environment of most legal writing, and is one of the principal reasons why so much of it is so bad.

But all rushes are not equal. Is it a rush to obtain agreement between bitter partisans, who might break off negotiations at any moment? Rush to file suit before an imminent deadline will bar it forever? Or is it the ordinary rush of the busy office? Get the paperwork done. What are we paying you for? Even under pressure, the professional remains a professional. Unflappable. A pause, for just a moment, to determine the nature of the "rush."

[1] Speed writing

Routine demands that important writing be done in a hurry usually come from those who have no understanding of writing, and no respect for the writer. They have no appreciation of the fact that *how* something is said determines *what* is said. *What* and *how* are inseparably joined, and when *how* gets drunk, *what* stumbles. The whip-crackers are unimpressed. They have an abiding faith that given a form book and a dictionary full of law words precise legal writing is automatic. This sort of tyrant ignoramus is also the first one to lay the blame on the writer when the writing collapses in a lawsuit.

Even under those unhappy conditions, something may yet be done.

[a] Haste makes words

This is the appeal to self-interest. The busy office (law, business, or government) thrives on "repeat business." The inquiry is, "Are we talking about 'quick' now, or 'quicker' later?" More time spent on writing now will save even more time later.

[b] Write in haste, repent in court

This is the appeal to self-interest plus fear of failure. "Maybe we're just repeating someone else's mistakes." More time spent on writing now will plug more holes.

[c] Last resort

Staple (do not clip) this memorandum to the copy of your writing that is delivered to client, senior partner, bureau chief, Member of Congress, Mr. President, the "boss."

MEMO

This was written in haste to meet an 8-hour deadline, now met. With more time, it would be more precise, shorter, and a lot clearer. I can live with this, but I'd rather not.

---

[2] Calculated ambiguity

Both sides to a negotiation may be eager to make a deal—a contract, a treaty, a statute, a majority for an appellate opinion. It is agreement now or maybe never. The alternative is too costly—strike, lockout, loss of tentative accord on some points that have taken months to work out, loss of a coveted property, disruption. The sticking point is substance not form, yet both sides would like to believe that some word magic will solve their problem. Let's not get bogged down in words. Though they may disavow it later, both sides are ready for the *calculated ambiguity.*

Ambiguity is sometimes limited to double meaning, as distinguished from *vagueness,* a general uncertainty. (On this distinction, see Dickerson, *The Interpretation and Application of Statutes,* 1975.) Lawyers commonly ignore the distinction, and use *calculated ambiguity* to refer to "the deliberate use of language which everyone recognizes as being easily misunderstood." In this sense, *ambiguity* is not a "disease of language" but an instrument chosen to avoid an impasse. We may never have to cross that bridge. Maybe others will. Maybe no one ever will. Whatever happens tomorrow, we must get something settled right now.

☐ **For example:**

Labor and management negotiators have hammered out agreement, except on *cost of living.* The sticking point is whether the negotiated wage shall be adjusted up and down, or only up. A strike deadline is imminent. Weary negotiators settle for a calculated ambiguity—*subject to a cost of living adjustment.* The problem of interpretation may never arise. If it does, one side will insist that clearly it means up *and* down, the other as vehemently, obviously only *up.* The controversy will be settled under circumstances different from those when the contract was negotiated. In the meantime, there has been labor peace.

☐ **For example:**

Negotiation of a contract for participation in a percentage of the *net profits* of a motion picture. How closely is *net* to be defined? Is a limit to be spelled out on the "overhead" that can be deducted in computing *net*? Or a maximum set for the producer's salary? Sometimes, it is negotiated down to a single sticking point. Beyond that, it is deliberately left undefined, for the sake of getting a picture produced before options run out on story, financing, services of actors.

If the picture flops, under any view, there is no problem. If the picture is a smash success, the result may be the triumph of good will (no lawsuit) or greed (lawsuit). The risks of ambiguity were calculated, as the calculated risks of D-Day invasion.

[3] Your side eager

In the rush that leads to the temporizing solution of the *calculated ambiguity,* anxieties tend to be equalized. Pressures change dramatically when the anxieties are unequal. It makes a tremendous difference whether you write for those who have the leisure and bargaining power to work out all the details, or for those who are oppressed with the burden of quick agreement. Whether *they* know it or not, we *have* to make this deal.

If it must be done quickly, consider in advance of the writing what your client will not give up, and what is legally necessary. The plan for writing must reflect those decisions. Within those limits, the strategy of quick agreement dictates the tactics of writing and re-writing. Here are some of them.

[a] Let them prepare the first draft

If the other side wants you to draw up something, ask for a memorandum from them of the points to cover. And work within that as closely as possible. Preferably, let them prepare the first draft. Maybe you can live with it, as is.

[b] Look charitably on the other lawyer's draft

[i] Avoid petty annoyance   Don't criticize the literary style. Don't improve on the punctuation if it doesn't affect the sense. Don't correct misspellings that affect only ego, unless that's all you're going to correct.

[ii] Keep changes to the bare minimum   Go to the heart. Knock out only what really hurts. Add only what you have to.

[c] Use whatever aids you have at hand

That includes a form, a formbook, an old file, even a telephone.

b. Durable

Legal writers, though acutely aware of how long it takes to write, rarely devote more than a strayed moment to consider whether *how* they write should vary with the anticipated life of *what* they write.

The ease of following all-purpose form blurs any distinction between writing for tomorrow and writing for the ages. It all tends to come out the same, a lot of words. So easy to forget that it is *not* a constitution that we are writing.

Here are some things that help decide when durability makes a difference, and what to do about it.

[1] How long is "durable"?

Like "short" and "long," "durable" is vague. The writing is durable if it lasts long enough. Still vague. Long enough if the writing serves out its purpose. A bit closer.

First thoughts of durability contrast writing for days with writing for the years, e.g., a lease for one month or 20 years.

☐ For example:
The details on assignment and subletting that might be desirable in a

119

long-term lease (mentioned on p. 103) are out of place in a lease for one month.

☐ **For example:**
Duration of a lease can affect matters of substance. A change of rent tied to changes in the purchasing power of the dollar may be critical long term, unimportant for the short term. Detailed specification of the "business days" a tenant must stay open may be critical in a long-term "percentage rent" lease, unimportant for the short term.

Fixed calendar time is the place to start. But calendar time fixed in a lease does not fix the durability of a relationship. A month-to-month lease, one either side could have ended in 30 days, frequently lasts for many years. People get along. With that sort of good feeling, on which a large proportion of business thrives, the short lease can be adjusted to suit the occasion. It need not be burdened from the start with the bric-a-brac typical of fixed long-term duration. Simplicity may even encourage trust, and durability.

Short or long fixed relationships are not always so congenial. To serve its purpose, the lease must be more durable than its calendar life. At a minimum, the writing carries a legal burden for the term of the lease plus time to bring suit (the statute of limitations) on troubles arising out of the lease. E.g., even for a short-term lease, while trying to keep the writing short, the writer will want to consider a provision for attorneys' fees in the event of suit. A matter of judgment.

If, by happy coincidence, writing time and lasting time are both short, the writer's task is simplified. Brevity takes stage center. Thus with the short-term lease, a small purchase, a quick notice—KEEP OUT.

Often, the pressure of the rush is coupled with a need for long-term durability. The writing itself may have to endure for years —a complicated transfer of real estate, the sale of a large business. Or the writing may have repercussions way down the line—a 90-day loan of $10,000,000, a presidential proclamation closing banks for a matter of days. When disparity between writing time and long-term effectiveness is substantial, the writer has a difficult public relations job —to sell policy makers on the need for a little more time to think out the possibilities, to avoid over-simplification that may defeat long-term durability. In the end, compromise. A little faster, but also a little longer, a little less precise, a little less clear. No absolutes. Not the best writing.

[2] A lawyer's vision of the future

Given adequate time to plan and write, the writer's natural inclination is to visualize all the possibilities of fact and law that can affect durability. All to the good. But the farsighted lawyer's vision of the future should not immediately loose a flood of detail. The precious leisure to plan gives opportunity to consider not only what can be put in but also what can be left out.

How far can one's vision reach? If I make the writing more precise, as things appear to me now, will it have the same crispness 10 years from now? Is it better to build in some looseness in the joints? The Constitution of the United States is a classic example of built-in durability, through the use of flexible words—*due process, equal protection, freedom of speech,* etc. Similar considerations affect less monumental writings.

☐ **For example:**

The *force majeure* (French, irresistible force) clause. Do you spell out all of the events you can think of that are "beyond control," that should extend a period fixed in a contract? War, piracy, riot, fire, flood, strikes, etc. Do you make it precise, tight; these events and no others.

Or do you make it flexible? *"Including but not limited to"* the listed events.

Do you want some flexibility, but not too much? The listed events *"or other events similar to those named."*

Or do you want it very flexible, concentrating not on crystal ball gazing but on the general nature of things that are "beyond control"? The listed events *"or other events beyond control, whether the events are similar or dissimilar to those named."*

Maybe short, maybe long; maybe precise, maybe not. Maybe clear, maybe not. Durability stands on its own merits. Pattern is not the answer.

[3] A judge's vision of the future

Most writers are beset by the healthy worry that they won't be read. The writer-judge suffers no such humbling agony. For a time at least, whatever the judge writes is law; readership not always meek but guaranteed. A tendency to write as though the whole world were waiting. Can pompousness be far away?

☐ **For example:**

The mantle of "the Fathers."

"But if the authors of those guarantees, fully aware of the potential conflicts between them, were unwilling or unable to resolve the issue by assigning one priority over the other, it is not for us to rewrite the Constitution by undertaking what they declined."

English translation. We like it this way.

121

Pompousness and verbosity go hand in hand, indifferent to readers. A touch of humility kills off verbosity.

☐ **For example:**

> "It appears inevitable that the Supreme Court will grant a hearing in this case to secure uniformity of decision. Therefore, since this opinion will be short-lived and our deathless prose promptly lost to posterity, we will attempt to be brief. . ."

> (Gardner, P.J., in *In re Mitchell,* 141 Ca. Rptr. 504 (1977), vacated—as predicted—in 22 Cal. 3d 946, 151 Ca. Rptr. 330, 587 P.2d 1144 (1978))

Pompousness, with some reason, is more common in majority opinions than in dissents. The dissenters have lost now; they will give the future something to hang its hat on. Unrestrained by trimming to win a majority, the dissenter can speak eloquently and sharply.

☐ **For example:**

Mr. Justice Stewart dissenting from a holding that an indigent could not file for bankruptcy without paying the filing fee:

> "The Court holds that Congress may say that some people are too poor to go bankrupt. I cannot agree."

> (*United States v. Kras,* 409 U.S. 434 (1973))

Too often dissenting opinions share the majority's vice of verbosity. But there are worse things.

☐ **For example:**

The dissenter who writes, "I dissent," and nothing more. This satisfies only ego, leaving the future to guess.

Even brevity can be overdone.

Point 2.

Outline

Outline before and after you write it out at length.
Outlining makes it easier to spot bad ideas,
and easier to keep good ideas from getting mislaid.

a. The working outline

[1] Why?

Your working outline will not be complete when you start using it. It can be very rough. You will want to change it, and depart from it. It need not be a masterpiece. The idea is to get something down on paper in some sort of orderly sequence. Here is what a working outline will do for you.

[a] It will compel you to tie floating thoughts together.
[b] It will be a checklist, giving you assurance that you will cover what you intend to cover.
[c] It will keep you from repeating yourself, and writing in circles.
[d] It will give you a feeling of progress, and an end in sight.
[e] It will give you a preview, enabling you to appreciate just how silly, how disjointed, and how briliant your ideas will look on paper.
[f] It will give you an opportunity to reorganize in logical order, before you have become completely intoxicated by the sight of your own words spread all over the page.

[2] The universal outline

When you start outlining, make it a real outline, and not a phony. A phony is a Universal Outline: a pile of generalized captions, numbered, lettered, indented, available for every topic under the sun. And good for nothing.

☐ For example:

OUTLINE FOR MY TOPIC [contract, opinion, statute, memorandum, brief, etc.]

   I.   *Introduction*
      A. Importance of the topic
      B. For whom?

   II. *Development of the Topic*
      A. General Considerations
         1. Background
         2. Today
      B. Special Considerations
         1. Today
         2. The Future

   III. *Conclusion*

b. The postmortem outline

Some people insist that they cannot write from a working outline. It inhibits their creative genius. They can deal with the most complex legal subject without an outline. This group has a special need for the postmortem outline. If you have written from a working outline, the postmortem is still useful.

Put what you have written into outline form. It may convince you that you are not through writing. You may discover that something has been left out. Or find that something has wandered in and out of your writing like a lost soul seeking salvation.

The postmortem outline is especially valuable in trying to make sense of the long, long sentence.

☐ **For example:**

Here is part of a statute giving the procedure for change-of-name. (Many people do it without lawyers.) This is the critical part, that is supposed to tell people where to publish a notice of their petition or application for the name change.

"**§3. Notice of Application**

Previous notice shall be given of such intended application, by publishing a notice thereof in some newspaper published in the municipality in which such person resides if such municipality is in a county with a population under 2,000,000, or if such person does not reside in such municipality, or if no newspaper is published in the municipality or if the person resides in a county with a population of 2,000,000 or more, then in some newspaper published in the county where such person shall reside, or if no newspaper shall be published in said county, then in some convenient newspaper published in this State. . . ."

Got it? If that's not crystal clear, try picking up the pieces with a postmortem outline. Remember; this is for your eyes only.

§3. Notice of Application

I. GIVE NOTICE OF APPLICATION IN A NEWSPAPER.

II. NEWSPAPER MUST BE *PUBLISHED:*

    A. *In municipality of residence IF* in co. under 2 million.

    B. *In county of residence IF*
       #1.   You don't reside in *A* (i.e., "such municipality"), OR
       #2.   No paper published in *A,* OR
       #3.   You reside in a co. of 2 mil. or more.

    C. *Anywhere in the State IF* no paper published in *B.*

Having tracked the statute the way it reads, you can now go back, to figure out what #1 means, i.e., not residing in "such municipality." You find that could be because:

a. No paper published there (covered in #2);

b. Co. of 2 mil. or more (covered in #3); or

c. Live in unincorporated area, i.e., in a county, but not a municipality. (That's all that #1 adds.)

Now you are in a position to generalize, and rewrite the statute, so that you and anyone else can see what it means:

§3. Notice of Application

a. A petitioner must give notice of intended application for change of name as stated in this section.

b. *General Rule.* Notice is to be in a newspaper published in the county of petitioner's residence; and if no newspaper is published there, in one published anywhere in the State.
   Exception. If residence is in a municipality in a county under 2,000,000, notice is to be in a newspaper published in the municipality. If no newspaper is published there, notice is to be as stated in the General Rule.

There are other ways of rewriting the original jumble. You could address the instructions to "you." The postmortem outline makes clarification possible.

RULE 7.

Cut!

Repeat the operation until you run out of time
or material. Don't say the same thing twice inadvertently.
Rewrite. Rewrite. Rewrite.

The one thing about legal writing that everyone agrees on is that there is too much of it. Everyone complains of everyone else's verbosity. All of the complainers are right. "The buck stops here."

Point 1.

Why Wordy?

The explanations for wordiness in legal writing
do not justify keeping it that way.

Most legal writers don't bother to explain away their own wordiness. That's the way it's done. More precise, you know. This is nothing but rationalization for sloppy writing.

There *are* explanations of why lawyers are wordy, more so than your ordinary long-winded neighbor. But the explanations are not justifications.

a. Old explanations

Here is a summary of the historical reasons for the wordiness part of lawsick. (For details, see Mellinkoff, *The Language of the Law*.)

The common law of England (which we inherited) grew up with a mixture of languages, chiefly Latin and older varieties of French and English. English was changing, absorbing from other languages, unstructured, plain disorderly. Habitually, sometimes necessarily, the law was expressed in more than one language. Law in highly inflected Latin was translated literally; that meant more words in English. The pace of life was slower. In and out of the law, verbose writing (especially tautology) was the fashion, with no modern notions of punctuation to interrupt the flow.

Legal procedure also encouraged verbosity. Cases were proved by documents, not by the testifying witness. Pleadings were hyper-technical and rigid, *the* word insisted upon in a growing body of forms. Life and property were in constant danger, and you departed from form at peril. Say it again and again; say it many ways; one of them might be right. If you missed out on the right word, or misspelled, your case was lost. Literal, hairsplitting logic gave lawyers the shakes, and encouraged ever finer distictions of literalness. Wordiness was a refuge from the harshness of the law.

Grosser sins played a part. Venality for instance. Documents paid for by the word; extra words, extra pay. Clerks supported by filing fees; more documents, more fees. Ignorance for instance. Following forms as a substitute for a legal education. Reasons unknown or unremembered; only the words.

Some of these old explanations are recognizable in the current practices of some legal writers. But no one today offers these old explanations as justifications for wordiness in legal writing. The force has gone. The words remain.

b. New explanations

How wordy legal writing came to be does not explain how it came to stay. There are other explanations why wordiness is not laughed out of court.

[1] Time pressure

Above all else, time pressure ("the rush," p. 116) of the twentieth century office leads to wordiness. It not only takes time to write shorter; it takes time to change habit. Without time, you grab for the nearest form, and stick with the old verbosity.

[2] Dread of omission

Legal writers, particularly lawyers, are schooled to an unholy dread that something has been left out. (See "the form disease," p. 101.) It is a phobia composed of one part tradition, one part the myth of precision, and one part playing the odds. Will I be in worse trouble by saying too much or too little?

[3] Dictated "writing"

In our electronic age, fewer and fewer scraps of writing are actually written, i.e., written out by a human being. Words are recorded, and disgorged automatically; and even in the first instance little is ever written. It is dictated "writing." It is "written" for the ear; it may even be pleasing to the ear. Any old ear (even a dictating "writer's") yearns for the reinforcement of repetition; ears don't glance back. You can re-play the tape, but that's not the same as reading (and scratching out) as you write. The ear of the "writer" needs more words, and the eye of the reader suffers with them.

[4] Abstract virtue

If you press a legal writer hard, you can squeeze out an admission that brevity is a virtue. "Sure, sure, I make it short when I can. It's a good thing." But it's an abstraction, unimportant. Sometimes a piece of legal writing comes out short. Good and short, or short and bad. Short by chance. The writer writes with no sense of the worth of brevity.

Before knuckling under to the clock, the machine, the old phobias, consider what you have to lose by verbosity and gain by brevity.

Point 2.

Shorter is Better

Unnecessary words increase the opportunities for you and your reader to go wrong.

a. Extra words, extra mistakes

Producing words by machine, following the form, is so fast, so effort-less, that one inclines to lavishness, and forgetfulness. One day some-one takes seriously words added mechanically against the old dread of omission.

☐ For example:
Seller used a form contract to take orders for, of all things, a "computer system." On its back the form bore 21 separate pieces of boilerplate—prepackaged form wording. When Buyer defaulted, Seller took ack the system, and sued for damages. But nestled in the boilerplate were words giving Seller a "security interest," that as a matter of law defeated Seller's claim for damages.

The wounded Seller: ". . .[N]o security agreement was ever intended. . .the provisions on the reverse of the contract were mere 'boilerplate'. . ."

" 'Boilerplate,' said the judge, "is, notwithstanding its reputation, language. . .If [Seller] intended no security interest, it should not have used language creating one."

Moral: You may be hoist by your own boilerplate.

Habitual use of too many words dulls the feeling for the sense of individual words.

☐ **For example:**
The Alaska Constitution requires a referendum. Art. XIII, Section 3 says:

> "If during any ten-year period a constitutional convention has not been held, the lieutenant governor shall place on the ballot for the next general election the question: 'Shall there be a Constitutional Convention?' "

How much of that do you put on the ballot? This would have been enough:

REFERENDUM

Shall there be a Constitutional Convention?
YES   _____
NO   _____

"[F]or some unexplained reason," the ballot said this:

REFERENDUM

As required by the Constitution of the State of Alaska
Art. XIII, Section 3

Shall there be a Constitutional Convention?
YES   _____
NO   _____

"Yes" won by less than 500 votes out of more than 79,000 cast. The result was thrown out by the courts because the extra words might have misled some voters into thinking that a "Yes" vote was "required."

(*Boucher v. Bomhoff,* 495 P. 2d 77, Alaska, 1972)

Moral: Every extra word is one more chance to goof.

b. Extra words, more ignorance

Here are two common ways in which extra words leave you worse off than when you started.

[1] Extra words destroy the original clarity

☐ For example:

(a) A statute might say:

" 'Harvest' means to cut and remove from the place where grown."

The sense is clear. Harvesting consists of two acts, cutting plus removal.

(b) A statute might say:

" 'Harvest' means to remove from the place where grown."

The sense is different, but still clear. Harvesting is one act, removal.

(c) The statute does say:

" 'Harvest' means to remove *or cut and remove* from the place where grown."

Whatever does it mean now?

You harvest by removing, whether or not you also cut, bind, or whistle "Yankee Doodle." The italicized words add nothing but confusion.

I could understand it at first, but now you've lawsicked it.

[2] Extra words make writer and reader forget

The long, long sentence not only talks about too many different things (Rule 3.3.b, p. 58). Often it also says the same thing too many times, and—for good measure—adds the completely unnecessary. No one, not even the writer, can keep it all straight, without taking it apart.

☐ For example:

A mobilehome park lease permits assignment on sale of the mobilehome, with a few hooks. It says this:

"(a) Removal on Sale: In the event Lessee sells the mobilehome located on the Space to a third party during the term of this agreement or any renewal or extension thereof, Lessee shall give Sixty (60) days notice to Lessor of his intent to sell the mobilehome as required by Section 798.59 of the California Civil Code and Lessee shall remove any mobilehome sold to a third party located upon the space on its sale, if that mobilehome is less than 10 feet wide or more than 20 years old, or more than 25 years old if manufactured after September 15, 1971 and is less than 20 feet wide, or both, or in a run-down condition or in disrepair. . . ."

Comment

(a) The sentence is bad enough without extra words. It has the typical disorder of the long, long sentence.

> *inverted chronology*—details of selling before anything about a notice of intended sale.
>
> *no pause between separate topics*—details of notice and details of removal.
>
> *misplaced modifiers*—"sold to *a third party located* upon the space"; "*sell the mobilehome as required* by Section 789.59."

(b) Now look at the repetitions.

> *"mobilehome"*
> *"located on the Space"*
> *"to a third party"*
> *"Sixty (60)"*—haphazard repetition; none for the other numbers.

(c) Now look at the words (in italics), completely unnecessary.

> [mobilehome] *located on the Space*. That's what the whole agreement is about. If the mobilehome isn't located on a Space in the park, what are we doing here?
>
> [sells] *to a third party*. That is to be distinguished from selling to yourself, or to the Lessor (who can waive a provision inserted for his benefit). Surplus.
>
> [sells] *during the term of this agreement or any renewal or extension thereof*. "Renewal" and "extension" are sometimes given independent meaning in the law of leases, but here the whole thing is surplus. If the sale is at any other time, it has nothing to do with this agreement.
>
> *his* [intent]. Whether or not "sexist," here it is needless.
>
> *as required by Section 798.59*. The Section does not require a notice of "intent to sell." For a different notice, it does require that the notice be "written," and "of not less than 60 days." Maybe that's what was intended here. You can add those items, while deleting the unnecessary.
>
> *California* [Civil Code]. If it's a California lease, that's the only "Civil Code."
>
> [run-down] *condition*. That's what "run-down" is. ("Disrepair" might be enough; some leases make a distinction.)
>
> *or both*. Does not fit in with anything.

A rewrite

(a) *Sale.* At least 60 days before sale of the mobilehome, Lessee must give

Lessor written notice of intent to sell. Lessee must remove the mobilehome when sold if it is described in any of these numbered subsections.

[i] In disrepair, or run-down.

[ii] Less than 10 feet wide.

[iii] Over 20 years old, if manufactured September 15, 1971 or earlier.

[iv] Both over 25 years old and less than 20 feet wide, if manufactured after September 15, 1971.

That's not quite cut in half, but it is a substantial cut. And makes twice as much sense. Trim the fat.

c. Extra words, wasted reading time

The reader of legal writing works under wraps. Skimming is dangerous. The guts may be buried in a heavy sheath of gibberish. So read and re-read. Look for the needles in the haystack.

Cutting legal writing down to essentials takes time for the writer. But it is the writer's message—easier and quicker for writer than reader to squeeze out the unessentials.

Point 3.
Wordiness is a Bad Habit.
Kick it.
Here's How.

Cold turkey is not recommended. The withdrawal symptoms are too severe, such as nightmares about your children not having enough words to eat. But you have lots of fellow addicts. And many writers have kicked the habit. You can too.

a. How to start cutting

[1] Birth control

The best way to start cutting out excess words is to stop them from happening. It's easier with a plan, and an outline. (See Rule 6, p. 114.)

[2] The blue pencil

The role of the hardboiled editor is easier when you are blue penciling someone else's writing. You make the cuts but you don't feel them. With practice, your blue pencil will work on your own writing. You become callous to the sight of blue. You become more critical of your own work. And the pain will ease.

Seize a blue pencil (or green, or a red pen, something vivid), and start cutting. Cut; do not hack. Know what you want to cut.

b. The cut list

Make your own list of words that you can do without. In the meantime, here is a list of 15 clusters of words to get you started. With some, just trim off the fat. Some, trim, and touch up what remains. Others cut completely. Taken individually, some of these cuts are insignificant. The cumulative body count is amazing. These are not the only cuts you will want to make, but these are sure-fire losers. They can all be made with ease, and without regrets.

The word clusters, some described in detail in other parts of the book, are listed here and briefly discussed. This is a *cut list* that will help you kick the habit of wordiness. When you spot the cluster, start cutting.

The Cut List
1. Old formalisms
2. Worthless Old and Middle English words
3. Coupled synonyms: junk antiques
4. Coupled synonyms: current stuff
5. Redundant modifiers
6. Inflation
7. Plain old repeating yourself
8. Circular platitudes
9. Hornbook law
10. Citations for hornbook law
11. Boilerplate introductions
12. Worthless definitions
13. Worthless labels
14. A choke of quotations
15. Footnotes loaded with text

[1] Old formalisms

Many of these phrases are reserved for oral use, and rarely get into print (see Rule 1.1.a[3], p. 5, and Appendix C). Too many do. Most can be cut completely.

☐ For example:

> *Be it remembered* and its stablemate *Know all men by these presents*
> —One of these is often the first line of a deed or contract. They
> add nothing to sense. Delete and start.
>
> *Further affiant sayeth* [or *saith*] *not*—often the last line of an affidavit.
> Adds nothing to sense. Delete and stop.
>
> *Whereas*—When used for anything but to express a contrary ("A says
> he was at home, whereas he was at the office"), *whereas* is worth-
> less. Often used to introduce "recitals," e.g., "Whereas, Septem-
> ber has 30 days." Delete. September still has 30 days.
>
> *Witnesseth*—a pause between the identification of a contract and the
> details. Adds nothing. Delete.

[2] Worthless Old and Middle English words

Some Old and Middle English words have simply outlived their use-
fulness (see Rule 1.1.a.[1], p. 3, and Appendix A); less confusion
when the sense is rendered in modern English—like *in this* instead of
herein. Some Old and Middle English needs no translation; completely worthless.

☐ For example:
Delete the italicized words; the meaning is unchanged.

> *the aforesaid* John Jones
> it is *hereby* ordered
> Al Spangle, *hereinafter* the Seller
> Enclosed *herewith*

[3] Coupled synonyms: junk antiques

These combinations are old fashioned habit (see Rule 1.1.a.[2], p. 4,
and Appendix B). All you have to do is make a choice. Pick one.

☐ For example:
Delete the italicized words; the meaning is unchanged.

> *in lieu, in place,* instead, *and in*
>   *substitution* of
> *last* will *and testament*
> *maintenance and* upkeep
> *null and* void

[4] Coupled synonyms; current stuff

Junk antique or not, a coupled synonym is excess. Again, make a
choice.

☐ **For example:**

Delete the italicized words; the meaning is unchanged.

> A choice made *intelligently, knowledgeably,* with his eyes open—try to imagine "intelligently (or knowledgeably) with his eyes closed."
>
> *in truth and* in fact—a saving of 3 words. (Even better, cut the whole cliché, and save 5.)
>
> there can be but one moment *of time* in the course of a trial
>
> over, *above, and in addition to*

[5] Redundant modifiers

☐ **For example:**

Delete the italicized words; the meaning is unchanged.

> *all* that *certain* lot
> *natural* life
> obtain *prior* approval before
> obtain prior approval *before*
> *surviving* widow
> *surviving* widower
> *true* facts
> *written* instrument

[6] Inflation

Let the hot air out of blown up expressions (Rule 3.2.b, p. 54).

☐ **For example:**

Delete the italicized words and substitute ordinary English; the meaning is unchanged.

inflated	corrected
gained entrance to the bar	admitted to the bar
his name was *stricken from the roll of attorneys*	he was disbarred
terminated his existence by an act of suicide	committed suicide

☐ **For example:**

Here is a pattern devised by the enterprising Justice Gerald Brown. Delete the italicized words; capitalize one word; the meaning is unchanged:

> "*This is an appeal from a conviction of* burglary. Appellant insists that his conviction was the result of. . ."

[7] Plain old repeating yourself

Unless you have a special reason to repeat (e.g., emphasis), saying it once is enough. The vice of repetition is bad enough in ordinary social intercourse. But you can't walk out on a boring statute.

☐ For example:

A statute makes it criminal to mutilate plants. It describes the plants:

> "any tree or shrub, or fern or herb or bulb or cactus or flower, or huckleberry or redwood greens, or portion of any tree or shrub, or fern or herb or bulb or cactus or flower, or huckleberry or redwood greens. . ."

On and on. In a single long, long sentence, those sad plants are listed 6 times.

List the plants once. After that, refer to them: "A listed plant (part or whole)."

[8] Circular platitudes

It says nothing. Cut completely.

☐ For example:

> "The negligence in the exercise of a duty of a lawyer to his client constitutes negligence."

[9] Hornbook law

Hornbook (or "black letter") law is basic law, familiar to anyone with the most modest legal training. Unless you are writing deliberately and carefully for those who are completely ignorant of the law, hornbook law is a time waster. Usually, it pads out opinions and articles; window dressing, not enlightenment. Cut hornbook law.

☐ For example:

Negligence is the failure to exercise due care.
Due care is the care of a reasonable man under the circumstances.

[10] Citations for hornbook law

If the sense of the writing requires a statement of hornbook law, then at least spare the reader long lists of cases supporting banal propositions. (See Rule 4.3.c.[2](b), p. 95.) Don't give a citation for hornbook law unless you want to quarrel with it.

[11] Boilerplate introductions

The typical drawn out form introduction serves no purpose except to clear your throat and cover the embarrassment of getting started.

Strike out boldly, call a will "WILL," or "WILL OF JANE DOE." Call a contract a "CONTRACT," or "AGREEMENT." See the examples of elimination of boilerplate, in a will (pp. 102-103), and in a contract (pp. 1, and p. 140).

[12] Worthless definitions

Definitions in a statute or contract can be useful, but they are hazardous (Rule 2.3.d, p. 24). When in doubt, don't define. Here are some that are pure waste, and should be cut.

[a] Definitions the writer ignores

Some definitions have become boilerplate, inserted mechanically, and ignored by the writer. Pity the reader. Cut.

☐ For example:
Words in the singular number include the plural and in the plural include the singular.

Without definition, "a person who" also means "persons who" (and vice versa), unless you have deliberately ruled that out. The definition is unnecessary, and those who use it ignore it, adding even more bulk by writing "A person or persons who." When you make good sense without definition, don't define.

[b] Definitions that don't fix meaning

A definition should fix meaning. If it doesn't, it simply adds confusion and words.

☐ For example:
An antique and still used definition of *reasonable doubt* (for jurors):

"It is not a mere possible doubt; because everything relating to human affairs, and depending on moral evidence, is open to some possible or imaginary doubt. It is that state of the case, which, after the entire comparison and consideration of all the evidence, leaves the minds of jurors in that condition that they cannot say that they feel an abiding conviction to a moral certainty, of the truth of the charge."

Do you now "feel an abiding conviction to a moral certainty?" that *reasonable doubt* has a fixed meaning? If you don't, cut the definition.

[c] Definitions that don't change meaning

☐ For example:
As used herein, *banana freckle* means a disease of the fruit and leaves of

the banana caused by an imperfect fungus (Macrophoma musae) producing brown or black spots.

Of course, *banana freckle* is *banana freckle.* That's what it says in my
dictionary. No need to pretend that it is something special in this contract
or statute. Cut the whole thing. At one stroke, you get rid of *herein* and the
definition of *banana freckle.*

[13] Worthless labels

Like definitions, labels can be useful but also hazardous (Rule 2.3.e,
p. 26). When in doubt, don't label. Some are pure waste, and should
be cut.

☐ **For example:**
The caption of any complaint identifies the parties.

XYZ CORPORATION,

Plaintiff,

v.

JOHN SMITH,

Defendant.

If there is only one plaintiff or only one defendant, it is surplus to re-identify
parties with labels they already have.

(a) Yet the complaint often says:

The XYZ Corporation, *hereinafter called the plaintiff.* . .John Smith,
hereinafter called the defendant.

Delete the surplus labels.

(b) Similarly, an opinion in the case will say:

Plaintiff *and appellant XYZ Corporation* appeals. . .

That's all an appellant ever does. Delete the italicized excess.

[14] A choke of quotations

Think twice before quoting anyone, even yourself, or me. Occasionally an apt quotation brings the reader quickly to the point. Some
quotations are indispensable (e.g., interpretation of writings). More
often, they obstruct the continuity of argument or exposition. Some
are little more than decorative substitutes for ideas; cutting and past-

ing instead of thinking and writing. Most quotations can be paraphrased, sharply cut down or eliminated completely, with considerable saving of space and reading time.

☐ **For example:**
Since the decision in *Miranda v. Arizona,* 384 U.S. 436, 86 S. Ct. 1602, 16 L. Ed. 2d 694 (1966), *Miranda warnings* (of constitutional rights) have become an important commonplace. Opinions by the bushel discuss the *Miranda Rule.* The case must be cited. Need it be quoted?

In 1980, a Circuit Court of Appeals reverses a conviction on evidence discovered after an officer put defendant in a police car and questioned him. The Court says this:

> "The Fifth Amendment question in this case is whether [he] could be questioned further, under these circumstances, without being advised of his constitutional rights. In *Miranda* the Court described the point at which the warnings must be given in the following language:
>
> 'The principles announced today deal with the protection which must be given to the privilege against self-incrimination when the individual is first subjected to police interrogation while in custody at the station or otherwise deprived of his freedom of action in any significant way. It is at this point that our adversary system of criminal proceedings commences, distinguishing itself at the outset from the inquisitorial system recognized in some countries. Under the system of warnings we delineate today or under any other system which may be devised and found effective, the safeguards to be erected about the privilege must come into play at this point.' The questioning of [defendant] was quite pointed and accusatory. . .''

The Circuit Court might have said this:

> "The Fifth Amendment question in this case is whether [he] could be questioned further, under these circumstances, without being advised of his constitutional rights. Adversary proceedings started, and *Miranda* warnings were required, when [he] was 'first subjected to police interrogation while . . . deprived of his freedom in any significant way.' The questioning of [defendant] was quite pointed and accusatory. . ."

If any quotation at all was thought desirable, that would have been enough to give the *Miranda* essence, with less interruption of the Circuit opinion. After 14 years of *Miranda* quotations, the Court might have struck a blow not only for liberty but brevity.

Did I quote too much?

[15] Footnotes loaded with text

Footnotes should be rigorously weeded out. (See the detailed discussion of footnotes in Rule 4.3.c, p. 94.)

Point 4.

Rewrite

Every time you rewrite you will find something to cut. Do not be disappointed if you also find something to add.

Whether or not you write from an outline, excess is inevitable. This Rule says, "Cut It in Half." For most legal writing that is a very modest beginning. It's also a convenient place to reorient yourself, think things over, talk things over. After you have cut that much or close to it, rewrite what you have left, and see how it looks. Start cutting again. Don't be afraid of wasting yellow paper.

After drafts one, two, three, you may feel that you can't go on. It's down to a scant nubbin. You say to yourself, "If I cut any more, there won't be anything left." Good! That is the moment the potential reader has been waiting for, a moment that few writers, let alone legal writers, have the courage to contemplate. "If that's all I have to say, maybe it's not worth saying." Don't worry too much about convincing yourself. Start cutting again.

Once you have made a cut, you are rid of words—for the moment. You may decide to restore something, or add something. But the cutting has served a purpose. You now see the core and form more clearly. Your final product will be leaner and sharper. So rewrite after each major operation to get a fresh view. Assess the gains and damage. Then start cutting again.

□ **For example:**

Here is a typical opener for a contract. In its own way, it serves the practical legal purpose of identifying the contract—naming the parties, and giving the date and place of making.

```
"THIS AGREEMENT, made and entered

into this 10th day of January, 1981, in

the City of Los Angeles, State of California,

by and between John Doak, hereinafter

sometimes referred to as and called the

Party of the First Part, and the Plotz
```

```
Corporation, a corporation duly organized

and existing under and by virtue of the

laws of the State of Delaware, hereinafter

sometimes referred to as and called the

Party of the Second Part,
    WITNESSETH:"
```

The cut list and blue pencil, please.

1. *Old formalisms*
   Cut: *WITNESSETH*

2. *Worthless Old and Middle English words*
   Cut: *hereinafter*
        hereinafter

3. *Coupled synonyms: junk antiques*
   Cut: [made] *and entered into*
        [under] *and by virtue of*

4. *Coupled synonyms: current stuff*
   Cut: *by and* [between]
        referred to as and [called]
        referred to as and [called]

5. *Redundant modifiers*
   Cut: *THIS* [AGREEMENT]
        this [10th day]
        the [Party of the First Part]
        the [Party of the Second Part]
        the [Plotz Corporation]
        duly [organized]

6. *Inflation*
   Cut: [10th] *day of* [January]
        the City of [Los Angeles]
        State of [California]
        the State of [Delaware]

7. *Plain old repeating yourself*
   Cut: [Plotz Corporation] *a corporation*

Enough for the moment. You've made a mess.

```
    "THIS AGREEMENT, made and entered

into this 10th day of January, 1981, in

the City of Los Angeles, State of California,

by and between John Doak, hereinafter
```

141

```
sometimes ~~referred to as and~~ called ~~the~~

Party of the First Part, and ~~the~~ Plotz

Corporation, ~~a corporation duly~~ organized

and existing under ~~and by virtue of~~ the

laws of ~~the~~ State of Delaware, ~~hereinafter~~

sometimes ~~referred to as and~~ called ~~the~~

Party of the Second Part,

     ~~WITNESSETH~~ : "
```

But you've cut it in half. With the debris cleared away, it looks like this:

```
"AGREEMENT, made 10th January, 1981,

in Los Angeles, California, between

John Doak, sometimes called Party of the

First Part, and Plotz Corporation,

organized and existing under the laws of

Delaware, sometimes called Party of the

Second Part."
```

Not bad. Start cutting some more. The cut list and blue pencil, please.

Old formalisms
  Cut: *Party of the First Part*
      Party of the Second Part

If you want a label, bring it into the twentieth century. "Doak," "Plotz," "Buyer," "Seller"—almost anything is shorter and better than what you have.

Worthless labels
  Cut: *sometimes called*
      sometimes called

Why only "sometimes"? If you label, stick with it.
    But why any label at all here? What's the matter with "Doak" and "Plotz Corporation"? In this agreement, there won't be any mistaking who they are, even if—without further ado—you talk about "Doak" and "Plotz."

Back up on the cut list. We missed something.

Boilerplate introductions
Cut: *organized and existing under the laws* [of Delaware]

That's standard boilerplate. What is its effect? Is Plotz representing proper organization and existence under Delaware law? Or are both Doak and Plotz agreeing that that is so? If the fact is of any consequence, it's too important to leave to an introductory and inconclusive recital. Put it into the agreement proper—one way or another.

With all that cut, you've got another mess.

```
"AGREEMENT, made 10th January, 1981,

in Los Angeles, California, between

John Doak, sometimes called Party of the

First Part, and Plotz Corporation,

organized and existing under the laws of

Delaware, sometimes called Party of the

Second Part."
```

But you've cut it in half again. With the debris cleared away, it looks like this:

```
"AGREEMENT, made 10th January, 1981,

in Los Angeles, California, between

John Doak, and Plotz Corporation, of

Delaware."
```

With the agreement stripped down like that, a point of law stares out at you. What about "made. . .in Los Angeles"?

Do you need it at all? Do you want it as an identifying handle on the agreement?

Or is it intended to describe the "place of making" as a factor in determining what law will govern the agreement—California law, Delaware, or some other place? Are you trying to fix the "choice of law," decide a "conflict of laws" point? If you want to be sure about what law governs, don't leave a "conflicts" point to an introductory and inconclusive recital; provide specifically what law is to govern.

If you decide that this introduction is just for identification, you now have enough. You might want to touch it up a bit, or vary the format.

It could look like this:

```
              AGREEMENT

                    January 10, 1981

                 Los Angeles, California

       JOHN DOAK and PLOTZ CORPORATION of

          Delaware AGREE:
```

Or, for a bit more identification, you might even add a few words:

```
              AGREEMENT

       FOR SALE OF THE "QUEEN MARY."
```

In any case, you've come a long way from the original.

This much painless brevity is achievable by blue penciling unnecessary words. The process applies to every kind of legal writing.

In some instances, you might decide that unscrambling unintelligible horror, and spelling out the details, are worth more than brevity. That goes back to planning (Rule 6, p. 114) and what you are trying to accomplish.

But don't sell brevity short.

PART TWO

Blunders and Cures

This Part gives you a series of practical demonstrations of how to go about analyzing and rewriting your own or someone else's legal writing. It shows you how to apply the Seven Rules. All of the examples taken apart and put together here suffer from more than one deficiency. All of the blunders are curable.

I

Guidelines That Don't Guide

A. BACKGROUND

The Copyright Act of 1976 (in 17 *United States Code* §101, at §107) permits "fair use" of copyrighted works, without special permission from the copyright owner. "Fair use" is deliberately vague, to allow for change and adaptation.

How much of a copyrighted work may teachers copy for classroom use? That daily puzzle has produced some *Guidelines* (House Report No. 94–1476, 5 U.S. Code Congressional and Administrative News 5681, 5682; 94th Congress, 2d Session, 1976).

To qualify for classroom use, the copying must pass various tests. One of them is the test for "Brevity," as defined in the *Guidelines*. Here is the heart of the definition.

B. THE SPECIMEN

```
1.  "Brevity

2.      (i) Poetry:  (a) A complete poem if less than 250

3.  words and if printed on not more than two pages or, (b)

4.  from a longer poem, an excerpt of not more than 250 words.

5.      (ii) Prose:  (a) Either a complete article, story or

6.  essay of less than 2500 words, or (b) an excerpt from any

7.  prose work of not more than 1,000 words or 10% of the work,

8.  whichever is less, but in any event a minimum of 500 words."
```

C. TAKING IT APART

As you go through the specimen, talk to yourself. Make notes.

1. First glance

a. It's short. That's good.

b. Not a law word in it. That's good.

c. Numbers seem to be uniformly rounded off—250, 2500, 1,000, 500; got to draw a line somewhere.

2. Look at those numbers again

a. Something wrong. Maybe they thought they were making them uniform, and rounded; but it doesn't work out that way.

    (1) First it's *"if less than 250."* That's 249, not 250. For a *complete* poem.

    (2) Then it's *"not more than 250."* That *is* 250. For an *excerpt* from a longer poem. (Or, as it says here, in lawsick, "from a longer poem, an excerpt."

    (3) Then it's back to *"less than 2500."* That's 2,499, not 2500. For some prose.

b. Violation of the *twofer rule* (Rule 2.3, p. 20), saying the same thing in two different ways. Inconsistent expression of a maximum.

    (1) Any reason for it?

    (2) Looks like they started with *less than*, got side-tracked by free association with *"not more than two pages,"* and then wobbled.

c. But it doesn't make sense.

    (1) Why would anyone want to permit copying of only *249* words *complete*, but *250* words for an *excerpt?*

    (2) If I take that seriously, it means that a poem *complete* in *250* words couldn't be copied in full. Doesn't meet either standard:

        (a) Not *complete* in *less than 250;* and

        (b) It is *complete, so not an excerpt.*

d. Probably none of that intended.

    (1) Looked like uniformity, and got snarled in the language.

    (2) Probably intended all the numbers to make the same neat dividing line. Carry that out:

        (a) Uniform at 250, and

        (b) Rounded at 2500.

3. Prose section. Wow!

a. Can't figure it out. Disorganized; too many different ideas run into each other. Word count not high, but it's the *long, long sentence* (Rule 3.3.b, p. 58). What modifies what?

b. *Prose (a)* get you thinking about something *complete.*
   (1) Quick. *Prose (b)* switches to *excerpt.*
   (2) But it's an excerpt *"from any prose work of not more than 1,000 words."* Cascading words carry me back to the length of the *complete* work; the *of* phrase tacked on to *work*, not to *excerpt.*
   (3) With a jolt, the next words *"or 10% of the work"* make you realize that both *1,000* and *10%* speak of excerpt.

c. Worse yet.
   "1,000 words or 10% of the work, *whichever is less*, but in any event a *minimum* of 500 words."
   (1) Now what does that mean? Fouled by the negatives of measurement (Rule 2.4.e.[3], p. 36).
   (2) Are they talking about two maximums?
   (3) Do they really mean a *minimum?* Ticket if you go less than 40 mph? Could they really mean that you *must* copy at least 500 words?

4. Discarding the absurd, still some peculiarities

a. Under *Poetry,* a complete short poem may be copied, but not an excerpt from it.
   (1) Maybe the poet would prefer it that way. It's so short; don't spoil it. Take all of me or nothing.
   (2) Possibly they thought that permission to copy *complete* included any part; but it sure doesn't say so.

b. Under *Prose:*
   (1) *Complete* part deals with "article, story or essay." *Excerpt* part deals with "any prose work." Perhaps intended. Says so distinctly, and not irrational.
   (2) *Complete* may be copied through *2500* [originally 2,499] words, but excerpt from same work limited to 500 words.
      (a) Maybe the author prefers it that way.
      (b) As with *Poetry,* possibly they thought that permission to copy *complete* included any part; but doesn't say so.

D. WHAT HAS TO BE DONE

Look over the original again. Mark it up.

"Brevity

                                       (1) (4)

    (i) Poetry: (a) A complete poem if less than 250 words

                (1) (4)   (3)   (2)

and if printed on not more than two pages or, (b) from a

                             (1)

longer poem, an excerpt of not more than 250 words.

                         (3)

    (ii) Prose: (a) ~~Either~~ a complete article, story or

           (1)   (3)   (2)

essay of less than 2500 words, or (b) an excerpt from any

                (1)

prose work of not more than 1,000 words or 10% of the work,

                    (5)

whichever is less, but in any event a minimum of 500 words."

(1) Make all of those uniform.

(2) Make uniform, and English.

(3) Apparently no difference intended; cut "either."

(4) Don't need this repeat. Make it "not more than 250 & 2."

(5) Work this over.

E. OUTLINE

Brevity

1. *Poetry*
   (a)   complete—max. 249 (change to 250); 2 pages.
   (b)   excerpt—max. 250 from longer poem.
   (c)   Note: can copy complete short poem, not excerpt it.
2. *Prose*
   (a)   complete
        (1)   ltd. to article, story, essay.
        (2)   max. 2,499 (change to 2500).
   (b)   excerpt
        (1)   any work
        (2)   max. 10%—
             EXCEPT:
                [a]   CAN copy 500.
                [b]   CAN'T copy over 1,000.
   (c)   Note:
        (1)   complete ltd. to specific works; excerpt any.
        (2)   can copy complete prose 2500; excerpt from it max. 500.

F. REWRITE

No. 1. Without much change in format, you can still shorten it a little, and make it clearer through some change of language and uniform usage.

BREVITY

     (i) Poetry (a) A whole poem complete in not more than 250 words and 2 printed pages; or

                (b) An excerpt of not more than 250 words from a longer poem.

     (ii) Prose (a) A whole article, story, or essay complete in not more than 2500 words; or

                (b) An excerpt of not more than 10% of any work, but you may always excerpt not more than 500 words and never more than 1,000.

No. 2. Since these are "guidelines," it would be worth some extra words and a much clearer format to really guide the audience that needs guidance badly—teachers. Tell them what you have discovered by taking apart the specimen.

BREVITY

     (i) Poetry

          (a) Complete poem - if not more than 250 words and was printed on not more than 2 pages; or

          (b) One excerpt - of not more than 250 words from a longer poem.

          (c) Note: The intended result of the limits in (a) and (b) is that a complete short poem may be copied but not an excerpt from it.

     (ii) Prose

          (a) Complete article, story, or essay - if not more than 2500 words; or

          (b) One excerpt - of not more than 10% of any work, with two exceptions:

[1] You may always copy not more than 500 words; and

[2] You may not copy more than 1,000 words.

(c) Note: The intended results of the limits in (a) and (b) are:

[1] No matter how short, a complete prose work may not be copied unless it is an article, a story, or an essay.

[2] A complete article, story, or essay, even though 2500 words, may be copied, but an excerpt from it has a top limit of 500 words.

No. 3. You may prefer the format of No. 2, and shorten it with a decision that the (c) Notes are not necessary.

II

Speaking of Corruption
(with a mouth full of mush)

A. BACKGROUND

Many federal and state laws attempt to keep government employment out of politics. This one is from California, part of a law dealing with "Political Activities of Public Employees." The expressions "local agency" and "state agency" are defined in another part of the law. Here is Government Code, §3204 (1976), titled *"Use of office, authority or influence to obtain change in position or compensation upon corrupt condition or consideration."*

B. THE SPECIMEN

1. "No one who holds, or who is seeking election or
2. appointment to, any office or employment in a state or local
3. agency shall, directly or indirectly, use, promise, threaten or
4. attempt to use, any office, authority, or influence, whether
5. then possessed or merely anticipated, to confer upon or secure
6. for any individual person, or to aid or obstruct any individual
7. person in securing, or to prevent any individual person from
8. securing, any position, nomination, confirmation, promotion, or
9. change in compensation or position, within the state or local
10. agency, upon consideration or condition that the vote or
11. political influence or action of such person or another shall
12. be given or used in behalf of, or withheld from, any candidate,
13. officer, or party, or upon any other corrupt condition or
14. consideration. This prohibition shall apply to urging or
15. discouraging the individual employee's action."

C. TAKING IT APART

1. Who is it for?

The title tells you that the law is against corruption. That's good. And despite the flow of words, you also gather that the law is about those who are "in" and those trying to get "in." So it ought to be addressed to all of those people; quite a varied bag (Rule 4, p. 66)."Clear to whom?" Influence peddlers, deal makers, as well as ordinary decent people trying to keep their politics separate from their jobs, trying to keep jobs, trying to get jobs. The ordinary job-seeker or government employee ought to know what is forbidden, better able to stand up to pressure. Wheelers and dealers, and ordinary candidates ought to be well warned. Also, the law has to be definite enough to be enforceable (Rule 2 and Rule 5, pp. 15 and 100).

2. Too many details to digest

So many ideas (and words) are thrown together in that first *long, long sentence* (Rule 3.3.b, p. 58) that it's impossible to separate the important from the fluff. Someplace, key words are hidden. Beat the bushes, and flush them out. As they break cover, grab them. Forget for the moment trying to figure it all out. Get one solid thought first. Then worry about the ramifications, including that little, lost second sentence.

D. WHAT HAS TO BE DONE

Step 1. Underline the Section to pick out the makings of a single topic.

Like this.

```
1.          "No one who holds, or who is seeking election or
2.    appointment to, any office or employment in a state or local
3.    agency shall, directly or indirectly, use, promise, threaten or
4.    attempt to use, any office, authority, or influence, whether
5.    then possessed or merely anticipated, to confer upon or secure
6.    for any individual person, or to aid or obstruct any individual
7.    person in securing, or to prevent any individual person from
8.    securing, any position, nomination, confirmation, promotion, or
9.    change in compensation or position, within the state or local
10.   agency, upon consideration or condition that the vote or
11.   political influence or action of such person or another shall
12.   be given or used in behalf of, or withheld from, any candidate,
13.   officer, or party, or upon any other corrupt condition or
14.   consideration.  This prohibition shall apply to urging or
15.   discouraging the individual employee's action."
```

The underlined words tie together to make a manageable sentence.

> NO ONE WHO HOLDS ANY OFFICE IN A AGENCY SHALL USE
> ANY OFFICE TO CONFER UPON ANY PERSON ANY POSITION WITHIN THE
> AGENCY, UPON CONSIDERATION THAT THE VOTE OF SUCH PERSON SHALL
> BE GIVEN IN BEHALF OF ANY CANDIDATE.

That is not nearly the whole section. What you now have is a bite size chunk. Everything else is complication, variations on a theme. As you look back over the original specimen, you can see why you couldn't digest it before. Acres of qualifications and multiplied instances.

Step 2. Compare the Step 1 extract with the parts of the original that are not underlined. On the extract, number and underline the words that are the keys to unraveling complexity.

>   1.   2.   3.   4.
> NO ONE WHO HOLDS ANY OFFICE IN A AGENCY SHALL USE
>   5.   6.   7.   8.
> ANY OFFICE TO CONFER UPON ANY PERSON ANY POSITION WITHIN THE
> 3.   9.   10.   7.
> AGENCY, UPON CONSIDERATION THAT THE VOTE OF SUCH PERSON SHALL
>   11.   12.   13.
> BE GIVEN IN BEHALF OF ANY CANDIDATE.

Step 3. Group the numbered words from Step 2 with the original adjacent words that complicate the story. See what can be deleted, generalized, consolidated, made uniform.

1. *Holds*—or who is seeking election or appointment. Make it uniform: HOLDING OR [who is] SEEKING. "Election or appointment" are incidents of "seeking"; delete them. "Seeking" = trying to get; it's sort of biblical, but probably generally understood.

2. *Office*—or employment.
   Not the same; need both.

3. *Agency*—state or local.
   Not the same; need both to start; then just *agency*. With the changes in #1, the section could now start: NO ONE HOLDING OR SEEKING ANY OFFICE OR EMPLOYMENT IN A STATE OR LOCAL AGENCY ... Not bad.

155

4. *Use*—promise, threaten or attempt to use.
—directly or indirectly.
So many ways of "using." Probably desirable to specify; but to keep the thought clear, hold the details for later.

5. *Office*—authority or influence, whether then possessed or merely anticipated.
This is "use *Office*," as distinct from "holds Office" in #2, but it's the same office. This "use *Office*" group boils down to two ideas: use of authority (that comes with office) and use of influence (of the broadest sort). Can omit *office*, but keep *authority* and *influence;* authority more direct than plain influence. If authority or influence are only *antici-pated,* when *used* either would be *influence. Anticipated* is surplus. That also makes *possessed* surplus. Delete both.

6. *Confer*—or secure for
—or to aid or obstruct in securing
—or to prevent from securing.
These are all ways of *affecting* someone's *Position* (#8). Why not say so, saving the details for later. Define *affect!*

7. *Person*—individual
—or another.
The *individual* qualifier is surplus. That's the only kind of *person* who gets a government job. Delete. The *or other* introduces a new concept; keep it.

8. *Position*—nomination, confirmation, promotion, or change in compensation or position.
All of this is "within the agency." *Position* is the blanket, used here to include office or employment. The ideas, not the wording, are essential. *Promotion* is a type of *change* of position; delete *promotion.*

9. *Consideration*—or condition.
—or upon any other corrupt condition or consideration.
—urging or discouraging the individual employee's action. [the second sentence].
Consideration and *condition* can be terms of art; probably not used that way here; but now tightened up with *urging* (not completely clear) to eliminate possible legal quibbles.

For example:

> *consideration:* "I'll do this *in exchange for* that."
> *condition:* "I'll do this *if* you do that."
> *urging:* "*Why don't you* do this? I could do that."

Or upon any other corrupt condition or consideration, just barely tacked on to the tail of the long, long sentence, is the critical theme of the law: *corrupt.* Everyone knows about that word. Coupled with *any other* it bluntly characterizes everything that has gone before. Keep the word, but move it up where it can be noticed. Later, give details.

10. *Vote*—or political influence or action. A facet of #9. Tie the details to *corrupt.* The crooked swap for votes, etc.

11. *Given*—or used.
    Given sufficient; delete *used* to eliminate confusion with *use* (#4).

12. *Behalf*—or withheld from.
    More details of the crooked swap. Keep with *corrupt.*

13. *Candidate*—officer or party.
    More details of the crooked swap. Keep with *corrupt.*

E. OUTLINE

You are now ready to organize the section.

1. **Forbidden: "Corrupt" use of authority or influence**
   A. By holders and seekers
       (1) of offices
                               } in state or local agencies
       (2) or jobs
   B. To *affect* other holders and seekers.

2. **"Corrupt" includes**
   A. What it usually does;
   B. Especially the crooked swap—
       (1) Using authority or influence to affect jobs; for
       (2) votes, political action, political influence given or withheld: candidates, officers, parties
   C. Something added: a near swap:
       (1) B. (1) to
       (2) urge or discourage B. (2).

3. **"Use" may be**
   A. Direct or indirect
   B. Varied—promises, threats, attempts.

4. **"Affect" means to help or hinder in getting:**
   A. Position
   B. Change of position
   C. Nomination to position
   D. Confirmation to position
   E. Change of pay.

F. REWRITE

No. 1.

No one holding or seeking office or employment in a state or local agency shall use authority or influence corruptly to affect another person's position in the agency.

(a) <u>Corruptly</u> includes, but is not limited to, for the consideration, on condition, or merely urging:

That the vote (or other political action or influence) of the person or someone else be given to (or withheld from) a candidate, officer, or political party.

(b) <u>Using</u> includes acting directly or indirectly, by promise, threat, attempt, or otherwise.

(c) <u>Affect</u> means to help or hinder the person in getting a position or change of position, a nomination or confirmation to a position, or a change of pay.

That cuts the word count and strips the law down to an understandable essence in one preliminary statement. For anyone in doubt, details are separately listed. That's all right for the books.

But that message won't get to everyone who needs it. It's still too long, says more than most people want to know, and it's inaccessible. To get to those who need it, the message ought to be shortened, posted in public offices, and passed out to job applicants and candidates. Try again.

No. 2.

```
                IMPORTANT NOTICE

                JOBS AND POLITICS


                    IF YOU

- HAVE A JOB                )
                                    IN A
- WANT A JOB               )
                              STATE OR LOCAL
- HOLD OFFICE              )
                                  AGENCY
- WANT TO HOLD OFFICE      )


               READ THIS:

IT IS AGAINST THE LAW TO USE YOUR INFLUENCE

          OVER A JOB OR AN OFFICE

     1. TO BUY VOTES OR OTHER POLITICAL ACTION.

            OR TO TRY TO.

     2. TO MAKE ANY OTHER CORRUPT DEAL.

            OR TO TRY TO.

(See California Government Code, Section 3204.)

                 * * *
```

That doesn't give all the details. It says enough.

III

The Orgy

A. BACKGROUND

A law, amended many times, prohibits "False Advertising." Though advertiser places false advertising in a newspaper, etc., the media do not become liable (§17502). The law also says that " 'person' includes any individual, partnership, firm, association, or corporation." The part of the law reproduced here is §17500 of the California Business and Professions Code, as amended in 1979.

B. THE SPECIMEN

```
 1.         "It is unlawful for any person, firm, corporation
 2.    or association, or any employee thereof with intent directly
 3.    or indirectly to dispose of real or personal property or to
 4.    perform services, professional or otherwise, or anything of
 5.    any nature whatsoever or to induce the public to enter into
 6.    any obligation relating thereto, to make or disseminate or
 7.    cause to be made or disseminated before the public in this
 8.    state, or to make or disseminate or cause to be made or
 9.    disseminated from this state before the public in any state,
10.    in any newspaper or other publication, or any advertising
11.    device, or by public outcry or proclamation, or in any other
12.    manner or means whatever, any statement, concerning such real
13.    or personal property or services, professional or otherwise,
14.    or concerning any circumstances or matter of fact connected
15.    with the proposed performance or disposition thereof, which
16.    is untrue or misleading, and which is known, or which by the
17.    exercise of reasonable care should be known, to be untrue or
18.    misleading, or for any such person, firm or corporation to so
19.    make or disseminate or cause to be so made or disseminated
```

```
20.    any such statement as part of a plan or scheme with the intent
21.    not to sell such personal property or services, professional or
22.    otherwise, so advertised at the price stated therein, or as
23.    so advertised.  Any violation of the provisions of this
24.    section is a misdemeanor punishable by imprisonment in the
25.    county jail not exceeding six months, or by a fine not exceeding
26.    two thousand five hundred dollars ($2,500), or by both."
```

C.   TAKING IT APART

1. Does it have to be like this?

Glancing through those 26 lines, the reader is not befuddled by law words. To be sure, there are some. Some old turkeys that don't help anyone—*thereto, thereof, therein.* Some, definitely legal, but known in a general way to non-lawyers—*firm, corporation, association, real property, personal property, misdemeanor.* Some that give hint of possible legal complications—*with intent, reasonable care.* But for a general understanding, nothing legal enough to completely baffle an ordinary person with an ordinary dictionary. The real trouble, the barrier to understanding, is not the law but lawsick writing.

2. Too many ORs

There are several reasons why that section is not clear. But the easiest way to visualize the impossibility of quick understanding is to circle every *or* (better in bright red).

```
1.        "It is unlawful for any person, firm, corporation
2.    (or) association, (or) any employee thereof with intent directly
3.    (or) indirectly to dispose of real (or) personal property (or) to
4.    perform services, professional (or) otherwise, (or) anything of
5.    any nature whatsoever (or) to induce the public to enter into
6.    any obligation relating thereto, to make (or) disseminate (or)
7.    cause to be made (or) disseminated before the public in this
8.    state, (or) to make (or) disseminate (or) cause to be made (or)
9.    disseminated from this state before the public in any state,
10.   in any newspaper (or) other publication, (or) any advertising
11.   device, (or) by public outcry (or) proclamation, (or) in any other
12.   manner (or) means whatever, any statement, concerning such real
13.   (or) personal property (or) services, professional (or) otherwise,
14.   (or) concerning any circumstances (or) matter of fact connected
```

161

15.   with the proposed performance (or) disposition thereof, which

16.   is untrue (or) misleading, and which is known, (or) which by the

17.   exercise of reasonable care should be known, to be untrue (or)

18.   misleading, (or) for any such person, firm (or) corporation to so

19.   make (or) disseminate (or) cause to be so made (or) disseminated

20.   any such statement as part of a plan (or) scheme with the intent

21.   not to sell such personal property (or) services, professional (or)

22.   otherwise, so advertised at the price stated therein, (or) as

23.   so advertised. Any violation of the provisions of this

24.   section is a misdemeanor punishable by imprisonment in the

25.   county jail not exceeding six months, (or) by a fine not exceeding

26.   two thousand five hundred dollars ($2,500), (or) by both."

The ORs overtax the mind. Of 260 words, 41 are ORs. The variations of meaning those ORs give to the section run into the hundreds. The mind flip-flops too fast, trying to grasp a shred of sense.

Some of the ORs join noun possibilities ("person, firm, corporation or association, or any employee"); some vary the verbs ("dispose . . . perform . . . induce"); some vary adverbs ("directly or indirectly"); some vary the adjectives ("untrue or misleading"). A little of that sort of variation may be expected in ordinary composition. But with ORs popping up all over it is difficult to keep track of what is tied to what. No warning that all ORs are not equal. No warning, for example, that the first OR in line 18 introduces a completely separate part of the law.

3. "It is unlawful," but what's "it"?

The ORs are bad enough. The long, long sentence (Rule 3.3.b, p. 58) makes matters worse. It forces reading and re-reading to gather the sense. "It is unlawful" all right, but just what is it that's unlawful?

It is unlawful for any person (line 1) to what? The search for a verb is on. Wade through *to dispose* (line 3), *to perform* (lines 3, 4), *to induce, to enter* (line 5), and then a whole swarm of verbs (lines 6-9) —*to make or disseminate or cause to be made or disseminated*, etc.

If you decide that *to make* is the key, start looking for an object. Layers of words, and then in line 12—*any statement.* Maybe that's it.

Way down in line 18, the whole thing starts up again—*or for any such person,* presumably referring all the way back to line 1—*it is unlawful.*

Too much crowded into one sentence, especially one so poorly organized.

D.   WHAT HAS TO BE DONE

Step 1. Mark up the original. Trim it. Watch for snags. Write notes to yourself.

1.   "It is unlawful for any person, ~~firm, corporation~~ ①

2.   ~~or association~~, or any employee ~~thereof~~ with intent directly ②

3.   or indirectly to dispose of real or personal property or to ⑧

4.   perform services, ~~professional or otherwise~~, ~~or anything of~~ ③ ④

5.   ~~any nature whatsoever~~ or to induce the public to enter into

6.   any obligation relating ~~thereto,~~ [to make or disseminate or ② ⑦

7.   cause to be made or disseminated before the public in this

8.   state, or to make or disseminate or cause to be made or ⑨

9.   disseminated from this state before the public in any state,

10.   in any newspaper or other publication, or any advertising

11.   device, or by public outcry or proclamation, or in any other

12.   manner or means whatever, any statement, concerning such real

13.   or personal property or services, professional or otherwise, ⑧ ③

14.   or concerning any circumstances or matter of fact connected

15.   with the proposed performance or disposition] ~~thereof,~~ ~~which~~ ②

16.   ~~is untrue or misleading~~, and which is known, or which by the ⑤

17.   exercise of reasonable care should be known, to be untrue or ⑩

18.   misleading, or for any such person, ~~firm or corporation~~ to so ①

19.   [make or disseminate or cause to be so made or disseminated] ⑦

20.   any such statement as part of a ~~plan or~~ scheme with the intent ⑪ ⑥

21.   not to sell such personal property or services, ~~professional or~~ ⑧ ③

22.   ~~otherwise~~, so advertised at the price stated ~~therein~~, or as ②

23.   so advertised. Any violation of the provisions of this

24.   section is a misdemeanor punishable by imprisonment in the

25.   county jail not exceeding six months, or by a fine not exceeding

26.   two thousand five hundred dollars ($2,500), or by both."

(a)   *Cut!* (Rule 7)

(1)   *firm, corporation or association* (lines 1–2)
firm or corporation (line 18)

The law already defines "person" to include all of those, and more. Besides the wordings are needlessly inconsistent.

(2)   *thereof* (line 2)—worthless.
thereto (line 6)—needs a substitute.
thereof (line 15)—worthless.
therein (line 22)—worthless.

(3)   *professional or otherwise* (lines 4, 13, and 21–22)

Services is broad enough. Unless some reason (unknown) for wanting to stress "professional," cut.

(4)   *or anything of any nature whatsoever* (lines 4–5)

This a foul ball. Grammatically, the sentence reads "to perform services . . . or anything." But that leads to a double puzzlement: (a) What do you perform in addition to "services"? and (b) The usage is inconsistent with the references elsewhere—"property" and "services" only. (Lines 13 and 21). Logically, sounds like a redundant goof, intended to follow not "perform" but "dispose of." Some research shows that from 1915–1941 that was the way it was. In 1941, the law was amended, with this appendage left untouched; and it has stayed that meaningless way ever since.

(5)   *which is untrue or misleading* (lines 15–16)

Redundant. The law calls for knowledge of the "untrue or misleading" character of the advertising; can't know it is untrue, etc. if it isn't.

(6)   *plan or* (line 20)

Redundant. Typical lawsick doubling of synonyms "plan or scheme." Choose one. (Rule 1.1.a.[2], p. 4)

(b)   *Tentative partial revision*

(7)   Lines 6–15 (the shaded area) sound very much like a long way around the barn to say *"advertising."* Shouting your wares "before the public" "in any . . . manner or means whatever" is the essence of advertising. Why not say so? Maybe *to advertise* would shorten it. This also applies to the reference to advertising in line 19.

(c)   *Watch these!*

(8)   In lines 3 and 12–13, the law says *real or personal property,* but in line 21 only *personal property.* That is not an unimportant or irrational difference. Keep it.

(9) If you puzzle over the grammar or sense of "or to make ... from this state before the public in any state" (lines 8–9), that was squeezed into an already overcrowded sentence in 1979. Without recasting the long, long sentence, the amenders added 21 words (4 of them ORs) to give the statute an effect beyond the California line.

(10) *untrue or misleading* (line 16).

  The two are not the same. Keep both.

(11) The reference of *any such statement* is not at all clear. How much of what has gone before does the *such* include? Perhaps a knowing "statement" in advertising —"know" or "reasonably should know." If it includes everything, why the latter part of the first sentence? This needs work.

Step 2. Write out the result of Step 1 cuts and revisions. Mark off the separate parts of the Section.

With the cuts made right now and the tentative revisions, you have much less to deal with. It is now possible to get the sense of the whole, and its separate parts.

```
        IT IS UNLAWFUL FOR ANY PERSON, OR ANY EMPLOYEE
WITH INTENT DIRECTLY OR INDIRECTLY TO DISPOSE OF REAL
OR PERSONAL PROPERTY OR TO PERFORM SERVICES OR TO
INDUCE THE PUBLIC TO ENTER INTO ANY OBLIGATION RELATING
[TO ANY OF THAT], [TO ADVERTISE OR DISSEMINATE ADVERTISING
OR CAUSE TO BE ADVERTISED OR DISSEMINATED IN THIS STATE
(WHETHER THE EFFECT IS HERE OR ELSEWHERE) SUCH REAL OR
PERSONAL PROPERTY OR SERVICES BY] ANY STATEMENT WHICH
IS KNOWN, OR WHICH BY THE EXERCISE OF REASONABLE CARE
SHOULD BE KNOWN, TO BE UNTRUE OR MISLEADING,

        OR FOR ANY SUCH PERSON TO SO [ADVERTISE OR DISSEMINATE
ADVERTISING OR CAUSE TO BE ADVERTISED OR DISSEMINATED BY]
ANY SUCH STATEMENT AS PART OF A SCHEME WITH THE INTENT
NOT TO SELL SUCH PERSONAL PROPERTY OR SERVICES SO
ADVERTISED AT THE PRICE STATED OR AS SO ADVERTISED.

        ANY VIOLATION OF THE PROVISIONS OF THIS SECTION IS A
MISDEMEANOR PUNISHABLE BY IMPRISONMENT IN THE COUNTY JAIL
NOT EXCEEDING SIX MONTHS, OR BY A FINE NOT EXCEEDING TWO
THOUSAND FIVE HUNDRED DOLLARS ($2,500), OR BY BOTH.
```

The specimen is now considerably shorter; the ORs are cut in half. It's still not in great shape. We've missed some things; it's not all worked out. At least you can see it better. And organize it.

E. OUTLINE

I. Unlawful to advertise
A. What
1. Services
2. Real property
3. Personal property
B. How
1. By statements advertiser knows (or reasonably should)
a. untrue, or
b. misleading.
2. Advertising includes:
a. what it usually means
b. disseminating it (media exempt)
c. causing others to advertise or disseminate.
C. Where
Acts here, with effect
1. here, or
2. in other states.
D. By whom
1. Person (as defined in code) advertising in this state
2. Employee doing it.
[3. Query: maybe combine this with B.2 and C.]
E. With intent
1. To perform services

directly

2. To dispose of the property

or

3. To induce public to obligate selves for #1 or #2

indirectly

II. Also unlawful to advertise
A. What
1. Services
2. Personal property
B. How
1. By statements advertiser knows (or reasonably should) part of scheme not to sell as advertised.

   2. Advertising includes:
       a. what it usually means
       b. disseminating it (media exempt)
       c. causing others to advertise or disseminate.
C. Where
    Acts here, with effect
    1. here, or
    2. in other states.
D. By whom
    1. Person as (defined in code) advertising in this state
    2. Employee doing it.
    [3. Query: maybe combine this with B.2 and C.]
E. With intent
    1. To sell at a price different from advertised price.
    2. To sell in some other way different from advertised.
    3. Not to sell an advertised item.

III. **Violations of I or II**
      A. Misdemeanor
      B. Maximum punishment
      1. 6 months—county jail
      2. $2500; or
      3. #1 and #2.

F. REWRITE

   (a) Advertising of services or real or personal property is unlawful if the advertiser knows, or reasonably should know, that the advertising contains an untrue or misleading statement. To be guilty under this subsection, the advertiser must have advertised with the intent to do one or more of these things, whether directly or indirectly:

   (1) Perform the services;

   (2) Dispose of the property;

   (3) Induce people to obligate themselves for either.

   (b) Advertising of services or personal property is also unlawful if the advertiser knows, or reasonably should

know, that the advertising is part of a scheme not to sell
as advertised. To be guilty under this subsection, the
advertiser must have advertised with one or more of these
intents:

    (1) To sell at a price different from that
          advertised;

    (2) To sell in some other way different from
          that advertised;

    (3) Not to sell an advertised item.

    (c) "Advertiser" means a person advertising
in this state, disseminating advertising here,
or causing someone else to do either, whether the effect
of any of those acts is here or in another state. For the
media exemption, see §17502.

    (d) Unlawful advertising makes the advertiser guilty
of a misdemeanor. The punishment is imprisonment in the
county jail for not longer than 6 months, a fine of not
more than $2500, or both.

IV

Deformed Building Contract

A. BACKGROUND

This is part of a contract to build a house. The contract starts off with a boilerplate agreement "by and between" and a "Witnesseth." Other parts of the contract describe the property, duties of the contractor, details of "Insurance," and the schedule of payments.

The house was built, but owners and contractor argued over price. Each side contended that the contract was unambiguously in its favor: $34,500 against $38,038. Those were 1968 dollars. Lawsuit.

The trial court agreed that the contract was unambiguous; $34,500. And if it were ambiguous, it was the contractor's fault; he drew it. Owners win. Appeal.

A majority of the state supreme court (in 1971) also agreed that the contract was unambiguous; $38,038. Contractor wins. A dissenter disagreed with everyone—litigants and judges. He called the contract "ambiguous." Like the trial court, he would resolve the ambiguity against the person responsible, the contractor, who had "copied the paragraph in dispute (No. 3) out of a form book."

An expensive difference of opinion.

Here is paragraph No. 3.

B. THE SPECIMEN

1.   In consideration of the performance by the said contractor

2.   of all the covenants and conditions contained in this agreement

3.   and contained in the plans and specifications the owners agree

4.   to pay to the contractor an amount equal to the amount of all

5.   material furnished by the contractor and the labor furnished by

6.   the contractor together with payroll taxes and Insurance, also

7.   together with the sum total of the net amount due the

8.   subcontractors performing work or furnishing work for said

9.   construction. The Owners also agree to pay to the contractor,

10. in addition to the amount specified hereinabove, a fee equal to
11. 10% of the actual cost of the said residence, said fee to be
12. paid after completion of said residence and acceptance thereof
13. by the Owners. It is specifically agreed by and between the
14. parties that notwithstanding the agreement hereinabove by the
15. owners shall not be required, under the terms of this agreement,
16. to pay to the contractor any amount in excess of the sum of
17. Thirty-four Thousand, Five Hundred Dollars ($34,500.00) which
18. is the estimated cost of construction, plus the fee provided
19. for herein.

C.   TAKING IT APART

Step 1. Analyze by postmortem outline (Rule 6.2.b, p. 123)

Owners To Pay Contractor ("C")

I.   **"In consideration of "** C's performance of covenants and conditions in:

   A.   Contract, and
   B.   Plans and specifications.

II.   **Miscellaneous cost items**

   A.   Materials C furnishes. ("amount = to the amount of all material. . .")?
   B.   Labor C furnishes + payroll taxes.
   C.   Insurance
   D.   Work of subs (1) performed or (2) furnished. ("sum total of the net amount")?

III.   **Fee to C** ("in addition to *the* amount specified hereinabove")?

   A.   10% of "actual cost" (10% of all of II?)
   B.   Payable on (1) completion and (2) acceptance by owners.

IV.   **Limit of owner's liability**

   A.   "NOTWITHSTANDING *THE* AGREEMENT HEREINABOVE" ("Notwithstanding" *what* agreement?)
     (1)   III—the closest. Would limit C's fee. *or*
     (2)   II—the remotest. Would not limit C's fee. *or*
     (3)   II and III—together "*the* agreement." Would limit C's fee.
   B.   *$34,500* (for everything). C bound by his "estimated cost." No "amount in excess" of: "the *sum*" of II+III=$34,500. *or*

    C.   *$34,500 + III.* The *figure* $34,500 ("estimated" for II) + III (10% of "actual"). Note line 18 comma. *or*

    D.   *$34,500 + 10% of $34,500.* 10% of "actual cost" (III) limited by *"notwithstanding"* (IV).

Step 2. Conclusions from the postmortem

1.   Pervasive carelessness

While the big trouble shows up most clearly in part IV, that is only a cumulative effect. Distant early warning of careless writing came in the opening boilerplate (see Background)—the coupled synonyms *by and between* (Rule 1.1.a.[2], p. 4), and the worthless old formalism *Witnesseth* (Rule 1.1.a.[3], p. 5).

2.   "In consideration of" (Rule 5.1, p. 101)

This boilerplate (beginning part I) goes back to a distant era that disqualified parties from testifying. The writing could "testify" for them; get it all in. Today, consideration is usually presumed in a writing, and a recital of consideration is not binding. Besides, as the Background tells us, the contractor's duties are already spelled out elsewhere. No need in any case to repeat it here. The whole of part I of the outline can be cut.

3.   Performance of covenants and conditions (Rule 5.1, p. 101)

Again in part I (lines 1 and 2 of specimen) form triumphs over thought, English, and law. *Covenant* at one time referred to an agreement under seal; today it rarely means more than *agree* or *agreement*. Sometimes, especially in leases, *covenant* distinguishes an *agreement* from a *condition.* But here, no refined usage. How do you *perform* a condition? A condition happens or doesn't happen. *If it rains* is a condition. *I agree to make it rain* is an agreement. It is possible to use *condition* in a completely non-technical sense, another word for *agreement.* If that is the usage here, *covenant and condition* is needless doubling.

4.   Twofers (Rule 2.3, p. 20)

More serious trouble shows up in part II A, and continues to the end. Different words for the same meaning and different meanings for the same word helped to bring on the litigation.

    The fundamental disagreement between owners and contractor is how much the house is going to *cost* the owners. To the owners, *cost* is the dent in the bank account, no matter how it got there —whether the *cost* of lumber or a contractor. Yet that nasty word is not used till part III—*actual cost*. Before that, *cost* is referred to indirectly as *amount* and *sum* (part II), with the special curiosity that part III speaks of *the* amount when two or three amounts are mentioned in part II.

Ignore the confusion of "amount equal to the amount of all material" (part II), which causes a moment's hesitation between the choice of *amount* as *quantity,* and *amount* as *dollars.* A more basic problem is that *amount* and *sum* are not only synonyms but share a joint duplicity. Each can mean a figure arrived at by a computation, or a fixed dollar figure.

That double role becomes critical with *sum.* When first used (part II C, line 7 of specimen), *sum* leads us to the language of arithmetic —*the sum total of the net amount.* When used again (part IV, line 17 of specimen) is *sum* still arithmetical, or is it simply a redundant label for a specific figure—$34,500? No "amount in excess of the sum of. . .$34,500. . .*which is* the estimated cost. . . , plus the fee" has the sound of arithmetic. Estimated cost + fee = $34,500.

The comma in line 18 after "estimated cost of construction" weighed heavily with the supreme court majority (but not at all with the trial judge or the dissenting justice). The majority thought it established $34,500 as the figure of "estimated cost," separate from the additional "fee." A comma before and after the clause would have been more persuasive (Rule 3.3, p. 56).

5.   The unnecessary negative (Rule 2.4, p. 28)

The postmortem outline makes clear that part IV contradicts a substantial—though ill-defined—portion of everything that has gone before. *Notwithstanding* (line 14) does it. Why say the owners agree to pay (II and III) and that they don't agree to pay (IV)? Last minute negotiation could account for the contradiction. But if that is what happened, the change was sufficiently important to require a rewrite. The limit on liability can be stated positively and clearly as part of the agreement to pay.

6.   Worthless Old and Middle English words (Rules 1.1.a.[1], p. 3, and 7.3.b.[2], p. 134)

The postmortem outline (parts III and IV A) also points up the traditional and misplaced reliance on the *herein* family for precise reference. Whether plain *herein* or *hereinafter* or—as in this case—*hereinabove,* they are simply not to be trusted. They give an old phony reassurance—"Well, that's been covered," and have been causing legal disasters for centuries. In this case, both references are further confused by the singular usage, *the* amount and *the* agreement, and no obvious singulars "hereinabove."

Turning from outline to specimen, you realize this *herein* is part of a pattern—addiction to archaic style, whether it does any good or not. *Said* contractor (line 1), *said* construction (line 8), *said* fee (line 11), though there is only one of each. Similarly, "acceptance *thereof*" (line 12) when "*its* acceptance" would be clearer; and a final "provided for *herein*" (lines 18–19) that adds nothing.

7. One afterthought

Labor and *work* (part II). It is not clear in the building trades that that is simply an old duplication ("work, labor, and materials"; "work, labor, and services") or a difference. Sometimes *labor* distinguishes work by the day, or the hour, from other types of work. *Services* is sometimes a separate category of work for higher pay, or by professionals. Here, the contract distinguishes between *labor* supplied by the contractor, and *work* supplied by the sub-contractors. Without more information, better let the distinction stand.

D. WHAT HAS TO BE DONE

The basic defect is no plan (Rule 6, p. 114).

Back up and start over. There is no single solution to the problems posed by the specimen because we don't know what was intended.

Go back to your clients, and ask them what they want, what the deal is. Then outline it. If you are still in doubt, ask again. This is not merely the solution of hindsight, but part of the planning that should be followed in any beginning. Don't just reach for a form (Rule 5.1.a, p. 101).

E. OUTLINE

No. 1—$34,500 includes everything

I. Owners' only liability for construction costs:
   A. Limited to $34,500 maximum.
   B. Over that, contractor bears.
   C. Contractor's fee included in maximum.

II. Within maximum, Owners to pay contractor for:
   A. Labor and materials supplied by contractor;
   B. Payroll taxes;
   C. Insurance;
   D. Work supplied by sub-contractors; and

E. Fee to contractor: 10% of items A–D.
   (1) Might be no fee.
   (2) If fee, payable when:
       (a) House completed and
       (b) Owners have accepted.

No. 2—$34,500 does not include fee

I.   Owners' only liability for construction costs:
   A. Limited to $34,500 maximum.
   B. Over that, contractor bears.
   C. Contractor's fee not included in maximum.
II. Within maximum, Owners to pay contractor for:
   A. Labor and materials supplied by contractor;
   B. Payroll taxes;
   C. Insurance;
   D. Work supplied by sub-contractors.
III. Owners also to pay contractor fee:
   A. 10% of items in II, even though items over maximum.
   B. Payable when:
       (1) House completed and
       (2) Owners have accepted.

No. 3—$34,500 does not include fee, but fee limited to 10% of $34,500.

I.   Owners' only liability for construction costs:
   A. Limited to $34,500 maximum.
   B. Over that, contractor bears.
   C. Contractor's fee not included in maximum.
II. Within maximum, Owners to pay contractor for:
   A. Labor and materials supplied by contractor;
   B. Payroll taxes;
   C. Insurance;
   D. Work supplied by sub-contractors.
III. Owners also to pay contractor fee:
   A. 10% of items in II, but maximum fee $3,450.
   B. Payable when:
       (1) House completed and
       (2) Owners have accepted.

F.   REWRITE

No. 1—following outline No. 1

Owners' only liability for construction costs, including the Contractor's fee, is limited to a maximum of $34,500;

anything over that will be borne by the Contractor. Within the maximum, Owners agree to pay Contractor for these items: Contractor's payroll taxes and Insurance for the job; labor and material supplied by the Contractor; work supplied by sub-contractors; and a Contractor's fee of 10% of the other costs just listed. If any Contractor's fee becomes payable, Owners agree to pay it after completion of the residence and its acceptance by the Owners.

No. 2—following outline No. 2

Owners' only liability for construction costs, exclusive of Contractor's fee, is limited to a maximum of $34,500; anything over that will be borne by the Contractor. Within the maximum, Owners agree to pay Contractor for these items: Contractor's payroll taxes and Insurance for the job; labor and material supplied by the Contractor; and work supplied by sub-contractors. Owners also agree to pay Contractor a fee of 10% of those costs, even though they exceed the maximum. Owners will pay the Contractor's fee after completion of the residence and its acceptance by the Owners.

No. 3—following outline No. 3

Owners' only liability for construction costs, exclusive of Contractor's fee, is limited to a maximum of $34,500; anything over that will be borne by the Contractor. Within the maximum, Owners agree to pay Contractor for these items: Contractor's payroll taxes and Insurance for the job; labor and material supplied by the Contractor; and work supplied by sub-contractors. Owners also agree to pay Contractor a fee of 10% of those costs up to a maximum fee of $3,450. Owners will pay the Contractor's fee after completion of the residence and its acceptance by the Owners.

V

Provided, Provided, Provided

A. BACKGROUND

The instalment auto sales contract is a well known feature of American life. The form of the contract has been regulated for years, with penalties for deviation. Some deviations may be corrected without penalty.

The retail seller of autos finances the stock in trade by turning over (sale, assignment) the instalment contract to a financier at a discounted price, or by giving the contract as security (e.g., a pledge) for a loan. As a result, various people at one time or another may "hold the paper" on the auto. The laws tell who is a *holder*.

Here is a short part of one of those laws telling when deviations from required form may be corrected.

B. THE SPECIMEN

```
 1.        Any failure to comply with any provisions of this chapter
 2.    (commencing with Section 2981) may be corrected by the holder,
 3.    provided, however, that a willful violation may not be corrected
 4.    unless it is a violation appearing on the face of the contract
 5.    and is corrected within 30 days of the execution of the contract
 6.    or within 20 days of its sale, assignment or pledge, whichever
 7.    is later, provided that the 20-day period shall commence with
 8.    the initial sale, assignment or pledge of the contract, and
 9.    provided that any other violation appearing on the face of the
10.    contract may be corrected only within such time periods.
```

C. TAKING IT APART

1. First glance

Only 10 lines, 106 words. How is it possible to pack so much confusion into such a small space? By violating every rule in the book.

2. The long, long sentence (Rule 3.3.b, p. 58)

This specimen doesn't set a record for the long, long sentence. But it is the traditional style of packing it all in and running it all together, which unfortunately doesn't seem silly to enough legal writers. Protracted negotiation—over legislation and contracts—encourages the style. Insert, but don't take out. No plan (Rule 6, p. 114). No concern for clarity of substance or format (Rule 4, p. 61).

3. Twofer (Rule 2.3, p. 20)

The sentence starts talking about *failure to comply* (line 1), forgets it, and drifts off into *violation—willful* (line 3), plain (line 4), and *other* (line 9). How many categories of sin do we have to deal with? Isn't *failure to comply* a *violation*, even though *failure* is Old French and *violation* Latin? Just because we have a peculiar, polyglot vocabulary (Rule 1.1., p. 2) doesn't mean we have to use all of it at the same time. If the distinction is between *willful* and *other* violations, stick to that. Easier to follow.

4. Clear to whom? (Rule 4, p. 61)

The law here is for the protection of consumers. It ought to be understandable to buyers of autos, and to those in the business of selling and financing autos. Well it's not clear to anyone right now, and the question is why not? Is there something about the law so complex as to defy simple exposition? Or is it lawsick that does it in?

5. Law (Rule 5, p. 100)

Law can't be ignored, but law words need not be taken on faith. Are law words the trouble?

a. *willful*—distinctively legal, but not a term of art, and not at all precise. It speaks of intentionally doing something; beyond that it is uncertain. Not clear that "*willful* violation" means intending to violate, or only intending to do something that turns out to be a violation. *Intentionally* would probably serve as well, but would still not remove the ambiguity. Unless we are re-legislating, or can find out what the policymakers want, we might as well leave *willful* alone. It seems clear enough to almost anyone that here it is intended to distinguish between the bad guys *(willful)* and the good, or at least better, guys (*other* violators).

b. *execution* "of the contract"—means doing what is necessary, not to kill it, but to bring the contract to life. Sometimes, just signing; sometimes, signing and delivery; etc. Not a term of art. *Making* would do as well. Probably those buying and selling are not misled.

177

c. *assignment*—technical, but not a term of art. Generally, a transfer of rights to someone else. Fairly common, and probably not misleading (Rule 4.2.g, p. 81).

d. *pledge*—delivery of personal property as security. A weak term of art, but known to anyone who ever "hocked" (i.e., pledged) a watch.

e. *holder*—defined elsewhere in this law; we need not bother with it here.

f. *on the face* "of the contract"—argot for apparent by inspection of the piece of paper. Not complicated.

g. *provided*—a word introducing a *proviso*, a qualification. Both now part of the common speech, but still closely associated with the law. Of all the law words in the specimen, this is the prime trouble-maker and the most unnecessary (Rule 5.1, p. 101).

The specimen starts with "Any failure to comply . . . may be corrected" (lines 1 and 2). This turns out to be a lie. A sad beginning.

The first *provided* (line 3) takes a big bite out of "may be corrected."

The second *provided* (line 7) nibbles away at the first *provided*.

The third *provided* (line 9) takes a second big bite out of "may be corrected," leaving more to exception than to the rule so confidently stated in line 1.

This is the vice of excessive qualification, the *ifs, ands,* and *buts* in the popular condemnation of legal writing. Wheels within wheels; in the same family with *notwithstanding*.

If you have a statement and an exception, let the exception stand out clearly. Don't burden the reader with a search mission. Cut *provided, provided, provided* (Rule 7, p. 126).

6.   Time (Rule 2.5, p. 38)

Excessive provisos are troublesome enough in any case, more so here because tied in with expressions of time. Time is tricky to express in any case, unclearer here because of the provisos.

D.   WHAT HAS TO BE DONE

Diagram the possibilities of correction. The variables are (1) willful violation, (2) not willful, (3) on face of contract, (4) not on face, (5) *time limit on correction [tl]*, and (6) *no time limit [ntl]*.

CORRECTABLE?

	WILLFUL	NOT WILLFUL
ON FACE	(a) *YES* (lines 3-5) *tl* (lines 5-8)	(b) *YES* (lines 9-10) *tl* (line 10)
NOT ON FACE	(c) *NO* (lines 3-5)	(d) *YES* (lines 1-3) *ntl*

All that is left of the general rule (lines 1–3) is in box (d); and that by default. Everything else has been made an exceptional case. This law encourages correction, as long as there has not been intentional wrongdoing. Violations on the face of the contract are readily detectable, and should be corrected without waiting too long; the time limits encourage compliance.

E. OUTLINE

Rules on holder's correction of violations

    I.   **Violations on face of contract**
        A. Correctable, within time limits.
        B. Time limits (at holder's choice)
            1. Within 30 days after contract executed; *OR*
            2. Within 20 days after first time it is either
                a. sold,
                b. assigned, or
                c. pledged.
    II. **Violations not on face**
        A. If willful—not correctable.
        B. If not willful—correctable at any time.

F. REWRITE

No. 1

        Rules on holder's correction of violations of this

Chapter.

        (a) Violations appearing on the face of the contract:

        May be corrected, but only within 30 days after

execution of the contract, or within 20 days after the first

time it is either sold, assigned, or pledged. The 30/20
alternative is at the holder's choice.

      (b) <u>Violations not appearing on the face of the contract</u>:

         (1) If willful, may not be corrected.

         (2) If not willful, may be corrected at any time.

No. 2

      (a) The holder of a contract may correct any violation
of this Chapter except a willful violation that does not appear
on the face of the contract.

      (b) On violations permitted to be corrected by
paragraph (a), these rules apply:

         (1) If not on the face of the contract, may be
corrected at any time.

         (2) If on the face of the contract, may be
corrected only within (i) 30 days after execution of the
contract, or (ii) 20 days after the first time it is either sold,
assigned, or pledged. Alternatives (i) or (ii) are at holder's
option.

No. 3

      If a violation of this Chapter is on the face of the
contract, the holder may correct it, but only during a limited
period. That period, at holder's option, is within 30 days
after execution of the contract or within 20 days after the
first time it is either sold, assigned, or pledged. If not on
the face of the contract, a willful violation may not be
corrected, but a non-willful violation may be corrected by
the holder at any time.

VI

Adam's Rib

A. BACKGROUND

In typical corporate elections, few shareholders show up at shareholders' meetings to vote in person. But the owner of shares (only the owner) may give someone a *proxy* (written authority to act) to vote the shares. Most shareholders do just that. If someone else solicits a proxy on the same shares (as frequently happens in battles for corporate control), the shareholder is free to give new proxies, the latest revoking all earlier proxies. A recurrent problem in corporation law is how to make proxies irrevocable.

Usually, a proxy may be revoked even though labeled "irrevocable." Usually, a "proxy coupled with an interest" is irrevocable. The catch then is in determining when a proxy *is* coupled with an interest, i.e., some interest in the corporation beyond the proxied shares. To eliminate that argument, some newer corporation laws say that a proxy can be made irrevocable *if* it is held by someone within a category specified in the corporation law.

This specimen is a part of one of those laws. In other parts of this particular law, some of the holders of irrevocable proxies are listed as *persons*, some according to legal role—*pledgee, creditor, beneficiary* of a trust.

B. THE SPECIMEN

[A proxy which states that it is irrevocable is irrevocable for the period specified therein . . . when it is held by any of the following or a nominee of any of the following:]

* * *

1.   A person who has purchased or agreed to purchase or holds

2.   an option to purchase the shares or a person who has sold a

3.   portion of such person's shares in the corporation to the

4.   maker of the proxy.

C.   TAKING IT APART

Clear sailing till the tail end of line 2, when the comma-less section runs into *person* trouble.

Why *person* in line 2 when you already have a *person* in line 1? Especially when, in such a short passage, line 3 includes the ambiguous reference to *such person's shares.*

A second and third *person* are not required for uniformity of language in the section. As the Background tells us, some of the other categories are described functionally.

The writer, under compulsion to make the section (the whole law) non-sexist, was appalled by the impending catastrophe of saying "or a person who has sold a portion of *his* shares," and took the easy, obscure way out with *such person's.*

But the catastrophe could have been avoided, and the law made considerably clearer, with a little effort. You can make something more out of *his* than a *person* (Rule 3.1.b, p. 47).

D.   WHAT HAS TO BE DONE

Step 1. List the cast in order of appearance.

"A person who":
    i.   "has purchased" [the shares]
    ii. "agreed to purchase" [the shares]
    iii. "holds an option to purchase the shares."

"a person who":
    iv. "has sold a portion of such person's shares in the corporation to the maker of the proxy."

Step 2. Translate.

    i.   "A person who has purchased"—*the buyer.*
    ii. "agreed to purchase"—*one who agreed to buy.*
    iii. "holds an option to purchase"—*one who holds an option to buy.*
    iv. "a person who has sold"—*the seller.*
        a. "a portion of such person's shares in the corporation" —*part of seller's shares* (seller has other shares in the corporation).
        b. "to the maker of the proxy"—*the buyer.*

E. OUTLINE

A proxy . . . is irrevocable . . . when it is held by:

1. Buyer of shares covered.
2. One who has agreed to buy.
3. One who has an option to buy.
4. Seller of the shares who retains other shares in the corporation.

F. REWRITE

[A proxy . . . is irrevocable . . . when it is held by . . .]

No. 1 *Adding a comma would help.* (Rule 3.3, p. 56)

A person who has purchased or agreed to purchase or holds an option to purchase the shares, or a person who has sold a portion of such person's shares in the corporation to the maker of the proxy.

No. 2 *Eliminating ambiguous reference to "person" helps more.* (Rule 3, p. 44)

A person who has purchased or agreed to purchase or holds an option to purchase the shares, or a seller who has sold a portion of the seller's shares in the corporation to the maker of the proxy.

No. 3 *A complete rewrite makes it clearer.* (Rule 4, p. 61)

The buyer of the shares covered by the proxy, one who has an agreement or option to buy them, or the seller of the shares if the seller retains other shares in the corporation.

No. 4 *Breaking up the long, long sentence and changing the format makes it even clearer.* (Rule 4.3, p. 91)

(a) A person who has bought, agreed to buy, or has an option to buy the shares covered by the proxy;

(b) The seller of the shares covered by the proxy, if the seller retains other shares in the corporation.

APPENDIXES

APPENDIX A

Ordinary Old and
Middle English Words

These words can be dropped from the legal vocabulary without any loss of precision, and with a gain in clarity. If you are ever tempted to use one of them, look in an ordinary English language dictionary for a current word. In this sampling, some of the words listed have more than one meaning; where a particular meaning is given in parenthesis, only that meaning of the word is recommended for oblivion.

aforesaid
behoof
bounden
foregoing
forswear
forthwith
henceforth
hereafter
hereby
herein
hereinabove
hereinafter
hereof
heretofore
herewith
hitherto
let (hindrance)
moreover
nowise
said (as an adjective)
saith
same (as a noun)
thence
thenceforth

thereabout
thereafter
thereat
therefor (as distinguished
    from *therefore*)
therefrom
therein
thereof
thereon
thereout
thereover
therethrough
thereto
theretofore
thereunder
therewith
to wit
whence
whensoever
whereas (to mean anything
    other than *on the
    contrary*)
whereat
whereby

wherefore
wherein
whereof
whereon
whereupon

whilst
witness (testimony: *in witness of*)
witnesseth

APPENDIX B

Coupled Synonyms

These coupled synonyms can be dropped from the legal vocabulary with a gain in precision, brevity, and clarity. In this sampling, some of the words have independent meanings when used alone, but when coupled as here in legal usage they are excess baggage. Once you decide exactly what you want to say, one of the coupled synonyms will say it better alone.

acknowledge and confess
act and deed
annul and set aside
authorize and empower
conjecture and surmise
covenant and agree
cover, embrace, and include
deem and consider
due and payable
each and all
each and every
entirely and completely
final and conclusive
fit and proper
fit and suitable
for and during
for and in consideration of
force and effect
fraud and deceit
free and unfettered
from and after
give and grant
give, devise, and bequeath
goods and chattels

have and hold
heed and care
hold and keep
hold, perform, observe, fulfill,
    and keep
in lieu, in place, instead, and in
    substitution of
in my stead and place
in truth and in fact
just and reasonable
keep and maintain
last will and testament
let or hindrance
lot, tract, or parcel of land
made and provided
made, ordained, constituted,
    and appointed
maintenance and upkeep
meet and just
mind and memory
modified and changed
null and void
null and void and of no force or
    effect

of and concerning
ordered, adjudged, and
    decreed
over, above, and in addition to
pardon and forgive
part and parcel
peace and quiet
remise, release, and quitclaim
rest, residue, and remainder
revoked, annulled, and held for
    nought

save and except
seised and possessed
shun and avoid
situate, lying, and being in
stand, remain, and be
truth and veracity
void and of no effect
void and of no force
void and of no value
void and of non effect
will and testament

APPENDIX C

Old Formalisms

These old formalisms can be dropped from the legal vocabulary without any loss of precision, and with gains in brevity and clarity. This sampling does not include those which rarely appear in writings except in transcripts of court proceedings (e.g., *approach the bench*).

are held and firmly bound
Be it remembered
Before me, a notary public
being first duly sworn, deposes
   and says
By virtue of the authority vested
   in me
came on for hearing
for such other and further relief
   as to the Court may seem
   meet and just
from the beginning of the world
   to the present
Further affiant sayeth not
Further deponent saith not
In Witness Whereof I have
   hereunto set my hand and
   caused the seal of . . . to be
   affixed
In Witness Whereof, the parties
   hereto have hereunto executed this agreement the
   day and year first above
   written.

Know All Men By These Presents
Plaintiff complains of defendant and for cause of action alleges:
respectfully submit
set down for hearing
ss
strangers to the blood
the undersigned
time is of the essence
To All To Whom These Presents Come, Greetings:
Whereas
Wherefore, defendant prays
   that plaintiff take nothing
without merit
WITNESSETH:

APPENDIX D

Law Latin, with English Equivalents

The law Latin words and phrases in this sampling are no more precise than their more intelligible English equivalents. Some of the "equivalents" are not literal translations, but convey in ordinary English the sense in which the Latin is used in the law. Law Latin that has been accepted as ordinary English is not included (e.g., *habeas corpus*). Law Latin terms of art are included in Appendix H.

ab initio—from the beginning

ad damnum—see *damnum*

arguendo—for the sake of argument (though not conceding the point)

cessante ratione legis cessat ipse lex—when the reason for the rule ceases, the rule itself ceases

cujus est solum, ejus est usque ad coelum et ad inferos—who owns the land owns it to the sky and to the depths of the earth

cum testamento annexo—with the will annexed; abbreviated *c.t.a.*

damnum—damage; *ad damnum*—the statement of damages (in a pleading)

damnum absque injuria—damage without injury (damage, but not of the sort for which the law gives redress)

de minimis non curat lex—the law does not concern itself with trifles; often shortened to *de minimis*

ejusdem generis—of the same kind

et al—and another (or, others)

expressio unius est exclusio alterius—when something, but not everything of the same category, has been expressed, one may infer that omissions were deliberate; often rendered with *inclusio* as the first word

ferae naturae—wild animals

in custodia legis—in custody (of the law)

in esse—in being

in haec verba—in the very words

in invitum—without consent

in pari materia—on the same topic

in propria persona —representing oneself (not by lawyer); abbreviated *pro per*

in re—in regard to; often abbreviated *re*

inclusio unius est exclusio alterius—same as *expressio unius est exclusio alterius*

inter alia—among other things

lex fori—the law of the forum (the law of the place where the court is)

lex loci— the law of the place

— — *actus*—of the act

— — *contractus*—of the contract

— — *rei sitae*—where the thing is located

mutatis mutandis—changing what ought to be changed; the same except for a change of details

nil—nothing

non obstante veredicto —notwithstanding the verdict (said of a judgment given by a court contrary to the verdict); abbreviated *n.o.v.*

nunc pro tunc—now for then (e.g., backdating)

per capita—per person (said of division of property by the number of individuals)

per curiam—by the court (said of an opinion or order not attributed to a specific judge)

per stirpes—by the stocks (said of division of property by representation of ancestors)

pro se—same as *in propria persona*

qui facit per alium facit per se —who acts through another acts himself (the principal is liable for the acts of the agent)

respondeat superior—let the superior answer (the principal is liable for the acts of the agent); another way of saying *qui facit per alium facit per se*

sub judice—under consideration by a court

sui generis—unique

sui juris—having legal capacity and responsibility

tabula rasa—a clean slate; as, in "We do not write upon a *tabula rasa,*" a cliché for: this ground has been worked over in other decisions.

terminus a quo—the starting point

vel non—or not

APPENDIX E

Law French, With English Equivalents

The law French words and phrases in this sampling are no more precise (sometimes less so) than their more intelligible English equivalents. Some of the "equivalents" are not literal translations, but convey in ordinary English the sense in which the French is used in the law. Law French that has been accepted as ordinary English is not included (e.g., *counsel*). Law French terms of art are included in Appendix H.

alien (verb)—to transfer (property)

assigns (plural noun) —assignees (those to whom something has been assigned)

cestui que trust—beneficiary of a trust

chose in action—a thing in action; right to sue for money—sometimes for personal property; or, the instrument—e.g., a note —embodying the right.

close (noun)—a piece of land

cy pres—as near as possible (to the intention of e.g., a testator)

demise—death; lease; convey; conveyance: the law French can mean any one of those.

de son tort—of his own wrong; as, a trustee *de son tort:* as part of a remedy, a fictitious trusteeship is imposed on someone who has acquired title to property by wrongdoing.

en ventre sa mere—in the womb; as, the rights of a child *en ventre sa mere*

feme covert—married woman

feme sole—a single woman (never married, now unmarried, and sometimes —only separated)

mesne—intermediate; as, *mesne* assignments

messuage (in other than historical usage)—a dwelling and the buildings and land that go with it

ordain—to appoint or order

presents (singular noun but requiring plural pronoun) —this legal document; as, *Know All Men By These Presents*

pur autre vie—for the life of another (said of the duration of an interest in property)

remise—release, as, in the tautology *remise, release, and forever quitclaim*

residue—all other property; as, in the tautology *rest, residue, and remainder*

save—except

seisin (in other than historical usage)—possession; title; ownership: the law French can mean any one of those; also spelled *seizin.*

specialty—a sealed contract

style (noun)—name

suffer—permit

APPENDIX F

Flexible Words

These are commonly used flexible words of the legal vocabulary. The words in this sampling are often useful. The only thing wrong is in using them as though they were precise.

about
abuse of discretion
adequate
    (- cause, - compensation,
    - consideration
    - preparation, - remedy
    at law, - representation)
adversely affected
and others
apparently
appropriate
approximately
arbitrary
as soon as possible
available
average
care
clean and neat condition
clear and convincing
clearly erroneous
commerce
comparable
compelling grounds
completion
contemporary community
    standards
convenient

custom and usage
discretion
due (- care, - diligence,
    - process)
excessive
existing
expenses
extra-hazardous
extraordinary (- compensation,
    - services)
extreme cruelty
fair division
few
fixture
gross (- profit; percentage
    of the -)
improper
in conjunction with
in regard to
inadequate
incidental
inconvenience
intention
intoxicated
it would appear to be
it would seem
lately

luxury
malice
manifest
material
mere
modify
moral turpitude
more or less
necessaries
need
negligence
neighborhood
net profit
nominal (- damages, -sum)
normal
notice
objectionable
obscene
obstruct
obvious
on or about
ordinary
overhead
palpable
possible
practicable
prejudicial
prevent
probative value
profits
promptly
proper
provide for
public (- interest)
reasonable (- care, - cause,
    - man, - speed, -time)
regular
relevant

remote
reputable
resident
respecting
safe
satisfactory
serious (- and willful,
    - illness, - misconduct)
severe
similar
slight
sound (- discretion,
    - mind)
structure
substantial
sufficient
suitable
taken care of
technical
temporarily
transaction
trivial
under the influence of
    (- a person, - liquor)
understand
undue (- delay, -influence,
    - interference, - restraint)
unreasonable
unsafe
unsatisfactory
unsound
unusual
usual
valuable
voluntary
welfare
willful misconduct
worthless

APPENDIX G

Legal Argot, with Ordinary English Equivalents

These are words and phrases of legal argot, some only one step removed from slang, some only one step removed from the precise and technical term of art. Often useful between lawyers, these expressions are unnecessarily unclear to others. This sampling does not include legal argot that is rarely written except in transcripts of court proceedings (e.g., *step down*), or of taped conversations between lawyers (e.g., Your client has been *dropping paper* all over town; if this one *bounces...*).

alter ego—a sham corporation; a corporation in name only used by the owners of the enterprise for a fraudulent purpose.

attractive nuisance—a dangerous condition of land or buildings likely to attract children at play.

Blackacre—a fictitious piece of real estate; as, "Suppose A owns Blackacre...".

case at bar—this case (now being tried).

case at bench—this case (now being tried); sometimes said to apply only to a case on appeal.

clean hands—free of wrongdoing that would cause a court to deny equitable relief, as in the maxim: "He who comes into a court of equity must come with *clean hands*."

cloud on title—a defect in the record title to property.

contract of adhesion—a take-it-or-leave-it contract, with one side having all the bargaining power.

court below—the court that is lower in the hierarchy of courts and previously dealt with this case.

exhaust the security—first try to get paid out of the debtor's security (before collecting from the debtor personally).

four corners of the instrument —within the confines of the writing.

horse case—an earlier case just like this one.

inferior court—a court lower in the hierarchy of courts.

John Doe—a fictitious person, abbreviated *Doe* (see Mellinkoff, "Who Is 'John Doe'"? 12 *UCLA Law Review* 79, 1964).

matter—a something on which attention is focused: a case, a proceeding, a problem, a claim, a point of law; etc., as "There is a *matter* I want to discuss," "We have a *matter* pending in Department 1."

negative pregnant—a denial in the very words of the charge, implying an admission of the substance of the charge. E.g., if a date is of no consequence, to the charge "You hit me on January 10," the *negative pregnant* denial is "I deny that I hit you on January 10."

off the record—not intended to be included in the reporter's transcript, even though the statement is made in court or in a judge's chambers.

on all fours—same as a *horse case.*

pierce the corporate veil —disregard the sham corporation (see *alter ego*) and hold the owners of the enterprise liable for what otherwise would be only a corporate obligation.

private attorney general—one who sues to right a wrong and can claim attorney fees for services in benefiting the public.

reasonable man—the hypothetical creature whose hypothetical action and lethargy are used to gauge the reasonableness of conduct of real people, as "What would a *reasonable man* have done under those circumstances?"

res ipsa loquitur—the thing speaks for itself; a Latin way of saying that usually it doesn't happen unless someone is negligent (applied in varying ways to affect the proof of negligence); as an adjective, often shortened to *res ipsa* (a *res ipsa* case) and sometimes to a slangier *resipsy;* abbreviated R.I.L.

sidebar—a conference between lawyers and the judge at the bench but outside the hearing of others in court, often *off the record;* also, something said at such a conference.

Whiteacre—a second fictitious piece of real estate, in a hypothetical proposition that has already used *Blackacre.*

APPENDIX H

Legal Terms of Art, with Short Explanations in Ordinary English

These samples of legal terms of art from many different areas of the law vary in degrees of sharpness and technicality. The term of art is short; it has no synonym in ordinary English. Often a full explanation would fill volumes. The "short explanations" here would ordinarily be enough to give a non-lawyer the general sense of what the technician means when using the term of art.

agency—a relationship in which one person, the *principal*, controls the acts of another, the *agent*, and the principal is liable for the acts of the agent in furthering the interests of the principal.

agent—see *agency*.

amicus brief—see *amicus curiae*.

amicus curiae (Latin, friend of the court)—someone not a party to the litigation, but usually favoring one of the parties, permitted to make an argument to the *court*, i.e., to the judge, not to a jury; the argument is usually made in a writing called an *amicus brief*.

appoint—see *power of appointment*.

cert—see *certiorari*.

certification (of a check)—an agreement by the bank on which a check is drawn *(drawee bank)* to pay the check when it is presented for payment, manifested by its appropriate writing on the check, e.g., "CERTIFIED—Bank of Banktown."

certiorari—a shortened form of *writ of certiorari*, abbreviated *cert*; it is one of the words of the older Latin form of the order *(writ)*, directing a lower court to send "up" the papers in a case, for review by the court issuing the writ; it is a form of "appeal" from a decision of a lower court, used when the higher court has a discretion to hear an appeal; the reviewing court *grants* or *denies* a *petition for a writ of certiorari*, i.e., agrees or refuses to hear the appeal.

demur—to file a written pleading called a *demurrer*.

demurrer—a written pleading filed in court saying that, whatever the facts may be, the pleading filed by the other side is no good as a matter of law; in many courts the same point is raised by filing a written pleading called a *motion to dismiss.*

double jeopardy—in *jeopardy* (danger) a second time for the same offense (forbidden by the United States Constitution); in this special sense of forbidden danger, generally a person is *in jeopardy* when put on trial in a criminal prosecution; there are legal exceptions to the general rule, such as: a defendant has not been in jeopardy when, after conviction, the defendant has obtained a new trial.

drawee bank—see *certification.*

estate in fee simple—see *fee simple.*

ex parte (Latin, on one side)—at the instance of one side only, without representation of the other side, and without advance notice to the other side; as, obtaining an *ex parte order* from a judge.

fee—see *fee simple.*

fee simple—shortened form of *estate in fee simple,* usually referred to as a *fee;* the most absolute form of ownership of property, usually applied only to real estate; the *fee simple* is owned without any limitation of time, with an indefinite succession of owners, each in succession free to transfer the estate, include it in a will, or —without a will—permit it to pass to those entitled under the laws of inheritance.

holding (of a case)—the precise issue or principle decided, as distinguished from *dictum,* something said in passing not essential to the decision.

in personam (Latin, against the person)—said of a lawsuit to make someone personally liable, as opposed to liability limited to property (see *in rem*); also said of the power of a court to make someone personally liable—*jurisdiction in personam,* based on some personal contact with the place where the court is, e.g., by being physically present there or doing business there; also said of the method of enforcing an order by holding the person in contempt of court for disobedience of the order.

in rem (Latin, against the thing)—said of a lawsuit to subject specific property to liability (as in a suit against a ship), as opposed to liability of the owner of the property (see *in personam*); also said of the power of a court where the property is located to make orders affecting the property—*jurisdiction in rem,* whether or not it has power over the owner (see *in personam*); also said of the means of enforcing a personal judgment against an owner (see *in personam*) by taking the owner's property.

intestate (Latin, without making a will)—said concerning someone who dies without having made any will or whose will was legally defective *(he died intestate)*, or whose will has not disposed of all the property (he died *intestate as to* Blackacre); also, the dead person (the children of the intestate live in Utah); also, said of the property left by the intestate (the *intestate property* consisted of . . .)

jeopardy—see *double jeopardy*

jurisdiction in personam—see *in personam*

jurisdiction in rem—see *in rem*

laches (law French, lax)—such excessive delay in asserting a claim that a court would deny the claim as a matter of the court's equitable discretion; to be distinguished from a definite period of time fixed by a particular *statute of limitations* after which the claim is barred.

mandamus (Latin, we command)—short for *writ of mandamus*, called *writ of mandate* or *mandate* in some jurisdictions; also, a verb, as "We *mandamused* them," i.e., we got a *writ of mandamus* against them; an order from a higher to a lower court, or from a court to an individual, a corporation, or a unit of government directing the performance of a public duty; called a "prerogative" or "extraordinary" writ, and issued in urgency, when the time for an appeal or an ordinary lawsuit would defeat the end sought. (see *prohibition*)

power of appointment—often shortened to a *power;* an authority given by a property owner permitting another person (*donee* of the power) to designate *(appoint)* someone *(appointee)* who will become the owner of the property or of a lesser interest in it; the authorization specifies the interest the appointee may acquire, how the appointment is to be made (the power *exercised*), and whether the appointee may be anyone (a *general power*) or only specified persons (a *special power*).

principal—see *agency.*

prohibition—short for *writ of prohibition;* an order from a higher to a lower court to stop further proceedings in a case over which the lower court has no jurisdiction (power); called a "prerogative" or "extraordinary" writ. (see *mandamus*).

statute of limitations—see *laches.*

supersedeas (Latin, you shall desist)—a shortened form of *writ of supersedeas;* it is one of the words of the older Latin form of the order *(writ)*, directing a lower court not to take any action to enforce a judgment.

APPENDIX I

The Plain Language Laws
(An Overview)

The "plain language movement" is the latest variation on the very old and never dead theme mentioned in the preface to this book. Ordinary people don't understand the language of the law; and don't like it—the language, the law, and being left out.

Any tally of plain language laws would be dated by the time you read this. A sufficient point of departure is that by 1980 the federal government and at least half the states were trying in more than 50 ways to regulate legal writing. That "trying" includes laws on the books, bills introduced, administrative regulations of all sorts.

To draw a sharper bead on what is continuation and what is new in the plain language laws, first take a quick look at their setting.

1. THE SETTING: EARLIER REGULATION

a. Public language

For centuries, government's principal response to protest against the unintelligibility of the language of the law was confined to some regulation of what may roughly be called "public language."

The first national control of legal language in England (1362) required courtroom pleadings (then oral) to be in English. The English language requirement was extended (late fifteenth century) to the statutes, and still later (seventeenth and eighteenth centuries) to written pleadings, law reports, and various papers publicly filed. Except during the period of the short-lived Commonwealth, "technical words" were still permitted.

In this country, English was made "official," and laws were to be published in English. Written pleadings by lawyers were required to be in "ordinary and concise language," "short and plain," "simple, concise, and direct"; lawyers nodded agreement, and went their accustomed way.

Other public legal language has also been subjected to some control. For example—ballot measures, jury instructions, traffic signs, and—above all—administrative regulations. The outpouring of regulations during World War II brought cries of outrage, even the coining of the word *gobbledygook*. An antidote was proposed. The expanded version of a memorandum for the Office of Price Administration, "The Simplification of Government Regulations" by David F. Cavers (8 *Federal Bar Journal* 339, 1947) is still an instructive critique. Intermittent efforts of bureaucracy to heal itself and its public writings continue. (See Rule 4.2.e., page 75.)

b. Private writings

i. Criticism

Criticism of the way private writings are written and put together is not new. For example, this century old, still pertinent, comment on insurance policies by the splendid Mr. Justice Doe of New Hampshire.

> "The study of them [policy provisions] was rendered particularly unattractive, by a profuse intermixture of discourses on subjects in which a premium payer would have no interest. The compound, if read by him, would, unless he were an extraordinary man, be an inexplicable riddle, a mere flood of darkness and confusion. Some of the most material stipulations were concealed in a mass of rubbish, on the back side of the policy and the following page, where few would expect to find anything more than a dull appendix, and where scarcely anyone would think of looking for information so important as that the company claimed a special exemption from the operation of the general law of the land. . . As if it feared that, notwithstanding these discouraging circumstances, some extremely eccentric person might attempt to examine and understand the meaning of the involved and intricate net in which he was to be entangled, it was printed in such small type, and in lines so long and so crowded, that the perusal of it was made physically difficult, painful, and injurious. Seldom has the art of typography been so successfully diverted from the diffusion of knowledge to the suppression of it. There was ground for the premium payer to argue that the print alone was evidence . . . of a fraudulent plot . . . As a contrivance for keeping out of sight the dangers created by the agents of the nominal corporation, the system displayed a degree of cultivated ingenuity, which, if it had been exercised in any useful calling, would have merited the strongest commendation."

> (*DeLancey v. Insurance Co.*, 52 N.H., 581, 587-588, 1873)

ii. Changing attitude toward regulation

As distinguished from criticizing, doing something about the style of private legal writing has traditionally been left in private hands. This has now changed.

The second half of this century has seen a sharp departure from the old concentration on public legal language as the target of government regulation. The interest in public legal language has not abated; it grows. But the style of private legal writings has become a prime target of government control.

Volumes will be written on the reasons for the change. Most immediate is the political pressure of a seething, spreading, nudging "consumer movement." Its own house of words not in order, government responds to consumer nudging by nudging business. Government nudging, consumer nudging, and a clear, dawning light of competitive self-interest have all stimulated private efforts to improve the "image" of business (See generally, Felsenfeld and Siegal, *Simplified Consumer Credit Forms,* 1978, and 1979, 1980, and 1981 Supplements.) In the background is a growing popular interest in language, especially in the language of the law.

iii. Regulation of private writings before the "plains" came

Until recently, government regulation of style in private contracts followed three relatively restricted channels—typography, specific wording of specified notices, and general clarity of specific parts of specific contracts. For example.

[a] **Typography**   One long regulated criterion is *legibility,* as affected by type size and inking—especially in insurance policies. A related, more pointed, criterion is *conspicuousness,* as affected by type and layout—insurance policies, warranty, warranty disclaimer, instalment credit terms; the prime exhibit here is the much litigated Regulation Z, under the federal Truth In Lending Act. (See discussion of typography in Rule 4.3., p. 91.)

[b] **Specific wording of specified notices**   Sometimes the required wording is brief—*full . . . warranty, limited warranty* in the federal Magnuson-Moss Warranty . . . Act. Sometimes the required wording is very detailed, such as the one that starts *Notice Credit History for Married Persons,* in Regulation B of the Federal Reserve Equal Credit Opportunity Regulations. (See discussion of required wording in Rule 4.1.a, p. 63.)

[c] **General clarity of specific parts of specific contracts** Here, the requirements have been embodied in a variety of flexible terms. *Meaningful disclosure* of credit terms (Truth in Lending Act);

makes plain that there is no implied warranty (Uniform Commercial Code); *simple and readily understood* warranty (Magnuson-Moss Warranty . . . Act); *clear and unmistakable* limitation on warranty (Magnuson-Moss Warranty . . . Act); *calculated to be understood by the average plan participant*—the summary of an employee retirement plan (Employee Retirement Income Security Act of 1974); etc.

2. THE SETTING: GENERAL LAW

A climate favorable to government control of private writings permitted the blossoming of the plain language laws, but the regulation of legal language has roots in specific areas of the general law. For example.

a. "Rules" on interpretation of writings

These "rules" (discussed in Rule 2.2, p. 16) apply to all kinds of legal writing. The "rule" most often invoked in discussion of the plain language laws is the one that says that if you made it uncertain, you are the one to suffer.

b. Basic contract law

The principle of contract as a relationship resting on consent underlies the arguments for plain language laws. It has been urged that the true basis of the laws is that without a "meeting of the minds" there is no contract. For the moment, the enacted plain language laws have not made that oversimplification their centerpiece.

c. Unconscionable contracts (equity)

A growing body of law is based on the old equitable rule refusing enforcement of what was offensive to the King's conscience. The rule finds various expression, e.g., in the Uniform Commercial Code §2302 (sale of goods), giving courts a broad discretion to refuse enforcement of *unconscionable* contracts or clauses. Of special pertinence here is the provision of the Uniform Consumer Credit Code (§5.108(4)(e)), that in determining unconscionability a court shall consider a knowing advantage taken of another's "ignorance, illiteracy, inability to understand the language of the agreement."

d. Contracts of adhesion

A blend of basic contract law and equitable notions of unconscionability has produced the label *contract of adhesion*. Take-it-or-leave-it contracts under conditions of gross disparity of bargaining power have been denied enforcement in numerous cases, typically in the mass market—e.g., automobile sales.

e. Standardized contracts

Whether or not they are contracts of adhesion, the form contract in the mass market has fostered growing reluctance of courts to enforce contracts where the normal expectation of the customer has been disappointed.

f. Insurance policies

These are often called contracts of adhesion, and standardized contracts, but they have a long history of close scrutiny that antedates those doctrines. (Refer to Mr. Justice Doe's comment, p. 206.) The "rule" of interpretation against the writer of the policy is frequently invoked. Insurance companies have become accustomed to dealing with regulation. In New Jersey, for example, a broad coverage plain language bill worried its way through the legislature, only to be temporarily sidetracked by a veto. Meanwhile, a much looser "Life and Health Insurance Policy Language Simplification Act," exempting those policies from other "language simplification standards," was enacted rather promptly. (*New Jersey Statutes Annotated*, §§17B:17–7 to 17B:17–25, 1979.)

g. Misrepresentation (fraud)

One rationale suggested for plain language laws is that unintelligible language is a species of fraud. A more direct approach, influenced by this branch of the law, is a special law requiring that, on request, a customer be furnished a copy of the contract—written in the foreign language in which the deal was negotiated. (See California Civil Code, §1632.)

h. Special rules for consumers

This broad rubric covers a rapidly growing body of law, concentrating on the mass market consumer. The protected consumer typically buys and borrows for personal, family, or household purposes, and is least able to understand or fight the market or the law. The laws and decisions are various and legion: expansion of strict tort liability of seller and manufacturer; required notice and hearing before seizure of property not paid for; curtailed application of theories of "holding-in-due-course" (which give lenders immunity from a customer's

209

defenses against the seller); expanded areas for class actions; etc. Increasingly, these laws take cognizance of the possibility that the ignorant may be imposed upon.

3. WHAT IS NEW

A part of the "consumer movement," the plain language movement is nonetheless distinct. Two elements, taken together, make the plain language laws unique.

a. A single-minded purpose to make the whole consumer agreement clear to signers by controlling the way it is written and designed.

In purest form, the plain language laws are not limited to particular points of an agreement—annual percentage rate, disclaimer of warranty, unusual provisions, etc.

In purest form, they are not complicated by legal considerations that are implicit in their origins. The laws deal with preparation of the contract, not with the capacity of a particular signer to cope with it. The contract is to be prepared in a prescribed way, presumably whether or not (a) it is unconscionable, (b) understood, (c) bargaining power is equal, (d) it is a form contract, (e) both sides are represented by lawyers. There is deviation from the model, especially on these latter two points. Also, the politics of legislation, have forced the concession that plain language regulation is not to conflict with other governmental regulation of language.

b. An attempt, at one stroke, to reach the broadest variety of consumer agreements in the mass market.

Generally, that means all mass market contracts for personal, family, or household purposes, including residential leases

The plain language laws fix the mass market by placing a top dollar figure on the contracts covered. This is $25,000 in Connecticut and Hawaii (neither has a dollar limit on residential leases); $50,000 in New York and New Jersey (except that New Jersey has no dollar limit on real estate or insurance contracts).

They are not limited to agreements that include (a) instalment payment, (b) borrowing of money, or (c) warranty. There is deviation from the breadth of the model to exclude some specifics, by untested interpretation (e.g., insurance policies: New York), or explicitly (e.g., insurance policies, real estate deeds, and writings about securities: Connecticut; life and health insurance: New Jersey).

Here (from a Maine bill not enacted) is an eloquent statement of the underlying purpose of the plain language laws.

"The purpose of this chapter is to enable the average consumer, who makes a reasonable effort under the circumstances, to read and understand the terms of so-called form contracts and the like without having to obtain the assistance of a professional."

While rejecting a broad gauge plain language law, Maine did adopt a plain language requirement for "Consumer Loan Agreements" up to a limit of $100,000. The act regulates form contracts of "supervised lenders." (10 *Maine Revised Statutes Annotated*, §§1121–1126, 1979).

4. TWO BASIC PATTERNS AND A VARIATION

Four states have now (Spring, 1981) enacted broad coverage plain language laws:

First, New York's *Requirements for use of plain language in consumer transactions* (General Obligations Law §5–702, 1978, amending—before it became operative—a law signed in 1977).

Second, Connecticut's *An Act Concerning Plain Language in Consumer Contracts* (Public Act No. 79–532, 1979).

Third, Hawaii's *Language of Consumer Transactions* (H.B. No. 721, H.D. 1, Act 36, 1980).

Fourth, New Jersey's *An Act concerning simple, clear, understandable and easily readable language in consumer contracts* (New Jersey Statutes Annotated, §§56:12.1 et seq.; P.L. 1980, Chapter 125, October, 1980).

Bills in various states, and plain language statutes of more limited scope, generally follow a New York pattern or a Connecticut pattern. The broad coverage law in Hawaii, as well as the Maine law on consumer loans *(supra)*, follow the New York pattern on the standards of "plain language." The New Jersey law is closer to the New York than the Connecticut pattern, but has some variations worth noting.

Similar in many details, the four broad coverage laws (New York, Connecticut, Hawaii, New Jersey) have a fundamental similarity in regulating both the way a contract is written and its topography.

Different in many details, the New York pattern and the Connecticut pattern also have a fundamental difference. New York establishes only general standards on what constitutes "plain language." Connecticut establishes both general and detailed standards. New Jersey has general standards, and some detailed "guidelines."

a. New York pattern

The covered agreements must be:
"1. Written in a *clear* and *coherent* manner using words with *common* and *every day* meanings;
2. *Appropriately* divided and captioned by its various sections." [italics added]

Comment

1. The writing standards, like the "plain language" title itself, are deliberately vague, following an old legal practice of built-in flexibility. None of the key words is precise.

Clear and *coherent* border on redundancy, but are not quite the same. Clarity cannot survive complete incoherence, though writing may hang together and yet not be clear. It bears emphasizing that things will be clearer if the parts have some logical connection.

Common and *every day* are redundant. It is unlikely that a contract would pass one test and not the other. It helps to recall that the New York standard is a stripped down version of an original that imposed an additional requirement—*"non-technical language."* It is now said that some *technical* words (e.g., *pay to the order of* in a check) are so commonly seen (whether or not understood) that they can pass muster as *common*, even if not a part of the *every day* vocabulary. That is a political rationalization, part of the growing up process by which a bill learns how to become a law.

2. The typographic (or design) standards governed by *appropriately* are again deliberately vague. The law bespeaks its background. It seems to be talking about form contracts, or long contracts, typically with "various sections," often absent in short, tailor-made contracts; yet it does not say so in plain language.

b. Connecticut pattern

i. "Plain language" test

The covered agreements must be:
"written in *plain language*. A consumer contract is written in plain language if it meets either the plain language tests of *subsection (b)* or the alternate objective tests of *subsection (c)*." [italics added]

Comment.

The *plain language* of the title is repeated as a positive requirement. Since it does not say that the *only* way to satisfy that requirement is by following the path of the subsections (which stretch into 5 times the length of the New York law), the Connecticut law contains an un-resolved ambiguity. If you write in language that is indubitably plain, need you be concerned with any further requirement? Whether the answer is "Yes," or "No," the law proceeds to lay out two standard ways of achieving plain language.

ii. Subsection (b) test

This is the more general route, and the language is *plain* if it only "substantially complies with" the listed details.

1. The writing standards resemble New York's in prescribing *everyday words*, "written and organized in a *clear* and *coherent* manner." Unlike New York, Connecticut also prescribes "*short* sentences and paragraphs," "*simple* and *active* verb forms," and references to parties to the contract by "personal pronouns, the actual or shortened names of the parties . . . or both."

Comment.
Plain, everyday, clear, coherent, substantially complies are all de-liberately vague. So too is *short*. Whether the requirement of "*simple . . .* verb forms" was deliberately chosen, it is vague. The outlawing of passive verbs makes a rule of what in many, but not all, instances is a preferred practice. The requirement of *active* verbs rules out such ordinary expressions as "the money was loaned," "the debt was paid," etc. The required reference to people by their names or pronouns (often useful) bans what is sometimes even more useful. For example, common functional labels such as *buyer* and *seller* often aid the reader's understanding. The ban on calling a party a *party*, though used in the law itself, is a Draconian approach to a good end.

2. The typographic (or design) standards require "type of readable size," "ink which contrasts with the paper," section and sub-division captions in "boldface type or which otherwise stand out *significantly*," and "layout and spacing" separating paragraphs and sections "from each other and from the borders of the paper."

Comment.
Deliberately vague.

iii. Subsection (c) test

The testing here is labeled "objective." The language is *plain* "if it fully meets all of the following tests, using the procedures described in section 8 of this act."

1. The writing standards follow subsection (b) on the required form of reference to the unmentionable "*parties* to the contract." Beyond that, the tests follow a variation of the sort of mechanical measurement popularized by Rudolf Flesch, *The Art of Readable Writing* (1949), and others, to test readability. The average number of words per sentence (less than 22), average of words per paragraph (less than 75), average number of syllables per word (less than 1.55) are all prescribed. A sentence cannot exceed 50 words, nor a paragraph 150. How you go about counting and computing are specified in greatest detail in Section 8. There are also definitions of *sentence, paragraph, syllable,* and *list.*

Comment.

By this mechanical route, language will be dubbed "plain," whether or not anyone can understand it. It holds out the bait of "certainty" of compliance, regardless of "certainty" of the language used. The intricacy of definition is such that evasion seems inevitable. If you don't write in *sentences,* as defined, the word count is thrown off. Among other requirements, a sentence must express a "complete thought."

2. The typographic (or design) standards leave no room for squirming variation. Detailed prescription is the rule: minimum typeface (8 points); minimum blank space between paragraphs and between sections (3/16 inch); minimum "borders" (1/2 inch); maximum average line length (65 characters). Sections are to be captioned, in a minimum 10 point boldface for printed contracts, underlined in typed contracts. More detailed typographical requirements are listed in Section 8.

Comment.

Again, the end is mechanical conformity whether or not the result is clarity. The large scale user of long lasting commercial forms may look upon this sort of regulation as freedom from consumer harassment. For anyone typing up a contract of the moment it can be an expensive, unproductive nuisance.

c. New Jersey variation

i. The basic standard

The covered agreements must be: "written in a *simple, clear, understandable* and *easily readable* way." [italics added]

Comment.

The key words are deliberately vague. *Simple, clear, understandable* are often used interchangeably (see p. 61). *Easily readable* could be redundant, or could point to factors of typography.

ii.

"Use of *technical terms* or *words of art* shall not in and of itself be a violation of this act." [italics added]

Comment.

This resolves the torment of legislators over what to do about legal technicality: deliberately flexible.

iii. Guidelines

In determining whether the basic standard *"as a whole"* has been met, a court or agency *"shall* take into consideration" the §10 *"guidelines."* Those are later split into §10.a. *"examples"* of guidelines that one *"may* consider," and §10.b. *"examples"* of guidelines that one *"shall* consider."

§10.a. *examples of guidelines:* (1) confusing cross references; (2) unnecessarily long sentences; (3) double negatives and "exceptions to exceptions"; (4) "confusing or illogical order" of sentences and sections; (5) words with obsolete meanings or with legal meanings different from the "common ordinary"; (6) "frequent use of Old English and Middle English words and Latin and French phrases."

§10.b. *examples of guidelines:* (1) logically divided and captioned sentences; (2) table of contents or index—in contracts over 3,000 words; (3) conditions and exceptions given *"equal prominence* with the main promise, *and* shall be in *at least 10 point type."* [italics added]

Comment.

1. *As a whole* discourages nit-picking, and reinforces the flexible treatment of technicality.

2. *Guidelines,* a vague word even when left alone, becomes vacuous with the alternation of more vague words—*shall* and *may.* You *shall* consider §10.a. guidelines that *may* be considered; and you *shall* consider §10.b. guidelines that *shall* be considered. Not "simple, clear, understandable."

3. *Examples* of the guidelines, mostly desirables, are left deliberately vague. "Equal prominence *and* . . . 10 point type" is confusing. (See pages 36 and 37.) Presumably, an agency or a court could establish *guidelines,* other than the *examples.*

iv. Administrative approval

New Jersey permits submission of proposed contracts to various state regulatory agencies. Approval eliminates liability for damages under the plain language law.

Comment.
Agency approval could be a quick way around the law, disapproval a hindrance to innovation. A variety of agencies could produce a variety of interpretations, or could produce a consensus of precedent.

v. Injunction.

As in the New York and Hawaii laws, the state "may seek injunctive relief." In addition, under the New Jersey law, that avenue is open to "any interested person."

vi. Effective date

The basic standard applies to consumer contracts made "on or after the *effective* date of this act. (§2).

Section 14 adds some detail:

"This act shall *take effect immediately, but* shall remain *inoperative* until *1 year* after its enactment, *except* that the act shall remain *inoperative* for *2 years* with regard to all contracts of insurance during which time a State regulator may receive and process requests for and render opinions as to whether consumer contracts comply with this act." [italics added]

Comment.
The basic standard and the guidelines apply to consumer contracts, but do not apply to "An act concerning simple, clear, understandable and easily readable language in consumer contracts."

5. WHAT HAS BEEN ACCOMPLISHED

a. Shock

The quiet passage of the New York plain language law (its author a Republican stockbroker named Sullivan) shocked the business community and its lawyers. They now live with the modified law, with only small anguish. Those who opposed it now prefer it to what might be worse, such as the Connecticut law, or further horribles. (Under both laws, good faith effort to comply is a defense; full performance is a defense; and a contract is not made void by a plain language violation;

damages, a small penalty are not too offensive.) But the enactment of four broad gauge plain language laws, a nationwide proliferation of bills, and a full bag of legislation and regulation reeking of the aroma of plain language are at the least unsettling. Most observers have become reconciled to the inevitability, if not the desirability, of similar legislation.

Among the opponents of plain language legislation, initial shock and outrage dissolved into protective strategies and calmer reflection. Some who despise federal regulation of any sort embrace the ogre of federal preemption as an alternative to the threat of state-by-state tinkering and variation. Some want a model uniform state law to freeze the plain language movement at its most innocuous level. Some would like to water down what has been enacted; New York and New Jersey are too uncertain; Connecticut too restrictive. Many are genuinely concerned that the efforts of some lawyers and some businesses (notably banks and insurers) to privately improve their own agreements will be hampered by bungling, amateur experiments with further regulation. Many wonder whether "plain language," in any case, does any good at all.

b. The mood of experiment

Haste to latch on to a cause suddenly politically popular helps account for the poor writing and poor thinking in some of the bills introduced in the wake of the New York law. (Refer to Rule 2.1, p. 15-16, and Rule 6, p. 115.) Such support will evaporate in the heat of some new frenzy to outlaw the semi-colon or tax the frisbee.

There are also signs that the New York, Connecticut, Hawaii and New Jersey laws have renewed the ancient dream that maybe something can be done about the obscurity of the law. Into the bubbling legislative pots have been tossed all manner of suggestions: agreements cannot be enforced unless written in plain language; deliberate violators to be fined up to $10,000; decision of what is "plain" to be left to the jury; decision of what is "plain" to be left to administrators (following steps in that direction by Maine and New Jersey); "plain" to be "plain" to those of "average intelligence," or a fixed level of schooling; etc. The mood is to experiment, above all to legislate, the "pass a law" solution to every problem.

The variety of suggestions is some evidence that *the* solution is not at hand. The ideal model has not been proposed. In that state of affairs, at the moment the New York pattern—for all its uncertainty —is a better, more flexible encouragement to self-improvement than the Connecticut pattern.

217

c. Long-term results

The plain language laws, the bills, the regulations have a common base in the age old frustration with legal language. That frustration reflects deeper frustrations with the complexity of law and of society itself. "Plain language" has yet to prove itself, prove that it will benefit those it is intended to benefit. Blackstone's comment on passage of a plain language law two centuries ago is still pertinent.

> "This was done, in order that the common people might have knowledge and understanding of what was alleged or done for and against them . . . Which purpose I know not how well it has answered, but am apt to suspect that the people are now, after many years' experience, altogether as ignorant in matters of law as before."
>
> (3 *Commentaries* *323)

But Blackstone was talking about another sort of law (English for public legal writings), and of a different age, where law did not reach out so intrusively, so persistently, into the daily lives of so many more or less literate people. If "plain language," across the board, in the daily agreements that ordinary people are asked to sign, has not proved that it yields positive benefit in late 20th century America, there are many possible explanations. Not the least is that "plain language" (however interpreted) has never yet been tried on that massive scale. Evidence that borrowers still have no bargaining power, even with Truth-In-Lending "clear and conspicuous" disclosure of credit terms, does not prove that plain language is a waste of time.

It would be better that legal writers mend their ways on their own; they can. But without the goad of some legislation, they won't. They need some encouragement, and not only on "consumer" agreements. The "plain language" movement may speed the disposal of much of the trash in the language of the law.

Addendum

Minnesota has now enacted a broad coverage *Plain Language Contract Act* (1981 Session, Chapter 274, §§1-9; Minnesota Statutes §§325G.29 - 325G.37; approved May 28, 1981). The Minnesota law generally follows the New York pattern, with a New Jersey-like wrinkle: A contract complies with the law if the state attorney general says so.

APPENDIX J

Selected Bibliography on Grammar, Word Usage, and Punctuation

GRAMMAR

Here are some books recommended for a quick refresher on English grammar. They may also help resolve an occasional doubt. They are not the place to learn English grammar from scratch.

English Grammar, by George O. Curme. New York, 1947. (Based in part on *College English Grammar,* 1925.)

Concise Index to English, by Eugene Ehrlich and Daniel Murphy. New York, 1974.

A Dictionary of Contemporary American Usage, by Bergen Evans and Cornelia Evans. New York, 1957. [A short, general article under the entry *grammar,* continues under the entry *parts of speech.* Other entries for individual parts of speech, and grammatical forms.]

The Grammatical Lawyer, by Morton S. Freeman. American Law Institute—American Bar Association Committee on Continuing Professional Education. Philadelphia, 1979.

WORD USAGE

The books listed are useful to anyone interested in using ordinary English words correctly. They are not always in agreement (nor am I in complete agreement with any of them). Like railroad timetables, correct usage is subject to change without immediate notice. The list is divided into American and British books, then into "Dictionaries" and "Style" (a loose classification). Within these latter categories, the listing is alphabetical by author.

[1] American books

[a] *Dictionaries*

Evans, Bergen and Cornelia Evans. *A Dictionary of Contemporary American Usage.* New York, 1957.

Webster's New International Dictionary of the English Language. 2d ed. Unabridged. Springfield: G. & C. Merriam Company, 1934.

Wentworth, Harold and Stuart Berg Flexner. *Dictionary of American Slang.* Second Supplemented Edition. New York: Thomas Y. Crowell Company, 1975.

[b] *Style*

Freeman, Morton S. *The Grammatical Lawyer.* Philadelphia, 1979.

Lanham, Richard A. *Revising Prose.* New York, 1979.

"   "   *Revising Business Prose.* New York, 1981.

Strunk, William Jr. and E.B. White. *The Elements of Style.* Third Edition. New York, 1979.

Wydick, Richard C. *Plain English for Lawyers.* Durham, 1979.

[2] British books

[a] *Dictionaries*

Fowler, H.W. *A Dictionary of Modern English Usage.* Second Edition revised by Sir Ernest Gowers. New York, 1965.

The Oxford English Dictionary. Oxford, 1933 to date. 15 volumes.

[b] *Style*

Gowers, Sir Ernest. *The Complete Plain Words.* Revised edition by Sir Bruce Fraser. London, 1973.

Quiller-Couch, Sir Arthur. *On the Art of Writing.* Cambridge: University Press, 1916.

PUNCTUATION

Despite considerable variation in the style of punctuation, there is general agreement on basic usage. These books are useful on punctuation generally and on individual punctuation marks.

Evans, Bergen and Cornelia Evans. *A Dictionary of Contemporary American Usage.* New York, 1967.

A Manual of Style. 12th ed., Rev. Chicago, 1969.

Strunk, William Jr. and E.B. White. *The Elements of Style.* Third Edition. New York, 1979.

Word and Phrase Index

(Asterisk: "Caution. Can be used as a term of art.")

225

General Index

†